Thinking with Tolstoy and Wittgenstein

Thinking with Tolstoy and Wittgenstein

Expression, Emotion, and Art

✦

Henry W. Pickford

NORTHWESTERN UNIVERSITY PRESS
EVANSTON, ILLINOIS

Northwestern University Press
www.nupress.northwestern.edu

Printed in the United States of America

10 9 8 7 6 5 4 3 2 1

Library of Congress Cataloging-in-Publication Data

Pickford, Henry W., author.
Thinking with Tolstoy and Wittgenstein : expression, emotion, and art / Henry W. Pickford.
pages cm
Includes bibliographical references and index.
ISBN 978-0-8101-3170-5 (cloth : alk. paper) — ISBN 978-0-8101-3172-9 (pbk. : alk. paper) — ISBN 978-0-8101-3171-2 (ebook)
1. Tolstoy, Leo, graf, 1828–1910—Criticism and interpretation. 2. Wittgenstein, Ludwig, 1889–1951. 3. Literature—Philosophy. I. Title.
PG3410.P48 2015
891.73'3—dc23
2015029413

∞ The paper used in this publication meets the minimum requirements of the American National Standard for Information Sciences—Permanence of Paper for Printed Library Materials, ANSI Z39.48-1992.

For Kuang-Yu

CONTENTS

ACKNOWLEDGMENTS

This book is in a way a record of my intellectual journey, at the way stations of which it was my great fortune to encounter people of outstanding intellect, erudition, generosity, and integrity, several of whom have become dear friends. As an undergraduate student at Dartmouth, I was introduced to Tolstoy's writings by Barry Scherr and to Wittgenstein's thought by Robert Fogelin. As a graduate student at Stanford, I was able to deepen my knowledge of Russian nineteenth-century literature with William Mills Todd III, who has continued to offer unstinting support of my work. As a graduate student at Yale, I honed my analytic skills and explored contemporary philosophy of language with Ken Gemes. As a graduate student at the University of Pittsburgh I was privileged to study Wittgenstein and much more with John McDowell: his influence on my thinking in this book is pervasive. As a visiting assistant professor at Northwestern University I was able to try out some ideas with Andrew Wachtel and Julia Borisova. As an assistant professor at the University of Colorado, Boulder, I was able to develop my thoughts about emotion and non-inferential knowledge with Robert Hanna.

Barry Scherr, William Mills Todd III, Timothy D. Sergay, and Robert Hanna each read chapters and offered invaluable criticisms and suggestions. Some initial lines of argument were published as an article in *Tolstoy Studies Journal*, whose editor, Michael Denner, provided very helpful suggestions. Earlier versions of parts of this book were presented in talks given at the University of Pittsburgh, New York University, Harvard University, Northwestern University, and at the annual conference of the American Comparative Literature Association; my thanks to these audiences. I am also grateful to two anonymous readers for the press, whose suggestions greatly improved the quality of the book. It was the late Helen Tartar who recommended Northwestern University Press and its fine editor Michael L. Levine to me for this project. Helen's commitment to innovative, interdisciplinary research in the humanities sustained the aspirations of books like this one, and it was completed in her remembrance.

The support of friends and colleagues has sustained me over the years of this project: Daniel Brudney, Daniel DelliBovi, David Ferris, Gordon Finlayson, John Frazee, Josef Früchtl, Ken Gemes, Zilla Goodman, Anil Gupta, Ben Hale, Robert Hanna, Johan Hartle, Karen Hawley, Saskia Hintz, Martin Jay, Janis Kaufman, Kathy Kiloh, Michael G. Levine, Iain Macdonald, Ruth Mas, John McDowell, Christoph Menke, David Pan, Larson Powell, Barry Scherr,

Jessica Schilling, Timothy D. Sergay, Kieran Setiya, Pam Shime, Martin Shuster, R. Clifton Spargo, Sonja Sutton, Rochelle Tobias, William Mills Todd III, Eric Walczak, Maureen Pickford, and the Ahrens family.

I would like to thank my new colleagues at Duke University for making me feel so welcome: Stefani Engelstein, Susanne Freytag, Kata Gellen, Michael Gillespie, Bryan Gilliam, Corinna Kahnke, Laura Lieber, Heidi Madden, Jakob Norberg, Thomas Pfau, Margaret Swanson, Dorothy Thorpe-Turner, and Ingeborg Walther. I am likewise grateful for the convivial support of colleagues from the University of North Carolina at Chapel Hill in the Carolina-Duke Graduate Program in German Studies.

Thinking with Tolstoy and Wittgenstein

INTRODUCTION

> There is *much* to be learned from Tolstoy's false theorizing about how a work of art conveys "a feeling."
>
> —Wittgenstein

> One could call Schopenhauer a quite *crude* mind. I.e., he does have refinement, but at a certain level this suddenly comes to an end & he is as crude as the crudest. Where real depth starts, his finishes. . . . One might say of Schopenhauer: he never takes stock of himself.
>
> —Wittgenstein

1. While the novels of his antipodal doppelgänger Dostoevsky enjoyed preeminence among philosophers inclined toward existentialism, Tolstoy's artistic prose and its unmatched psychological realism have often served as true north for philosophers writing on the nature of mind, emotions, moral psychology, and value theory.[1] Indeed, one contemporary philosopher has confessed of *Anna Karenina* that "some of us come away from the book with the sense that there is at least as much to learn from Tolstoy about how we should live as can be learnt from Aristotle or from Kant. If this is right, philosophy will be poorer if philosophers stay away in their professional compartment and ignore Tolstoy and other novelists."[2] One philosopher who did not ignore Tolstoy is Ludwig Wittgenstein, who famously admitted to having read few thinkers: chiefly Frege, Russell, and Schopenhauer.[3] Recent scholarship has concluded that Tolstoy should be added to this narrow pantheon. Ray Monk writes of the young Wittgenstein's fascination with Tolstoy's *The Gospel in Brief*: "It became for him a kind of talisman: he carried it wherever he went, and read it so often that he came to know whole passages of it by heart . . . 'If you are acquainted with it,' he later told a friend, 'then you cannot imagine what an effect it can have upon a person.' "[4] And several memoirs by colleagues attest to his enthusiasm for Tolstoy's later writings in general, including the treatise *What Is Art?*, with some conclusions of which, Engelmann reports, Wittgenstein said he agreed.[5] While Tolstoy's importance for Wittgenstein has been acknowledged in the literature, most often that importance is relegated to Wittgenstein's supposed emulation of Tolstoy in his personal life and outlook. Representative of this view is Davison, who claims that "the root of Tolstoy's appeal for Wittgenstein lies in an essential

affinity of character and spirit which is reflected in some biographical similarities,"[6] such similarities including teaching in rural schools, forsaking family fortunes for a life of simplicity, and so on. While these biographical similarities are compelling (indeed, both Tolstoy and Wittgenstein are often viewed as leading somewhat "saintly" lives),[7] I think that Tolstoy's artistic and essayistic texts—his images, ideas, and thoughts—are far more deeply implicated in Wittgenstein's thought than has hitherto been acknowledged.[8] In this book I endeavor to show how a certain line of reasoning in Wittgenstein can be seen to be responding to problems mooted in Tolstoy's texts. In so doing I will show how Wittgenstein can elucidate Tolstoy, help us understand his theory of art and help us see how it ultimately fails. Moreover, enlisting further philosophical insights by Wittgenstein, I will develop a revisionary account of Tolstoy's idea of aesthetic expression that, I hope, will merit renewed consideration.

2. My reading of Tolstoy via Wittgenstein, however, also has a second aim. "Deconstruction," based on the philosophy of Jacques Derrida, has profoundly influenced literary theory and several generations of scholars in a wide variety of fields. While some scholars have argued for apparent affinities between Derrida's semiological critique of meaning and Wittgenstein's (later) philosophy, I join others who see that Wittgenstein can offer a powerful rebuttal to deconstructive arguments for meaning skepticism.[9] In the first chapter I lay out how such a Wittgensteinian rebuttal might look, drawing on its key move, the claim that there are instances of understanding that do *not* require an act of interpretation *qua* justification. That claim recurs in Tolstoy's later writings, literary and essayistic, and tracing it out in some detail in subsequent chapters reveals new insights into some of Tolstoy's best-known writings: *Anna Karenina*, *What Is Art?*, and *The Kreutzer Sonata*. We will also come to see how Tolstoy's study of Schopenhauer's philosophy raised a problem for his conception of immediate understanding in his aesthetic theory, and how, in trying to resolve it, he fell behind his own best insights. This in turn suggests how a revised aesthetic theory, modified in accordance with Wittgenstein's philosophy including his implicit criticism of Tolstoy, might be worth our renewed attention today. The final chapters of the book draw on lessons learned in previous chapters in order to situate a modified Tolstoyan aesthetic expressivism in the contexts of today's vigorous debate in philosophy of mind surrounding the philosophy of emotions in general and of moral emotions in particular, and the equally lively debate in philosophical aesthetics surrounding the nature of aesthetic expression.

3. This book is thus an extended essay and a reconstruction in several senses. *First*, it is a rational reconstruction of Tolstoy's thought, drawing on various texts he wrote in his later years. My general claim here is not that I am positivistically re-creating what Tolstoy was thinking when he put pen to paper.

Rather I am fashioning, from the materials of his texts and my understanding of Wittgenstein, a rationally compelling account I believe his texts can suggest to us. This endeavor in rational reconstruction is guided by the principle of charity towards Tolstoy's writings: trying to make sense out of them with a view to the reasonableness, coherence, and consistency of their author.[10]

Second, the first chapter is a rational reconstruction of two arguments by Derrida, which I lay alongside a similar argument by Saul Kripke in his influential reading of central passages in Wittgenstein's *Philosophical Investigations*. By construing Derrida's arguments in this context, I hope to bring out how Wittgenstein offers a telling refutation to them. Admirers of Derrida might claim that I have twisted the master to suit my purposes; my response is to request the same principle of charity that I bring to my readings.

Lastly, if I can show how to revise Tolstoy's aesthetic expressivism, then such a revised aesthetic theory would constitute a qualified reconstruction of Tolstoy in answer to Derrida-inspired deconstruction. Moreover, elaborating that reconstruction in the light of Wittgensteinian perspectives in contemporary debates surrounding emotion and aesthetic expression enhances its plausibility.

Plan of the Book

In chapter 1 I introduce the central line of inquiry through a critical presentation of what could be considered a platitude in contemporary literary theory: that any act of understanding (of a text, of spoken words, of a person) requires an act of interpretation *qua* justification. This platitude may be called the *interpretivist* assumption. What often follows this assumption is the conclusion of meaning skepticism, either in an epistemological vein (we can never be certain of having correctly or conclusively understood an expression's determinate meaning) or a metaphysical vein (there is no such thing as determinate meaning). I juxtapose arguments for this conclusion by Saul Kripke in his reading of Wittgenstein and by Jacques Derrida, and then show how their arguments for meaning skepticism can be construed as versions of one horn of a general dilemma (whose other horn is meaning Platonism) that issues once the interpretivist assumption has been made, by way of an alternative reading of Wittgenstein indebted to John McDowell. This alternative reading holds against the Cartesianism of the interpretivist assumption that there are instances of understanding that are *not* acts of interpretation, where one's understanding is immediate, non-inferential, and without recourse to what could be called a justification in any robust sense.

In chapter 2 I turn to Tolstoy at the time of his "spiritual crisis" and locate a similar notion of immediate, non-interpretive understanding at work in his novel *Anna Karenina*, specifically functioning within a larger frame of his avatar Levin's skepticism about the meaning of life. I here introduce a few thoughts from Wittgenstein in order to tease out how skepticism, understanding, and the will may be related in Tolstoy's novel.

In chapter 3 I interpret Tolstoy's major treatise on aesthetics, *What Is Art?*, to show how he develops this notion of immediate understanding into a central concept in his expressivist aesthetic theory: a successful work of art will "infect" immediately and universally its recipients with a distinct "feeling," and a good work of art will convey the right types of feelings, namely those that foster either Christian brotherhood or universal communion.

In chapter 4 I explore how Schopenhauer's ethical and aesthetic theories might inform Tolstoy's later writings. In doing so I unfold what I call the "Nietzschean threat" implicit in this model of ethico-aesthetic understanding, based on an interpretation of Schopenhauer's theory of the influence of music together with his theory of action and moral psychology. I conclude by showing how Tolstoy's theory in *What Is Art?* appears to be susceptible to this threat.

In chapter 5 I turn to the novella *The Kreutzer Sonata*, which Tolstoy wrote concomitantly with *What Is Art?*. I read the novella as Tolstoy's attempt to work out precisely the Nietzschean danger, that is, as an obstacle to the ethical ambitions Tolstoy has for his aesthetic theory. Here again some thoughts on ethics by Wittgenstein, themselves likely derived from his study of Schopenhauer, inform my discussion. I then return to the last chapter of *What Is Art?* and suggest that it was added to the treatise in an attempt by Tolstoy to avert the Nietzschean threat he had come to realize inhabited his aesthetic theory and its ethical aspirations. In order to guarantee the ethical aims of his aesthetic theory Tolstoy uses precisely the metaphor of rules as rails that he had criticized so savagely in his earlier writings, and the same metaphor that Wittgenstein famously uses to trope meaning Platonism. In so doing we see that Tolstoy ultimately falls behind his own best insights.

The final three chapters outline a reconstruction of Tolstoy's theory sufficient to constitute a viable alternative to "interpretist" accounts of aesthetic understanding that derive from Derridean principles. Such a reconstruction must negotiate three areas of vigorous debate: current controversies in the philosophy of emotions in general, and of moral emotions in particular, and debates about the nature of aesthetic expression. Chapter 6 identifies constraints on the ontology and epistemology of emotions from my earlier interpretations of Tolstoy's writings, and argues that a conception of central emotions as sui generis states inseparably composed of cognitive, conative, and affective (physiological, phenomenological and behavioral-dispositional) dimensions best fulfills those constraints. This view of emotions is defended against rival theories including non-cognitive "affect theory," which rest on causal accounts that cannot incorporate the intentionality and normativity of moral emotions.

Chapter 7 extends the examination of emotions to specifically moral emotions, and demonstrates that the amalgam account resolves a fundamental tension in metaethics between moral judgment as cognitive belief on the one hand, and motivating desire on the other. The chapter also argues that a "sensibility theory" of moral emotions best fulfills the epistemological constraint, as opposed to a purely causal-dispositional account or an overly cognitive inferentialist account. Lastly, the chapter provides an account of an individual's development of the cognitive dimension of moral emotions sufficient to explain how aesthetic experience might contribute to one's moral upbringing.

Chapter 8 locates a version of the causal-normative distinction within various theories in philosophical aesthetics surrounding the emotional expressiveness of artworks. Surprisingly, these debates reproduce some of the positions that were identified and evaluated in chapter 1 regarding meaning skepticism, so that it is possible to discern a theoretical account of an artwork's expression of emotion that parallels the account given of meaning and understanding at the outset of this study. In this way I intend to show that Tolstoy's theory, suitably reconstructed and developed, constitutes a viable position within these debates today. The book's conclusion unifies the arguments of the previous chapters in order to offer just such an account of aesthetic expressivism.

A Note on Texts, Translations, and Typographical Conventions

Whenever possible currently available English translations of the works discussed have been consulted and cited. English translations of Tolstoy's works have been checked against the Jubilee edition of his works,[11] and those of Schopenhauer and Wittgenstein against their respective collected works.[12] Unless otherwise noted, all translations are my own, and quotations of original Russian are rendered in a modified Library of Congress transliteration scheme.

In keeping with current philosophical conventions, reference to words will be made using quotation marks, while concepts will be indicated by the use of small caps. Thus "fear" refers to the word, while FEAR refers to the concept.

Chapter 1

Meaning Skepticism in Derrida and Wittgenstein

> Something surprising, a paradox, is a paradox only in a particular, as it were defective, surrounding. One needs to complete this surrounding in such a way that what looked like a paradox no longer seems one.
>
> —Wittgenstein

In this chapter I shall lay out some lines of argument and positions surrounding the question: what is it to understand or know the meaning of an expression? Reconstructions of certain arguments by Derrida and Wittgenstein regarding the role of *interpretation* in knowledge of meaning will ultimately prove to be crucial. Once we understand the lineaments and layout of thoughts in this region, we will better appreciate how Wittgenstein might help us to understand and evaluate Tolstoy's theory of aesthetic expression.

1. Suppose someone correctly understands the meaning of the expression "Add 2." Then such understanding naturally entails that, when that person is demonstrating her understanding and has enumerated, for instance, "996, 998, 1000," that she should next say, "1002," and that any other expression, such as "1004" or "zebra," would be an *error*, or a *misapplication* of the rule underlying how one is to apply the concept or rule ADD2. That is, it is natural to think that the understanding of "Add 2" has a normative reach, extending forward to numerals in the enumeration which have not yet, or perhaps ever, been actually spoken, and that to understand "Add 2" entails that, if one understands the meaning, then one's relevant behavior must accord with the rule of that expression's application. Such *normativity* of meaning seems to be essential to what it means to grasp or understand meaning. Our arithmetical example is clearly simply an illustration for a general requirement on understanding meaning; one manifests an understanding of "red," for instance, when one judges correctly, of red things before one, "this is red." But the arithmetical example possesses the virtue of simplicity: one's behavior must accord only with the relevant understanding, whereas in the case of a descriptive term like "red," correct accord requires not only

correctly understanding the meaning of the term, but also correctly perceiving the empirical world. (Compare someone who understands the meaning of "red" in terms of inferential relations, so knows that "this is red all over" is incompatible with "this is blue all over" and entails "this is colored," and so on, but who is color-blind and so cannot correctly identify red things.) So the arithmetical example brings to the fore the general link between understanding meaning and behavior that is correct or incorrect in relation to the meaning understood, that is, behavior that either does or does not accord with the meaning grasped.[1]

2. This normative relation between the meaning understood and the relevant behavior can be further specified by contrasting a merely *descriptive* or *causal* relation. Understanding meaning cannot consist simply in the *disposition* to behave in ways that accord with the meaning, for in that case it would be correct, rather than merely an anthropomorphizing indulgence, to attribute understanding of "Add 2" to an electronic calculator. Clearly the calculator can be described as performing addition, as tested by exercising its disposition to causally produce the next number in the series when "Add 2" is provided as input. But consider a case in which there is a glitch in the wiring, and the calculator malfunctions, always an empirical possibility. To even register that the machine is *mal*functioning, one must already have the idea of the correct performance, such that the actual, empirical, dispositional behavior can be seen to diverge from this normatively correct, expected behavior. In §§192–95 of *Philosophical Investigations*, Wittgenstein introduces the image of a super-rigid "machine-as-symbol" to capture this normative notion that the future applications of a word are already somehow determined, "in a mysterious sense—already *present*." But he notes that this machine-as-symbol is *not* any actual, empirical machine, for the latter could have moved differently, whereas the former, as it were by normative stipulation, cannot:

> But when we reflect that the machine could also have moved differently it may look as if the way it moves must be contained in the machine-as-symbol far more determinately than in the actual machine. As if it were not enough for the movements in question to be empirically determined in advance, but they to be really—in a mysterious sense—already *present*. And it is quite true: the movement of the machine-as-symbol is predetermined in a different sense from that in which the movement of any given actual machine is predetermined.[2]

Therefore the understanding of meaning cannot consist in actual dispositional facts about one's performance. A dispositional account of meaning may provide a *description* of performance, but it cannot provide a *justification* of performance, because a disposition is not something to which its exercises can be said to accord or not to accord.[3] The dispositional account cannot accommodate the normativity of meaning. As Wittgenstein states in §192, the dispositional account and the normative account constitute two different pictures of meaning; we get the idea of a super-rigid machine "as the result of the crossing of different pictures." His most memorable image of this crossing of different pictures occurs shortly thereafter, when he tropes normative *rules* as *rails*:

> Whence comes the idea that the beginning of a series is a visible section of rails invisibly laid to infinity? Well, we might imagine rails instead of a rule. And infinitely long rails corresponds to the unlimited application of a rule.[4]

We shall have occasion to encounter this image again in Tolstoy's later writings.

3. At this point in the dialectic we have specified an essentially normative aspect of grasping the meaning of an expression, namely grasping the normative reach of the expression, its correct application in appropriate circumstances. We have also argued that this normative relation cannot be captured by a purely causal or dispositional account of meaning, for such an account presupposes a normative account in the assumption that the disposition is functioning correctly. And now one is tempted to claim that it must be some kind of *occurrent* mental state in which meaning consists and which accounts for how one's behavior accords with the meaning. Thus I imagine a red image and consult it to determine whether a given object before me is red and thus warrants the predication "___ is red." Or I imagine the series of even integers up to the last numeral enumerated and imagine the next in order to determine the proper answer to "Add 2." Or I call up from memory the correct rule for performing an addition (e.g., placing them in a column, moving right to left, carrying digits as necessary, etc.) and use it to determine the correct sum, and so on. The occurrent mental state then, be it image, sensation, rule, or principle, constitutes a meaning fact, as it were, appeal to which justifies one's behavior as being in accord with the meaning of the expression in question.

4. And at this point, according to Kripke's reading of Wittgenstein, skepticism seems unavoidable, for the skeptic asks: when you advert to the rule of addition to justify your response to "Add 2" as correct, hence to justify that "Add 2" means addition, how do you know to reach for the rule of addition rather than some other rule, and moreover, a rule the application of which might accord with the rule of addition in all actual cases of "Add 2" which you've hitherto treated, but which diverges from the "Add 2" series in some future case?[5] For example, suppose another rule, call it QUADD2, which, like the

rule ADD2 for "Add 2," produces a series of numbers, say: 2, 4, 6, 8, . . . and so on, but which diverges at some point further along the series, a point past which you have never in fact thought of the series. Thus in all your behavior in response to the request "Add 2," your answers have accorded with *both* the rule ADD2 and the rule QUADD2. And therefore it is always possible that you have not understood the meaning of "Add 2," since all along you took it to mean QUADD2 rather than ADD2. But this *epistemic* skepticism in turn gives rise to *metaphysical* meaning skepticism.[6] No matter what mental state you invoke to justify your grasp of the meaning of an expression, it is always possible to interpret that mental state differently in the future. McDowell's exposition is especially lucid here:

> Whatever piece of mental furniture I cite, acquired by me as a result of my training in arithmetic, it is open to the skeptic to point out that my present performance keeps faith with it only on one interpretation of it, and other interpretations are possible. So it cannot constitute my understanding "plus" in such a way as to dictate the answer I give. Such a state of understanding would require not just the original item [in my mind] but also my having put the right interpretation on it. But what could constitute my having put the right interpretation on some mental item? And now the argument can evidently be repeated.[7]

The upshot of this argument is what Kripke calls Wittgenstein's "skeptical paradox": there is no fact of the matter that could constitute my having attached one rather than another meaning to "Add 2" or any other expression.[8]

5. There is a temptation to recoil from the skeptical paradox by asserting that there is a regression-stopper, a "final interpretation" that constitutes and justifies meaning, and lays down, objectively, the normative reach of meaning. In *The Blue Book* Wittgenstein gives voice to this temptation: "What one wants to say is: 'Every sign is capable of interpretation; but the *meaning* mustn't be capable of interpretation. It is the last interpretation.'"[9] And in *Philosophical Investigations* §218, as we saw, Wittgenstein captures this notion using the imagery of *rules* as *rails*, the image, for instance, of the arithmetical series that accords with "Add 2" running out to infinity (2, 4, 6, 8, and so on): "We might imagine rails instead of a rule. And infinitely long rails correspond to the unlimited application of a rule."[10] Contemporary philosophical parlance—for instance in mathematical realism—names this idea of an independent, objective fact of meaning "meaning Platonism."[11] David Pears provides a useful gloss: "The idea is that in all our operations with language we are really running on fixed rails laid down in reality before we even appeared on the scene. Attach a name to an object, and the intrinsic nature of the object will immediately take over complete control and determine the

correct use of the name on later occasions."[12] On the one hand, it captures the idea that there is an objectively correct normative standard of application of an expression with which one must accord if one understands the expression in question. On the other hand, it induces the skeptic to ask: how can such an infinitely applicable meaning be *present* in one's mind?

> "But I don't mean that what I do now (in grasping a sense) determines the future use *causally* and as a matter of experience, but that in a *queer* way, the use itself is already present."—But of course it is, "in *some* sense"! Really the only thing wrong with what you say is the expression, "in a queer way."[13]

The invocation of addition as a Platonic idea does not solve the skeptic's problem, for granted the objective existence of such an idea, the skeptic may still inquire: how do you know that your mind has grasped *that* idea, *that* particular rule? What constitutes your having grasped the Platonic idea ADD2 rather than the Platonic idea QUADD2? Thus, Kripke concludes: "for Wittgenstein, Platonism is largely an unhelpful evasion of the problem of how our finite minds can give rules that are supposed to apply to an infinity of cases. Platonic objects may be self-interpreting, or rather, they may need no interpretation; but ultimately there must be some mental entity involved that raises the sceptical problem."[14]

6. It is this conception of meaning as meaning Platonism which constitutes the target of Derrida's recognizably "deconstructive" arguments. In Husserl's *Logical Investigations*, Derrida claims to uncover a tacit "metaphysical presupposition": "the original self-giving evidence, the *present* or *presence* of sense to a full and primordial intuition" which he subsequently elaborates as "self-presence in consciousness—where 'consciousness' means nothing other than the possibility of self-presence of the present in the living present."[15] And in "Différance" Derrida equates intentional meaning (*vouloir-dire*) with self-awareness in consciousness:

> What does "consciousness" mean? Most often in the very form of "meaning" ["*vouloir-dire*"], consciousness in all its modifications is conceivable only as self-presence, a self-perception of presence. And what holds for consciousness also holds here for what is called subjective existence in general. Just as the category of subject is not and never has been conceivable without reference to presence as *hupokeimenon* or *ousia*, etc., so the subject as consciousness has never been able to be evinced otherwise than as self-presence.[16]

In *Limited, Inc.*, Derrida again locates his target in self-conscious intentional meaning as determined by what he calls the positive values "of an exhaustively definable context, of a free consciousness present to the totality of the operation [that is, open-ended application], of an absolutely meaningful speech [*vouloir-dire*] master of itself: the teleological jurisdiction of an entire field whose organizing center remains *intention*."[17] And in *Of Grammatology* he explicitly identifies *Cartesianism* as providing the basis for the idea that "the determination of absolute presence is constituted as self-presence, as subjectivity."[18] If to understand the meaning of a word is to know, in the Cartesian sense of intentional self-consciousness, the normative reach of the word, its correct usage in future applications, then Derrida's target would appear to be meaning Platonism transposed into a Cartesian model of self-consciousness. That model holds that the contents of one's mind are transparently available to introspection or "inner sense," so that the inner, mental realm is one of limpid self-knowledge, whereas across the Cartesian divide, knowledge of the external world via "outer sense" is always susceptible to skeptical doubt, since the deliverances of outer sense may be mistakenly identified, or misinterpreted.[19]

7. We can reconstruct arguments from Derrida's writings that target meaning Platonism on either side of the Cartesian divide and that in both cases lead to a skeptical paradox similar to Kripke's reading of Wittgenstein.[20] Derrida's arguments turn on "quasi-transcendental infrastructures," to use Rudolphe Gasché's helpful term,[21] which Derrida claims are both the conditions for the possibility of meaning and the conditions for the impossibility of meaning, where meaning is understood as meaning Platonism.

Quasi-transcendental infrastructure is Gasché's general term for differential relations which constitute the possibility of signification, that is, for a signifier to bear meaning. The classic locus for this way of thinking is Saussurean linguistics, where the meaning-bearing property of a phoneme is grounded in that phoneme's being different from but related to other phonemes that likewise thereby can bear meaning. Thus the phoneme /b/ in English is meaning-bearing because its differential relationships to other phonemes such as /p/ are minimally necessary to ground the semantic difference in the words "bat" and "pat." But the meaning-bearing possibility of /b/, according to Saussure and Derrida, resides wholly in its systematic (structural) differentiation from other phonemes. Derrida's move is to claim that any potentially meaning-bearing entity—phoneme, word, concept—likewise has as its condition of possibility its differential relationship to other potentially meaning-bearing entities of its type:

> In fact, even within so-called phonetic writing, the "graphic" signifier refers to the phoneme through a web of many dimensions which binds it, like all signifiers, to other written and oral signifiers, within a "total" system open, let us say, to all possible investments of sense. We must begin with the possibility of that total system. . . . Even

> before it is linked to incision, engraving, drawing, or the letter, to a signifier referring in general to a signifier signified by it, the concept of the *graphie* [unit of a possible graphic system] implies the framework of the *instituted trace*, as the possibility common to all systems of signification.[22]

The "trace"[23] is therefore the condition of possibility for "the play of signifying references that constitute language," "that is to say the origin of *meaning* in general."[24] Thus, whatever word (or concept) may be occurrently present to consciousness, its conditions of possibility include its differential relationships to other words (or concepts) *not* occurrently present to consciousness.

This understanding of the trace forms the basis of our first reconstructed deconstructive argument, which attacks meaning Platonism *within* Cartesian consciousness by arguing that such a conception of meaning could never be wholly epistemically accessible to such a consciousness. Since a necessary condition for signification is the given semantic item's differential relationship to other semantic items, those other items, although not present as the intentional content of one's self-awareness, are nonetheless somehow "present" through their very relatedness to the given semantic item which is the intentional content of one's self-awareness. Thus there is always a "supplement" or "remainder" that is not available to intentional consciousness and yet is necessary for its determinate, meaningful content. Moreover, Derrida claims that these differential relationships are themselves not intentional, not "motivated," and hence prior to while enabling of the purview of intentional consciousness. Determinate differential relationships are made possible by just this "possibility of the trace" or "arché-writing": "Difference by itself would be more 'originary,' but one would no longer be able to call it 'origin' or 'ground,' those notions belong essentially to the history of onto-theology [which understands being as presence], to the system functioning as the effacing of difference";[25] "it [arché-writing] is that very thing which cannot let itself be reduced to the form of *presence*."[26] Differentiality as such, as the condition for determinate differential relationships which themselves are conditions for determinate signification, Derrida calls *différance*:

> It is not the question of a constituted difference here, but rather, before all determination of the content, of the *pure* movement which produces difference. *The (pure) trace is différance* . . . Although it *does not exist*, although it is never a *being-present* outside of all plenitude, its possibility is by rights anterior to all that one calls sign (signified/signifier, content/expression, etc.), concept or operation, motor or sensory . . . [*différance*] founds the metaphysical opposition between the sensible and the intelligible, between the signifier and signified, expression and content, etc. If language were not already, in a sense, a writing, no derived "notation" would be possible; and the

> classical problem of relationships between speech and writing could not arise. Of course, the positive *sciences* of signification can only describe the *work* and the *fact* of différance, the determined differences and the determined presences that they make possible. There cannot be a science of différance itself in its operation, as it is impossible to have a science of the origin of presence itself, that is to say of a certain non-origin.[27]

The enabling but unmotivated operation of *différance*, anterior to intentional consciousness, Derrida calls *play*: "One could call *play* the absence of the transcendental signified as limitlessness of play, that is to say as the destruction of onto-theology and the metaphysics of presence. . . . The immotivation of the trace ought now to be understood as an operation and not as a state, as an active movement, a demotivation, and not as a given structure."[28]

This picture of the quasi-transcendental infrastructure as a necessary condition for signification in general justifies Derrida's next claim: that intentional consciousness, understood in the Cartesian model as an occurrent mental state fully accessible to the subject, cannot bring to awareness these differential relationships underlying the determinate meaning content of intentional consciousness:

> Différance is what makes the movement of signification possible only if each element that is said to be "present," appearing on the stage of presence, is related to something other than itself but retains the mark of a past element and already lets itself be hollowed out by the mark of its relation to a future element. This trace relates no less to what is called the future than to what is called the past, and it constitutes what is called the present by this very relation to what it is not, to what it absolutely is not; that is, not even to a past or future considered as a modified present.[29]
>
> The first consequence to be drawn from this is that the signified concept is never present in itself, in an adequate presence that would refer only to itself. Every concept is necessarily and essentially inscribed in a chain or a system, within which it refers to another and to other concepts, by the systematic play of differences.[30]

We have to be more careful here, for the argument as it stands is enthymematic, relying on a tacit assumption which Martin Stone has called the interpretivist premise: that to understand any semantic item (word, concept, etc.) requires *interpreting* it.[31] That is, our argument works only so long as we assume that to know or understand the intentional content (meaning) of one's occurrent mental state requires that one interpret that content as the (correct) meaning. Since the content can never, by Derrida's lights, be brought to complete ("absolute") self-presence in consciousness, it can never definitively be interpreted. Rather, *différance* ensures that once we try to interpret the semantic item under our mind's eye, we are liable to set off on a potentially infinite quest for the determinate differential relationships, "the indefinite drift of signs, as errance and change of scene, linking re-presentations one to another without beginning or end."[32] Therefore we can never absolutely, fully, know what we mean by any semantic item we entertain in consciousness, because the quasi-transcendental infrastructures that are a necessary condition for the possibility of meaning are likewise a condition for the impossibility of meaning (where meaning is understood as full presence to consciousness of determinate semantic content).[33]

We can now provide the reconstruction of this first deconstructive argument in more perspicuous form:

> 1. Assumption: to understand any semantic item (word, concept, etc.) is to interpret it.
> 2. A necessary condition for signification is the semantic item's differential relationship to other semantic items.
> 3. The differential relationship between these items entails that those other than the intentional content of consciousness are nonetheless "present" or implicated through their relatedness. Thus there is always a "supplement" or "remainder" that is not immediately available to intentional consciousness and yet is a necessary condition for it.
> 4. Therefore the supplement is a condition for both the possibility and impossibility of meaning (determinate intentional content).
> 5. Therefore interpretation is interminable, since the requirement of interpretation (premise 1) and the nature of meaning content (premise 3) entails the possibility of unending "drift" or "deferral" (*différance*).
> 6. Therefore there is no determinate meaning (skeptical paradox).[34]

8. This first reconstructed deconstructive argument is, however, liable to a telling objection, namely that the argument operates with conceptual materials that are not yet *sufficient* to speak of *meaning*, because these conceptual materials do not include the notion of the *normativity* of meaning. Derrida clearly asserts that at the level of *différance* and related infrastructures (mark, trace, spacing, supplement, remainder, etc.), such relations are not motivated, not bound by intentionality or any other normative constraint, and therefore they operate at a level below, as it were, the "bedrock" at which justifications for meaning come to an end: "If I have exhausted the justification I have reached bedrock, and my spade is turned. Then I am inclined to say: 'This is simply what I do.'"[35] The idea of the objection is to concede that differential relationships among semantic items are indeed necessary for meaning, but to

deny that they are sufficient: the notion of meaning comes into the picture only when the normative reach of the semantic item is taken on board, and such normative reach in turn constrains the claimed-for infinite deferral of sense. Since the possibility of such deferral does not allow the notion of *error* or *mistake* to play a role, that possibility operates below the level at which one can speak of meaning at all:

> Someone asks me: What is the colour of this flower? I answer: "red."—Are you absolutely sure? Yes, absolutely sure! But may I not have been deceived and called the wrong colour "red"? No. That certainty with which I call the colour "red" is the rigidity of my measuring-rod, it is the rigidity from which I start. When I give descriptions, *that* is not to be brought into doubt. This simply characterizes what we call describing.
>
> (I may of course even here assume a slip of the tongue, but nothing else.)
>
> Following according to the rule is FUNDAMENTAL to our language-game. It characterizes what we call description.[36]

The sign "red" and the concept RED are differentially distinct from related semantic items, like the signs "led" and "bed" and the concepts BLUE and YELLOW, but those differential constitutive relationships operate below the level of "rigidity"—normativity—that is definitive of meaning at all. Therefore the contingency or potentially open-ended network of differential relationships cannot ground meaning skepticism. An analogy may be helpful here. Consider a flat surface composed of regular squares, alternately light and dark colored, and a pile of variously shaped bits of wood. It is true that the squares of the flat surface and bits of wood are in part individuated—repeatedly recognizable—through their differences from other similarly typed entities. But this differential relationship cannot constitute the basis for raising skeptical doubts about whether these entities constitute the determinate game of chess, say, because a necessary feature of the game of chess—normative rules about how chess should be played—are not yet in view. The identity of a given bit of wood as a "bishop," say, already imports the idea of normativity (because "the bishop" is in part defined as that bit of wood that moves only diagonally, or has a value of three points, etc.). Hence if the skeptic asks, "Given that this bit of wood is individuated only in its differential contrast to differently shaped other bits of wood, what justification can you provide for claiming that it represents a bishop?", one can respond that the skeptic cannot use the term "bishop" without already presupposing the normative notions (what constitutes a correct and incorrect move in chess, for example) that answer his question: the bishop is that bit of wood that *may move like this but not like that.* Likewise Derrida's "semiological critique" of determinate meaning as self-presence to consciousness cannot reach upward to meaning, as it were, from the level at which the critique operates, because the critique lacks the conceptual resources to speak of meaning: normativity. If normativity—following according to the rule of an expression's application—is fundamental to meaning, then the differential relationships that operate below this normative "bedrock" of meaning cannot yet be considered meaningful, since they do not of themselves carry normative significance.

9. Although the first deconstructive argument fails to reach its conclusion of meaning skepticism, a second deconstructive argument explicitly addresses the normativity constraint inherent in the notion of meaning, in order to argue for meaning skepticism. This argument can be reconstructed from Derrida's *Limited, Inc.*, where he introduces another quasi-transcendental infrastructure, that of "iterability," meant to syncopate the notions of repeatability and alterity.[37] Derrida claims that the meaning of an expression must be at once identical, that is, repeatable across contexts, and different, that is, applicable to new contexts, since each context is (ever so slightly, perhaps) different. Therefore, when confronted with new circumstances, one must judge, that is, interpret, whether the expression correctly applies to those circumstances, in effect possibly extending the range of application of the item. Thus to know what "red" means is in effect to be able to apply "red" correctly to novel red things one encounters in future contexts. Thus the meaning of "red" and RED extends in an open-ended way to new circumstances of application in the future. Because of the logical possibility of novel circumstances of application, there can be no knowledge "of an exhaustively defined context, of a free consciousness present to the totality of the operation, and of absolutely meaningful speech [*vouloir-dire*]."[38] Derrida explains:

> Let us not forget that "iterability" does not signify simply . . . repeatability of the same, but rather alterability of this same idealized in the singularity of the event, for instance, in this or that speech act. It entails the necessity of thinking *at once* both the rule and the event, concept and singularity. There is thus a reapplication (without transparent self-reflection and without pure self-identity) of the *principle* of iterability to a *concept* of iterability that is never pure. There is no idealization without (identificatory) iterability; but for the same reason, for reasons of (altering) iterability, there is no idealization that keeps itself pure, safe from all contamination.[39]

Derrida inscribes within the structure of the expression representing a concept the conditions of its "normative reach": each application or recognition of a concept's use in principle necessarily requires the subject to interpret the concept, to decide whether it falls under the rule of its application. The condition that makes it possible for a concept to apply in novel circumstances is the same condition that makes the idea of a fixed, ideal meaning impossible. In other words, the application of a concept in part determines its meaning; since the former is in principle underdetermined vis-à-vis possible future circumstances, so too is the latter.[40] Derrida analyzes this underdetermination of meaning specifically in terms of the normativity of meaning: the meaning of an expression being underdetermined entails the possibility of misapplication, error, or mistake. This has dire consequences *only* if we think of meaning as "fixed" or "ideal": that if one knows the meaning of an expression, then one somehow already knows all the correct applications of the expression in a potentially infinite number of infinitely variable circumstances. The conclusion of meaning skepticism emerges from Derrida's claim that error—hence the elimination of fixed or ideal meaning—is "a necessary possibility"[41] inscribed into the nature of the expression by its iterability. To treat error and misunderstanding as only accidental, external to the expression's use, is precisely to presuppose a metaphysical-normative idealization of meaning, of a concept's application reaching out to all of its possible circumstances. Hence "the condition of the possibility of these effects [of meaning] is simultaneously . . . the condition of the impossibility of their rigorous purity," which succinctly names the deconstructive version of the skeptical paradox.[42]

We can understand the second reconstructed deconstructive argument as follows:

> 1. Assumption: to understand an expression is to interpret it.
> 2. Any expression possesses the property of *iterability*: both repeatable (capable of correct application) in new circumstances and alterable (capable of misapplication or radically new interpretation).[43]
> 3. Therefore the necessary conditions of possibility for the meaning of an expression are also the conditions for the impossibility (error, misapplication) of the meaning of an expression. The risk of misapplication and misunderstanding is a "necessary possibility" of meaning.[44]
> 4. Therefore there can be no infallible and full (i.e., Cartesian) understanding of intentional meaning.[45]
> 5. Therefore there is no determinate meaning (skeptical paradox).[46]

It is clear that once again Derrida's target is the form of meaning Platonism found in Husserl: full intentional self-presence of meaning, what he in *Limited, Inc.*, calls "absolutely meaningful speech [*vouloir-dire*]."[47] Wittgenstein's image of rules as rails is here rendered vulnerable, historical, contingent:

> To account for a certain stability (by essence always provisional and finite) is precisely not to speak of eternity or of absolute solidity; it is to take into account a historicity, a nonnaturalness, of ethics, of politics, or institutionality, etc. If recalling this is to put radically into

> question the stability of contexts, then, yes, I do that. I say that there is no stability that is absolute, eternal, intangible, natural, etc. But that is implied in the very concept of stability. A stability is not an immutability; it is by definition always destabilizable.[48]

In our first reconstructed deconstructive argument, we saw how Derrida endeavored to show how within the Cartesian mind, meaning as intentional self-consciousness is susceptible to the drift of *différance*, such that the Cartesian ego can never completely grasp the supposed meaning of an expression. In this second argument Derrida offers a critique from the other side of the Cartesian divide. The normative reach of an expression is in principle always, as a "structural possibility," vulnerable to misapplication, misunderstanding, radical reinterpretation, and so on. This possibility of normative failure exceeds the normative constraints of context, be they external (the circumstances of correct application can never be completely known or stated) or internal (the possibilities of failure or reinterpretation exceed one's intentional meaning [*vouloir-dire*]). While according to Derrida the philosophical tradition—including Austin in his theory of speech acts—relegates the possibility of mishap to accidental, or marginal or parasitical cases, Derrida claims that such possibility of mishap inheres in the very metaphysical structure of any expression in virtue of the infrastructures discussed above:

> In the description of the structure called "normal," "normative," "central," "ideal," this possibility [of misunderstanding] must be integrated as an *essential* possibility. The possibility cannot be treated as though it were a simple accident—marginal or parasitic.[49]
>
> The relation of "mis" (mis-understanding, mis-interpreting, for example) to that which is not "mis-," is not at all that of a general law to cases, but that of a *general possibility inscribed in* the structure of positivity, of normality, or the "standard." All that I recall is that this *structural possibility* must be taken into account when describing so-called ideal normality, or so-called just comprehension or interpretation, and this possibility can be neither *excluded nor opposed*. An entirely different logic is called for.[50]

Thus we can see that both of our reconstructed deconstructive arguments by Derrida for the skeptical paradox of meaning rely on a Saussurean construal of the "structure of the sign" together with the interpretivist assumption that understanding a sign, or any semantic item, *always* requires an act of interpretation.

10. Both Kripke and Derrida offer meaning-skeptical arguments that appear to conclude in versions of a skeptical paradox, that is, that there is no such

thing as determinate meaning, no fact of the matter as to what an expression means. We have also seen that their arguments commence from the tacit assumption that understanding the meaning of an expression requires interpreting the expression. We can now recast their thinking in the form of a dilemma: an argument that leads to an alternative between two false or undesirable conclusions.

Kripke's Dilemma

1. Assumption: understanding an expression requires interpreting the expression.
2. Problem: what fact constitutes my having given some expression (e.g., "plus") an interpretation with which only certain uses of it would conform?
3. First Horn of Dilemma = skeptical paradox. Any fact I identify as indicative of my having given some expression a determinate interpretation is itself susceptible to the skeptic's query: couldn't that fact be interpreted differently? If so, what makes my interpretation the right one? Result: regress of appeals to interpretation.
4. Second Horn of Dilemma = meaning Platonism. Understanding an expression is possessing an interpretation that cannot in turn be interpreted (a regression-stopper). The instruction one received in learning the expression guarantees the future use one makes of it, because to understand the expression is to know all its possible correct applications.

This presentation of Kripke's thinking brings out how the skeptical paradox and meaning Platonism are related, as possible responses to the problem generated by the skeptic once the assumption of understanding as interpretation is taken on board.[51]

Derrida's thinking also lends itself to presentation as a dilemma.

Derrida's Dilemma

1. Assumption: understanding an expression requires interpreting the expression.
2. Problem: any expression is part of a system of differential relationships with other expressions, and therefore in some sense refers to these other expressions. So what fact constitutes my having given the expression a determinate interpretation?
3. First Horn of Dilemma = skeptical paradox. The conditions of possibility of an expression being determinately meaningful are

> likewise conditions of impossibility of an expression's having a determinate meaning. Interpretation is potentially endless, and involves the essential possibility of normative failure (misunderstanding).
>
> 4. Second Horn of Dilemma = meaning Platonism. Understanding an expression is possessing an interpretation that cannot in turn be interpreted (a regression-stopper), an "ideal unity" of the expression's meaning present to intentional consciousness (Husserl's Cartesianism).

Here too this presentation emphasizes how meaning skepticism and meaning Platonism can be seen as two responses to the problem that emerges once we assume that to understand an expression is to interpret it.

11. It will prove valuable later, in section 4 of chapter 8, to note here that Kripke and Derrida diverge in their respective responses to the dilemma outlined above. To the "scepticial paradox" he reads in Wittgenstein Kripke offers what he calls a "sceptical solution." It is a sceptical solution because it "begins . . . by conceding that the sceptic's negative assertions are unanswerable."[52] That is, Kripke's solution accepts the metaphysical conclusion of the "sceptical paradox," that there is no such thing as a meaning fact, no truth-conditions for the meaning of an expression or the extension of a concept for an individual; hence "the sceptical solution does not allow us to speak of a single individual, considered by himself and in isolation, as ever meaning anything. . . . Wittgenstein holds, with the sceptic, that there is no fact as to whether I mean plus or quus [i.e., something like QUADD2] . . . if we suppose that facts, or truth conditions, are of the essence of meaningful assertion, it will follow from the skeptical conclusion that assertions that anyone ever means anything are meaningless."[53] Instead, to explain the normative reach of an expression or concept, Kripke holds we should invoke a weaker notion of justification or assertability conditions, roughly understood as the conditions under which a community of speakers would accept a given assertion of an expression or predication of a concept as acceptable. Kripke understands these assertability conditions to be the "inclinations" of the community to license or reject given utterances, and hence to accept or reject a potential member of the community:

> In fact, our actual community is (roughly) uniform in its practices with respect to addition. Any individual who claims to have mastered the concept of addition will be judged by the community to have done so if his particular responses agree with those of the community in enough cases, especially the simple ones. . . . An individual who passes such tests is admitted into the community as an adder; an individual who passes such tests in enough other cases is admitted as a normal speaker of the language and member of the community.

> Those who deviate are corrected and told (usually as children) that they have not grasped the concept of addition. One who is an incorrigible deviant in enough respects simply cannot participate in the life of the community and in communication.[54]

This is a descriptive account of the communal recognition of meaning, and it amounts to a communal form of the causal-dispositional account that Kripke rejected in the case of an individual's grasp of meaning. In effect, the normativity of meaning is now equated to whatever the community is inclined or disposed to accept; it is conceptually impossible, on this account, for the community to be wrong about the meaning of an expression. The position that Kripke attributes to Wittgenstein—the view of "Kripkenstein," as it were—accepts metaphysical meaning skepticism and elevates the dispositional account from the context of the individual to the context of the community; but just as a dispositional account fails to capture normativity for an individual's understanding of an expression, so too does the dispositional account fail to capture normativity for a community's understanding of an expression.

Derrida, on the other hand, embraces metaphysical meaning skepticism for its political potentialities. If meaning is fundamentally underdetermined, if there is no meaning fact as to what rule of application a concept has, or what the normative reach of an expression is, then it is always possible for conventions and institutions to radically change or be changed, for them to "invent" a new rule of application or alter the normative reach of an expression, for it is the "structural possibility" inscribed in the metaphysical nature of the sign, as he writes in *Limited, Inc.*

12. Presenting Kripke's and Derrida's arguments in the form of a dilemma focuses our attention on the assumption that gives rise to it, the assumption that understanding an expression necessarily involves interpreting the expression. It is this assumption which Wittgenstein interrogates in passages like the following:

> A rule stands there like a sign-post.—Does the sign-post leave no doubt open about the way to go? Does it shew which direction I am to take when I have passed it; whether along the road or the footpath or cross-country? But where is it said which way I am to follow it; whether in the direction of its finger or (e.g.) in the opposite one?—And if there were, not a single sign-post, but a chain of adjacent ones or of chalk marks on the ground—is there only *one* way of interpreting them?—So I can say, the sign-post does after all leave no room for doubt. Or rather: it sometimes leaves room for doubt and sometimes not. And now this is no longer a philosophical proposition, but an empirical one.[55]

In this passage Wittgenstein emphasizes precisely the questionable move that both Kripke and Derrida make, that of isolating and hypostatizing the semantic item (rule or expression) and then claiming that it has no intrinsic determinate meaning, is liable to multiple interpretations, a conclusion to which meaning Platonism can be seen to respond.[56] But both positions—meaning skepticism and meaning Platonism—issue from and in response to the interpretivist assumption. Wittgenstein develops the point further along in the *Philosophical Investigations*:

> "But how can a rule shew me what I have to do at *this* point? Whatever I do is, on some interpretation, in accord with the rule."—That is not what we ought to say, but rather: any interpretation still hangs in the air along with what it interprets, and cannot give it any support. Interpretations by themselves do not determine meaning.
>
> "Then can whatever I do be brought into accord with the rule?"—Let me ask this: what has the expression of a rule—say a sign-post—got to do with my actions? What sort of connexion is there here?—Well, perhaps this one: I have been trained to react to this sign in a particular way, and now I do so react to it.
>
> But that is only to give a causal connexion; to tell how it has come about that we now go by the sign-post; not what this going-by-the-sign really consists in. On the contrary; I have further indicated that a person goes by the sign-post only in so far as there exists a regular use of sign-posts, a custom.[57]

I take it that one of the things that Wittgenstein is doing here is objecting to the move by Kripke and Derrida of abstracting an expression from the practice in which it has normative significance and then, in the voice of the skeptic, to demand an account of the expression's normative significance when so isolated. Wittgenstein's response is that it is *only* in the context of that very practice, custom, institution that one can speak of normative significance in the first place:

> To obey a rule, to make a report, to give an order, to play a game of chess, are *customs* (uses, institutions).
>
> To understand a sentence means to understand a language. To understand a language means to be master of a technique.[58]

Wittgenstein is also careful to hold apart the *historical-causal* account of one's learning the technique from the *normative* account of the technique itself. Thus, in response to the skeptical question "why should you follow the sign-post in *this* way?" one is justified in providing a historical-casual account, namely, "That is the way my parents taught me" as well as a normative account, namely, "That is the correct way to follow signs around here (in our community)."[59]

Moreover, Wittgenstein in §199 acknowledges that any interpretation of an expression "still hangs in the air along with what it interprets," and cannot provide the kind of justification ("support") demanded by the skeptic. But rather than invoke a form of meaning Platonism which he has already savaged, Wittgenstein diagnoses the problem as emerging from the tacit assumption that to understand is to interpret:

> This was our paradox: no course of action could be determined by a rule, because every course of action can be made out to accord with the rule. The answer was: if everything can be made out to accord with the rule, then it can also be made out to conflict with it. And so there would be neither accord nor conflict here [i.e., the skeptical paradox].
>
> It can be seen that there is a misunderstanding here from the mere fact that in the course of our argument we give one interpretation after another; as if each one contented us for a moment, until we thought of yet another standing behind it. What this shews is that there is a way of grasping a rule which is *not* an *interpretation*, but which is exhibited in what we call "obeying the rule" and "going against it" in actual cases.
>
> Hence there is an inclination to say: every action according to the rule is an interpretation. But we ought to restrict the term "interpretation" to the substitution of one expression of the rule for another.[60]

Wittgenstein's diagnosis acknowledges *one* kind of legitimate use of "interpretation": "the substitution of one expression of the rule for another," where the alternative expressions of the rule function at the same level, so to speak, where the understanding of the rule is presupposed. Wittgenstein is challenging instead a notion of interpretation that as it were *justifies* or *grounds* the understanding of the rule in the first place (elsewhere he speaks of it as a "shadow" accompanying particular correct applications of the rule).[61] At this level, the level of bedrock, the interpretivist assumption is misplaced.[62]

13. The diagnoses of the dilemmas of Kripke and Derrida reveal their tacit assumption of the *interpretivist* premise that understanding an expression always requires the act of interpreting the expression. Adopting such an assumption leads to the two horns of the dilemma: meaning skepticism and meaning Platonism. Meaning skepticism draws the counterintuitive, paradoxical conclusion that meaning is indeterminate: there is no fact of the matter that justifies an expression's having a determinate meaning. Meaning Platonism halts the interpretive regress, but itself is stymied by an implicit *Cartesianism*: either meaning Platonism exists in some transcendent, supernatural world (Plato's heaven of the Forms) in which case it seems impossible to account for how we humans can grasp meanings (Kripke's response to

meaning Platonism), or *ex hypothesi* the human mind possesses such "ideal unities" but then confronts the "necessary possibility" that any actual utterance, or application of the meaning-entity, is liable to circumstances of failure (Derrida's response to Husserl's meaning Platonism).

Wittgenstein's solution to meaning skepticism as adumbrated here is to reject the interpretivist assumption, that is, to hold that there are cases of understanding the meaning of an expression that are *not* acts of interpretation or inference in the sense of justification. In this line of thought Wittgenstein had an unlikely literary predecessor: Leo Tolstoy, who at the height of his literary fame succumbed to a debilitating spiritual crisis prompted by radical skepticism.

Chapter 2

Tolstoy's Crisis: *Anna Karenina*

> "I noticed that he was out of humor." Is this a report about his behavior or his state of mind? . . . Both; not side-by-side, however, but about the one *via* the other.
>
> —Wittgenstein

1. We have seen in the previous chapter how *Cartesianism* and *interpretivism* lie at the heart of the reconstructed meaning-skeptical dilemmas whose horns are meaning Platonism (rules as rails) on the one hand, and the meaning skeptical paradox (there is no determinate meaning) on the other. This chapter will explore aspects of the problem of meaning skepticism as they are broached in several texts from the later period of Tolstoy's production, that is, around the time of his "crisis," the onset of which preceded by several years his beginning to write *Anna Karenina* and which he presented to the public in *A Confession*, and which scholars believe was at least in part triggered by his reading of Schopenhauer.[1] Tolstoy's thought about meaning and action, and their implications for aesthetic experience, developed throughout his long writing life and were more often expressed in literary than discursive works. Those thoughts, however, became more direct, and directly expressed, during and after his "spiritual crisis." For that reason, and because out of this crisis emerged the work with which we are principally concerned, *What Is Art?*, we shall consider works from the author's "late" period, beginning with *Anna Karenina*. While some scholars claim a full break between *Anna Karenina* and Tolstoy's later, overtly religious works, I shall trace certain conceptual and lexical characteristics in his later writings to their ostensible origin in *Anna Karenina*, and—in subsequent chapters—show how they are developed more fully in later texts such as *What Is Art?* and *The Kreutzer Sonata*.[2]

My general approach to Tolstoy's writings of this period derives both from the larger project of the book—to explore a set of problems common to him and Wittgenstein in the context of a critique of Derrida's meaning skepticism—and from a hint offered by Tolstoy himself. In a letter (April 23–26, 1876) to his friend Nikolai Strakhov, Tolstoy propounded his understanding of the unity and coherence of *Anna Karenina*, which was often perceived as consisting of two unrelated plots (Anna and Vronsky on the one hand, Kitty and Levin on the other) by its early critics.[3] In his letter Tolstoy spoke of "inner linkages" connecting scenes and chapters of the novel:

> In everything, almost everything that I have written, I have been guided by the need to collect thoughts that are linked between each other in order to express myself, but each thought expressed separately in words loses its meaning, is terribly coarsened, when it alone is separated from its linkage. That very linkage is created not by thought (it seems to me), but by something else, and to express the essence of that linkage directly in words is impossible; it is possible only indirectly, by describing images, actions, situations, in words.[4]

Several critics subsequently have explored this idea of "linkage" at the linguistic, symbolic, thematic, biographical, and serial-compositional levels.[5] I here undertake something similar, exploring such linkages, ranging from the lexical to the biographical levels, but *across* writings extending from *Anna Karenina* to *A Confession*, *Kreutzer Sonata*, and *What Is Art?* to the late tales. In his writings Tolstoy meditated and elaborated upon the same problems of existential importance to him, and so we find related topics, images, and *Denkfiguren* (thought-figures) recurring in the writings from this late period. A strand of an argument from *What Is Art?* will be embodied in a character or plotline in *Kreutzer Sonata*; Levin's solution to a problem will tacitly be revisited in *A Confession*, and so on. Tracing out and articulating these relationships will reveal more coherence and sustained consideration of the problem of meaning skepticism by Tolstoy than his readers have hitherto surmised.

2. Four years before Tolstoy began writing *Anna Karenina*, he succumbed to his infamous "spiritual crisis" on September 2, 1869, while traveling in the town of Arzamas, and perhaps precipitated by his reading of Schopenhauer that summer.[6] He became overcome by dread, terror, and melancholy at the prospect that life is in fact without meaning, and that all that awaited him was a senseless death. He arguably suffered such doubts later in his life as well, and certainly described the initial malaise in detail in his unfinished story, "The Memoirs of a Madman," which he began in 1884 and was published posthumously in 1912; we shall consider a specific linkage with this story later in the chapter. For now, it suffices to note that several aspects of that crisis are thematically treated in *Anna Karenina*: the conclusion that neither modern science nor unrevised church doctrine can provide a "guidance for life"; skepticism regarding the "meaning of life" and concomitant thoughts of suicide; the pernicious falsity of polite society; the relationship between sex and procreation in marriage, and so on.

One way of looking at the novel—one of the "inner linkages" of which Tolstoy spoke—is as a comparative portrayal of individuals' relationships to social mores. Indeed, the novel traverses the Cartesian divide between inner intentionality and outer behavior through implicitly comparative portraits of characters' interior mental lives—or lack thereof—and their outward social behavior, conceived as habits, codes, norms, roles, rules, and, as we shall later see, metaphorically as *rails*. For example, the narrator wryly describes the behavior of the Scherbatskys abroad in native/foreign permutations of the contingent relationship between inner attitude and outer behavior:

> The prince and princess held completely opposite views on life abroad. The princess found everything wonderful, and, despite her firm position in Russian society, made efforts abroad to resemble a European lady—which she was not, being a typical Russian lady—and therefore had to pretend [*pritvorialas'*], which was somewhat awkward for her. The prince, on the contrary, found everything foreign vile and European life a burden, and kept to his Russian habits [*privychki*] and deliberately tried to show himself as less of a European than he really was.[7]

Both characters' responses to European social mores involve forms of pretense, denying one's provenance in one case, exaggerating it in the other. And such possible pretense is of course entailed by the presupposed Cartesian divide: that one's mental states and motives may be completely divorced from one's observable behavior. Because the Scherbatskys' attitudes presuppose such social codes as completely contingently related to people's interior mental states and motives, those attitudes also tacitly reinforce Cartesianism rather than submitting it to critical scrutiny, as I will claim Tolstoy does. For after all, the Scherbatskys are minor secondary characters in the novel, and the narrator's presentation of the inner and outer lives of the main protagonists, as we shall see, proffers several different accounts which qualify, if not deny, the Cartesian divide.

3. We can start to explore this Cartesian territory through contrasting Tolstoy's portrayal of his primary characters. The narrator first introduces Oblonsky by way of his relationship to his moderately liberal newspaper:

> Stepan Arkadyich subscribed to and read a liberal paper, not an extreme one, but one with the tendency to which the majority held. And though neither science, nor art, nor politics itself interested him, he firmly held the same views on these subjects as the majority and his paper did, and changed them only when the majority did, or, rather, he did not change them, but they themselves changed imperceptibly in him.

> Stepan Arkadyich chose neither his tendency nor his views, but these tendencies and views came to him themselves, just as he did not choose the shape of a hat or a frock coat, but bought those that were in fashion. And for him, who lived in a certain society [*obshchestve*], and who required some mental activity such as usually develops with maturity, having views was as necessary [*neobkhodimo*] as having a hat. If there was a reason why he preferred the liberal tendency to the conservative one (also held to by many in his circle), it was not because he found the liberal tendency more sensible, but because it more closely suited his manner of life [*obraz zhizni*]. The liberal party said that everything was bad in Russia, and indeed Stepan Arkadyich had many debts and decidedly too little money. . . .
>
> And so the liberal tendency became a habit [*privychkoi*] with Stepan Arkadyich, and he liked his newspaper, as he liked a cigar after dinner, for the slight haze it produced in his head. He read the leading article, which explained that in our time it was quite needless to raise the cry that radicalism was threatening to swallow up all the conservative elements, and that it was the government's duty to take measures to crush the hydra of revolution; that, on the contrary, "in our opinion, the danger lies not in the imaginary hydra of revolution, but in a stubborn traditionalism that impedes progress," and so on.[8]

The fluidity of Oblonsky's character, derivative and expressive of the momentary reigning social opinions, reaches a delicious irony in his habitually espousing the liberal condemnation of habitual thinking. His lack of an interior life contrasts with Vronsky's more deliberative relationship to social custom and propriety, which nonetheless also functions within a structure of external behavior and internal self:

> In his soul he did not respect [his mother] and, without being aware of it, did not love her, though by the notions of the circle in which he lived, by his upbringing, he could not imagine to himself any other relation to his mother than one obedient and deferential in the highest degree, and the more outwardly obedient and deferential he was, the less he respected and loved her in his soul.[9]

It is precisely this structure of external, public behavior and internal, private motivation that leads to the skeptical interpretive questions articulated in the previous chapter. Moreover, outward behavior can exhibit a looping effect on intentionality: the norms of polite society (*svet*) not only permitted but encouraged Vronsky's seduction of Anna:

> He knew very well that in the eyes of Betsy and all society people he ran no risk of being ridiculous. He knew very well that for those

> people the role [*rol'*] of the unhappy lover of a young girl, or of a free woman generally, might be ridiculous; but the role [*rol'*] of a man who attached himself to a married woman and devoted his life to involving her in adultery at all costs, had something beautiful and grand about it and could never be ridiculous, and therefore, with a proud and gay smile playing under his moustache, he lowered the opera-glasses and looked at his cousin.[10]

> Vronsky's mother, on learning of his liaison [*sviaz'*], was pleased at first—both because nothing, to her mind, gave the ultimate finish to a brilliant young man as a connection [*sviaz'*] in high society, and because Anna, whom she had liked so much, who had talked so much about her son, was after all just like all other beautiful and decent women, to Countess Vronsky's mind.[11]

The imbrication of affair and polite society is reinforced at the lexical level: social connections and adulterous affairs are both called "liaisons" [*sviazi*].[12] And we can now see Vronsky's affair with Anna as an inversion of the valences of the external/internal structure: his problem is not the affair itself, whose external behavioral codes are implicitly sanctioned by polite society (for a heterosexual male, at any rate), but in investing it with internal, private motivation.

Conversely, Anna's husband Karenin allows himself to perceive only the external behavior in his confrontation with her and demands of her only that outward appearances be maintained:

> Despite all he had seen, Alexei Alexandrovich still did not allow himself to think of his wife's real situation. He saw only the external signs. He saw that she had behaved improperly and considered it his duty [*svoim dolgom*] to tell her so.
>
> . . .
>
> "But I demand that the outward conventions of propriety shall be observed until"—his voice trembled—"until I take measures to secure my honor and inform you of them."[13]

Thus Tolstoy exposes the structure of external/internal by cycling through its possible permutations in the men orbiting Anna, until they come to exchange roles—or perhaps "jump tracks" would better accord with the imagery—when Anna, on her sickbed, bids her husband to forgive Vronsky:

> After his conversation with Alexei Alexandrovich, Vronsky went out to the porch of the Karenins' house and stopped, hardly remembering where he was and where he had to go or drive. He felt himself shamed, humiliated, guilty and deprived of any possibility of washing away his humiliation. He felt himself knocked off of the track

> [*vybitym iz toi kolei*] he had been following so proudly and easily till then. All the habits and rules of his life [*privychki i ustavy ego zhizni*], which had seemed so firm, suddenly turned out to be false and inapplicable. The deceived husband, who till then had seemed a pathetic being, an accidental and somewhat comic hindrance to his happiness, had suddenly been summoned by her and raised to an awesome height, and on that height the husband appeared not wicked, not false, not ludicrous, but kind, simple and majestic. Vronsky could not but feel it. The roles [*roli*] had been suddenly exchanged. Vronsky felt Karenin's loftiness and his own abasement, Karenin's rightness and his own wrongness. He felt that the husband had been magnanimous even in his grief, while he had been mean and petty in his deceit.[14]

With this realization Vronsky resolves to commit suicide, but after the failed attempt falls back into his tracks, his "ruts":

> By this act he had washed himself, as it were, of the shame and humiliation he had felt previously. He could think calmly now of Alexei Alexandrovich. He recognized all his magnanimity and no longer felt himself humiliated. Besides, he fell back into the old rut of his life [*popal v prezhniuiu koleiu zhizni*]. He saw the possibility of looking people in the eye without shame and could live under the guidance of his habits [*rukovodstvuias' svoimi privychkami*].[15]

Here Tolstoy motivates the plot through a reversal of motivation in the structure: rather than internal (intentional) belief driving external behavior, it is rather a reappraisal of the external behavior (inversion of roles) that drives intentionality (Vronsky's shame and resulting resolve to kill himself). Of course this structure of external/internal, social code/private intentionality is not new to Tolstoy: indeed, it is one of the defining characteristics of the "society tale" genre of the 1820s and 1830s.[16] But Tolstoy combines the permutations this structure offers with realistic psychological descriptions of the consciousness of characters such that both extremes emerge and threaten autonomy: external roles, ruts, duties, customs devoid of intentional meaning—Karenin's fulfilling the requirements of officialdom—and intentionality collapsed upon itself, unable to realize itself in any socially recognized role—Karenina's final journey to the train station.

Several of the terms used in *Anna Karenina* to refer to codified behavior—*koleia*, *doroga*, *reil'*, and so on—either name or evoke railways, and readers have long interpreted the role of rails in the novel in relation to Tolstoy's criticism of railways, itself echoed by Levin[17], and which was widespread among Russian cultural conservatives at the time.[18] For our purposes the observation by Gary Jahn is particularly apt: "several particular qualities of the 'social' are suggested by the use of the railroad as its sign . . . The social involves rules and orderliness as suggested by the tracks along which the train must run and in the mechanical (that is, also, logical) nature of the object."[19] Even better, "rail" as social "rule" is in fact a *figura etymologica*: "rail" derives via Middle English ("reyle, raile") and Old French ("reille" ["iron rod"]) from Latin "regula" meaning "straight stick, rod, bar, pattern," itself related to "regere" ("to rule") and "rex" ("king"), from which comes "rule."[20] The connection between "rails" and "rules" is made explicit—together with the Cartesian picture underwriting it—at one point in the novel, when the narrator observes of Vronsky: "though the whole of Vronsky's inner life was filled with his passion, his external life rolled inalterably and irresistibly along the former, habitual rails [*po prezhnim, privychnym reil'sam*] of social and regimental connections [*sviazi*] and interests."[21]

One of the two other metaphorical uses of "rails" in Tolstoy's later writings (the last instance will be discussed in chapter 5) works within precisely the same Cartesian structure. The first-person narrative "The Memoirs of a Madman"[22] (written in 1884, but published only posthumously in 1912) strips the comic elements from Gogol's 1835 tale of the same title and artistically recapitulates the crisis that befell Tolstoy in Arzamas in 1869. The narrator, a wealthy landowner like Tolstoy, suffers acute attacks of what he calls "spiritual melancholy" (*dukhovnaia toska*): depression and mortal dread because his skepticism leads him to fear that life is meaningless and suicide the only reasonable response.[23] Only praying seems to help him, and eventually he comes to embrace the teachings of the Gospel and the lives of the saints, and undergoes the revelation "that the peasants, like ourselves, want to live, that they are human beings, our brothers, and sons of the Father as the Gospels say."[24] This conversion to universal love and Christian piety the narrator calls his "madness," presumably because this is what his fellow gentry landowners would term his conversion.[25]

But during the period after his first attack, which he quelled by praying without truly believing his words, and with the fear of a relapse hanging over him, he writes that "I had to live without stopping to think, and above all to live in my habitual conditions. As a schoolboy repeats a lesson learnt by heart without thinking, so I had to live to avoid falling under the power of that awful melancholy."[26] He develops the description of his survival strategy:

> I . . . continued to live as before, only with this difference, that I began to pray and went to church. As before—it seemed to me, but now I remember that it was not so—I lived on what had been previously begun. I continued to roll along the rails already laid down by my former strength [*prodolzhal katit'sia po prolozhennym prezhde reil'sam prezhnei siloi*], but I did not undertake anything new. And I took less part in those things I had previously begun. Everything seemed dull and I became pious. My wife noticed this and scolded and nagged me on account of it. But my anguish did not recur at home.[27]

Here, as with the earlier passage about Vronsky, external, fixed behavior is divorced from internal intentional states. Tolstoy deftly portrays the gradual conversion of the narrator in terms of his withdrawing his belief from one set of external behaviors (acquisitive landowner, traditional husband) and eventually investing it in another set of external behaviors. In the tale this motion is concretized by his first speaking his prayers without endorsing (believing in) them, to ultimately endorsing his prayers and certain religious texts, where that endorsement amounts to the commitment to change his life. The conceptual structure that allows the narrator's internal self to alienate itself from one set of outward behaviors and gradually find itself at home in a radically different set of outward behaviors is just the Cartesianism that invites meaning skepticism. It is also the same conceptual structure that we encounter at the very outset of the tale, when the post-conversion narrator tells us how he successfully evaded being certified as insane by a medical board:

> They disputed and finally decided that I was not insane—but they arrived at this decision only because during the examination I did my utmost to restrain myself and not give myself away. I did not speak out, because I am afraid of the lunatic asylum, where they would prevent me from doing my mad work. So they came to the conclusion that I am subject to hallucinations and something else, but am of sound mind.
>
> They came to that conclusion, but I myself know that I am mad.[28]

Skepticism about meaning issues from this kind of conceptual structure, the structure that allows the narrator of the story to believe himself quite mad (from the perspective of those who have not undergone the spiritual conversion he has), while also believing he had successfully deceived the doctors who examined him.

4. Besides exploring the ways in which outward behavior and internal mental states can diverge and affect each other in *Anna Karenina* as we have seen, Tolstoy deepens his analysis of Cartesianism in the novel by exploring ways in which the Cartesian divide is surpassed, and it is these explorations that move Tolstoy's novel from the realm of society tale into something closer to philosophy of mind and more properly Wittgensteinian concerns. I will show how Tolstoy illustrates at least four different ways in which inner and outer, mind and world are joined, thereby denying the absolutism of the Cartesian divide, which itself is presupposed by interpretivism. Therefore, this aspect of *Anna Karenina* prepares the way for Tolstoy's larger claims in later texts to the effect that aesthetic experience and understanding do not require interpretation. We can helpfully subdivide the four ways in which mind and world are joined along the following lines. In this section I will discuss two ways in which inner state and outer behavior are of a piece, where the emphasis

is on the manifestation or expression of mental states. In the next section I will examine the other two ways, where the emphasis is on the communication or intelligibility of one's mental states by others. Common to all these ways in which mental states or attitudes are manifested is the *lack of will*. Tolstoy consistently presents these forms of anti-Cartesianism as will-less expressions.

Let us once again turn to the very beginning of the novel, and the character of Oblonsky, for our entry into this problematic. Oblonsky's wife Dolly has just found a note indicating his infidelity and confronted him:

> What happened to him [Stepan Arkadyich Oblonsky] at that moment was what happens to people when they are unexpectedly caught in something very shameful. He had not managed to prepare his face for the position he found himself in with regard to his wife now that his guilt had been revealed. Instead of being offended, of denying, justifying, asking forgiveness, even remaining indifferent—any of which would have been better than what he did!—his face quite involuntarily [*sovershenno nevol'no*] ("reflexes of the brain," thought Stepan Arkadyich, who liked physiology) smiled all at once its habitual, kind and therefore stupid smile.
>
> That stupid smile he could not forgive himself. Seeing that smile, Dolly had winced as if from physical pain, burst with her typical vehemence into a torrent of cruel words, and rushed from the room. Since then she had refused to see her husband.[29]

This tragicomical scene owes much of its pathos to the drama playing across the canvas of the married couple's faces. Oblonsky's habitual facial reaction preempts, as it were, the formation of an intentional, purposive attitude towards his wife. This can be considered the obverse of pretense and pretending, where a person's outward behavior conceals her intentional state; both possibilities turn on the Cartesian divide. But Oblonsky's "stupid smile" is not intentional: it is a physiological "reflex of the brain," and occurs causally, not intentionally, hence not *normatively*.[30] Thus Oblonsky simultaneously rebukes himself for not expressing what he *should have expressed*. Moreover, the narrator in turn explains Oblonsky's involuntary action not simply in terms of physical causation, but in terms of customs or habits, typical of those who find themselves in such circumstances. The narrator likewise explains Dolly's action as habitual, as "her typical vehemence," but then metaphorically likens it to a physical-causal reaction: she "had winced as if from physical pain." There are thus two levels of involuntary expression described in this brief scene: physical-causal expressions (i.e., wincing in pain, reflexes of the brain) that are not susceptible to normative constraint, and habitual-customary expressions which are susceptible to normative constraint. Involuntary actions, responses, expressions, in short, involuntary behavior is the genus, of which there are at least two species: *physiological reflexes* (which occur according to causal-dispositional laws of nature), and *habitual behavior* (which occur according to second nature, that is, the inculcation of cultural dispositions). Early in the novel Tolstoy establishes that this problematic will also be essential for Levin, who on a visit to Moscow observes his half-brother engaged in argument with a well-known professor of philosophy:

> The professor was engaged in heated polemics with the materialists. Sergei Koznyshev had followed these polemics with interest and, after reading the professor's last article, had written him a letter with his objections; he had reproached the professor with making rather large concessions to the materialists. And the professor had come at once to talk it over. The discussion was about a fashionable question: is there a borderline between psychological and physiological phenomena in human activity, and where does it lie?
>
> . . .
>
> Levin had come across the articles they were discussing in magazines, and had read them, being interested in them as a development of the bases of natural science, familiar to him from his studies at the university, but he had never brought together these scientific conclusions about the animal origin of man, about reflexes, biology and sociology, with those questions about the meaning of life and death which lately had been coming more and more often to his mind.
>
> Listening to his brother's conversation with the professor, he noticed that they connected the scientific question with the inner, spiritual ones, several times almost touched upon them, but that each time they came close to what seemed to him the most important thing, they hastily retreated and dug deeper into the realm of fine distinctions, reservations, quotations, allusions, references to authorities, and he had difficulty understanding what they were talking about.[31]

We shall see later that Levin discovers his own solution to this problematic, but for now it suffices to establish the problematic—the delineation of the borderline between the physical and the intentional in one's mental life—and Tolstoy's exploration of it in terms of physical causation and habit formation.

There is a further distinction which Tolstoy draws, possibly in consideration of his reading of Schopenhauer. It appears that Tolstoy countenances psychophysical causation, in the sense that the unconscious or simply "excitement" (*volnenie*) or "feeling" (*chustvo*) can express itself involuntarily as well, most usually in contrast to "reason" (*razum*). Thus in part 6 of *Anna Karenina*, Sergei Ivanovich and Varenka embark on the pretense of mushroom picking in order to fulfill society's expectations that he shall propose to her, for he had reasoned that she was a good match, and she had tacitly encouraged such reasoning.[32] Each knows what is expected, and yet each, involuntarily, acts contrary to the expectations. Rather than maintaining the quiet decorum social etiquette requires, to give the suitor the chance to broach an intimate topic, Varenka "against her will, as if inadvertently [*no protiv svoei voli, kak budto nechaianno*]," continues to talk about mushrooms. Likewise Sergei "wanted to bring her back to her first words about her childhood; but, as if against his will [*kak by protiv voli svoei*], after being silent for awhile, he commented on her last word." The scene continues:

> He also repeated to himself the words in which he wished to express his proposal; but instead of those words, by some unexpected consideration that occurred to him [*po kakomu-to neozhidanno prishedshemu emu soobrasheniiu*], he suddenly asked: "And what is the difference between a white boletus and a birch boletus?"
>
> Varenka's lips trembled as she answered:
>
> "There's hardly any difference in the caps, but in the feet."
>
> As soon as these words were spoken, both he and she understood that the matter was ended, and that what was to have been said would not be said, and their excitement [*volnenie*], which had reached its highest point just before then, began to subside. . . .
>
> Varenka was both hurt and ashamed, but at the same time she had a sense of relief.
>
> On returning home and going through the arguments, Sergei Ivanovich found that his reasoning had been wrong [*chto on rassuzhdal nepravil'no*]. He could not betray the memory of Marie [his childhood love who had died].[33]

In this subtle study of psychology, both parties are in fact relieved not to have acted as their reason and conscious will had dictated, coming to recognize their unconscious, will-less[34] actions as in fact the authentic expressions of their unconscious. In this case their self-interpretations prove to be short-circuited by their actual expressions.[35]

5. We have sampled some instances where Tolstoy portrays a will-less expression of mental states which undercuts the Cartesian divide presupposed by interpretivism: expressions that are physically caused (such as blushing, wincing) and those that are habitual-cultural reactions. Such forms of involuntary expression undercut the supposed gulf from the mental realm of intentionality to the outer realm of observable behavior. Tolstoy likewise develops forms of will-less expression from the other side of the putative divide: instances or acts of immediate, will-less understanding of one character by another, and I submit that these forms of immediate, non-inferential, and will-less understanding in *Anna Karenina* constitute the germination of thoughts that will be more fully developed in *What Is Art?* (as we shall see in chapter 3).

Indeed, I would claim that such instances constitute one of the major "linkages" of the novel, connecting the two narratives of Anna and Vronsky on the one hand, and Kitty and Levin on the other, in an inverse relationship: for at the outset of the novel Anna and Vronsky experience immediate, involuntary mutual understanding, which subsequently deteriorates into misunderstanding, skeptical doubt, and (failed) interpretation, and likewise initially Kitty and Levin misread each other before eventually achieving that same immediate mutual understanding. This is how Tolstoy portrays the first encounter between Anna and Vronsky:

> In that brief glance Vronsky had time to notice the restrained animation that played over her face and fluttered between her shining eyes and the barely noticeable smile that curved her red lips. It was as if a surplus of something so overflowed her being that *it expressed itself beyond her will*, now in the brightness of her glance, now in her smile. She *deliberately* extinguished the light in her eyes, but *it shone against her will* in a barely noticeable smile.[36]

And when Anna and Vronsky meet again:

> Each time he spoke to Anna, her eyes flashed with a joyful light and a smile of happiness curved her red lips. She *seemed to be struggling with herself to keep these signs of joy from showing, yet they appeared on her face of themselves.* "But what about him?" Kitty looked at him and was horrified. What *portrayed itself so clearly* to Kitty in the mirror of Anna's face, she also saw in him. . . .
>
> And on Vronsky's face, always so firm and independent, she saw that expression of lostness and obedience that had so struck her, like the expression of an intelligent dog when it feels guilty.
>
> Anna smiled, and her smile passed over to him. She lapsed into thought, and he too would turn serious.[37]

And when Anna encounters Vronsky at the Moscow train station, "his first words involuntarily told her just what he thought."[38] Tolstoy's preferred term for the immediate understanding of another's mental state (feelings or thoughts) is "communion" (*obshchenie*), and the verb describing the act of such immediate (that is, non-interpreted, non-inferential), involuntary understanding is "to communicate itself" (*soobshchat'sia*). Here are some examples from Anna and Vronsky.

His perception of her shame:

> Shame at her spiritual nakedness weighed on her and communicated itself to him.[39]

His perception of her horror at being ostracized from polite society:

> "What happiness?" she said with loathing and horror, and her horror involuntarily communicated itself to him. [40]

But, precisely as their relationship deteriorates under the pressure of Anna's social ostracism, such involuntary "communications" begin to be *misunderstood, misinterpreted.*

Regarding news of her pregnancy:

> But she was mistaken in thinking that he understood the significance of the news as she, a woman, understood it. At this news he felt with tenfold force an attack of that strange feeling of loathing for someone that had been coming over him; but along with that he understood that the crisis he desired had now come, that it was no longer possible to conceal it from her husband and in one way or another this unnatural situation had to be broken up quickly. Besides that, her excitement [*volnenie*] communicated itself physically to him.[41]

And Vronsky's immediate perception of her anxiety (after her husband's denial of her petition for divorce), without however understanding the reason or justification for it:

> In her presence he had no will of his own: not knowing the reason for her anxiety, he already felt that this same anxiety had involuntarily communicated itself to him.[42]

Vronsky's relationship to his steeplechase horse, Frou-Frou, prefigures the fatal misunderstandings he will have with Anna, down to the lexical level:

> To Vronsky at least it seems that she [the horse] understood everything that he was feeling now as he looked at her. . . .
>
> The horse's excitement had communicated itself to Vronsky [*Volnenie loshadi soobshchilos' i Vronskomu*]; he felt the blood rushing to his heart and, like the horse, he wanted to move, to bite; it was both terrifying and joyful.[43]

Although Vronsky involuntarily and immediately understands Frou-Frou as easily as he does Anna, he will commit a fatal error in anticipating the horse's movement during a jump and break its back with dire consequences. An early symptom of fissures developing in Anna's and Vronsky's relationship is the emerging necessity for them to interpret or "read" each other's expressions:

> But she was not listening to his words, she was reading his thoughts in the expression of his face. She could not have known that his expression reflected the first thought that occurred to him—that a duel [with Karenin] was now inevitable. The thought of a duel had never entered her head and therefore she explained the momentary expression of sternness differently.[44]

This deterioration of mutual understanding finally leads to Anna's having to not only interpret, but *guess* the meaning of Vronsky's outward behavior:

> But the look that flashed in his eyes as he spoke those tender words was not only the cold, angry look of a persecuted and embittered man. She saw that look and correctly guessed its meaning.
>
> "If it is like this, it is a disaster!" said the look. It was a momentary impression, but she never forgot it.[45]

What these scenes suggest is, perhaps, that the failure of will-less immediate understanding is not the result of but the *condition for* the Cartesian divide. That is, something has to have gone wrong in our everyday concourse with each other for internal intentional states and outward appearance to diverge such that the specter of Cartesianism, and the interpretivism it entails, first arises.

Tolstoy devotes more attention to describing scenes of immediate, involuntary understanding between Kitty and Levin that inversely parallel the growing mistrust and misunderstandings—the incipient skepticism—between Anna and Vronsky.[46] Here too the verb of choice is "to communicate itself" (*soobshchat'sia*):

> She [Kitty] wrinkled her forehead, trying to understand. But as soon as he [Levin] began to explain, she understood.
>
> "I understand: you must find out what he's arguing for, what he loves, and then you can . . ."
>
> She had fully divined and expressed his poorly expressed thought. Levin smiled joyfully: so striking did he find the transition from an intricate, verbose argument with his brother and Pestsov to his laconic and clear, almost wordless, communication [*soobshcheniiu*] of the most complex thoughts.[47]

The crowning scene of their immediate and will-less mutual understanding occurs during their wedding ceremony. The church ceremony seems devoid of meaning for Levin, and his mind becomes closed in on itself, disconnected from the people and actions around him. Soon thereafter precisely Cartesian skeptical doubts arise in his mind:

> "But do I know her thoughts, her desires, her feelings?" some voice suddenly whispered to him. The smile vanished from his face as he fell to thinking. And suddenly a strange sensation came over him. He was possessed by fear and doubt, doubt of everything.[48]

The salving response is *not* a reasoned argument that proves such doubts unfounded, but rather the memory of her immediate understanding of his mind: "She told him that she loved him because she thoroughly understood him, that she knew what he must love and that all that he loved, all of it, was good."[49] As the wedding ceremony continues, both Kitty and Levin become confused and make errors in the rituals they are to follow. Although Kitty cannot understand the words of the benediction, "a smile of joy, which involuntarily communicated itself to everyone who looked at her, shone on her radiant face," and:

> Levin looked at her and was struck by the joyful glow of her face; and the feeling [*chuvstvo*] involuntarily communicated itself [*nevol'no soobshchilos'*] to him. He felt just as happy as she did. . . .
>
> The spark of joy that flared up in Kitty seemed to have communicated itself to everyone in the church. To Levin it seemed that both the priest and the deacon wanted to smile just as he did.[50]

The artificiality and obscurity of the church prayers elicit from both Kitty and Levin the will to interpret them and frustrates that will, whereas the happiness of Kitty is immediately involuntarily understood and shared by all those who see her, without any need to interpret her appearance or behavior. This is the third way in which the inner and outer of the Cartesian divide is preempted, as it were; and it is, *in nuce*, the role that Tolstoy will attribute to "genuine art" in *What Is Art?*, as we shall see in the next chapter.

In *Anna Karenina*, the form of immediate understanding and communication lexically marked by the verb "to communicate itself" (*soobshchat'sia*) is implicitly contrasted to another verb, "to infect" (*zarazhat'*), which constitutes the fourth and final way Cartesianism is denied in the novel, and which will be developed into a fundamental aesthetic concept in *What Is Art?*. Whereas "to communicate itself" seems restricted to cases where the perceiver immediately understands and shares the mental state of the person perceived, "to infect" refers to immediate social-physiological mimicry, either exemplified by or likened to the infectiousness of a yawn or laughter:

> And Betsy obviously tried to restrain herself but failed and burst into the infectious laughter [*tem zarazitel'nym smekhom*] of people who laugh rarely. "You'll have to ask them," she said through tears of laughter.

> "No, you're laughing," said Anna, also involuntarily infected with laughter [*tozhe nevol'no zarazivshaiasia smekhom*], "but I never could understand it. I don't understand the husband's role in it."[51]

> And Levin saw that [the peasant] Yegor was also in a rapturous state and intended to voice all his innermost feelings. "My life is so remarkable. Ever since I was little, I . . ." he began, his eyes shining, obviously infected [*zarazivshis'*] by Levin's rapture, just as people get infected by yawning [*tak zhe kak liudi zarazhaiutsia zevotoi*].[52]

And late in the novel, in part 6, "infectious laughter" becomes a virtual leitmotif of the minor comic character Veslovsky, the young, fat, gregarious nobleman accompanying Oblonsky who misfires his hunting rifle and chases peasant girls:

> Veslovsky began by being so naively upset and then laughed so good-naturedly that it was impossible not to laugh with him.[53]

> [Veslovsky] was sitting in the middle of the cottage, holding on with both hands to a bench from which a soldier, the brother of the mistress of the house, was pulling him by the slime-covered boots, and laughing his infectiously gay laugh [*smeialsia svoim zarazitel'no veselym smekhom*].[54]

> Stepan Arkadyich was saying something about the girl's freshness, comparing it to a fresh, just-shelled nut, and Veslovsky, laughing his infectious laugh [*smeias' svoim zarazitel'nym smekhom*], repeated something, probably what the muzhik had said to him.[55]

These uses of the verb "to infect" (*zarazhat'*) seem to signify simply a *causal* relation: involuntary mimicry that may not transmit any meaning content at all. That is, consider the paradigmatic cases of the "infectious" effect, yawning or laughing: the recipient may not think himself tired, or judge something to be funny, but the effect comes off nonetheless. As a causal relation, infection occurs will-lessly *not* because the will to interpret has been stilled, but simply because the will cannot be involved in the first place, the reaction is involuntary, and there is no normative relation possible. "To infect," therefore, seems to be the reception counterpart to the involuntary causal-physiological production we examined in the previous section: it occurs *regardless* of one's will, and is involuntary in that sense. But "to communicate itself" (*soobshchat'sia*) seems reserved for a more complex relation, for in the cases we have examined it occurs where one's skeptical doubts, one's will to interpret, has not been elicited, *although it could*. And whereas "infection" can come off in the absence of a particular mental state conveyed, what "communicates itself" is a distinct mental state, often a feeling or excitement, but also at times a thought or belief. And it appears that these distinct mental states are liable to the normative constraint elaborated earlier. It is in principle possible to be mistaken in what is communicated, or—as we saw with Vronsky and Anna—to understand the feeling conveyed but not understand its reason or motive. These distinctions will play an important role in our reading of subsequent works by Tolstoy.

6. In *Anna Karenina* Levin, like Tolstoy, seeks salvation from the metaphysical meaning skepticism attending the Cartesian structure. If his friends described Tolstoy as "the greatest of skeptics,"[56] we recall Levin confessing on the eve of his wedding, "My chief sin is doubt. I doubt everything and for the most part live in doubt."[57] Levin, who like Tolstoy "think[s] railways [*dorogi*] are useless,"[58] arrives, like Wittgenstein, at a "therapeutic solution"; he overcomes his crisis by quieting his *will* to pose the skeptical question after he experiences cases of understanding that do not require the step of interpretation between external behavior and internal intentional state, cases of immediate, will-less understanding, most famously when he and Kitty try to perform the code that institutionally consecrates their bond to each other during the wedding ceremony.

Unlike other characters in the novel, Levin embarks upon a wholly *individualistic* and indeed *nominalistic* relationship to rules and roles. That is, whereas other characters and their plotlines depend on the possibilities afforded by the internal/external, mental state/behavior structure, Levin and his plotline place the structure itself in question. Levin's increasing skepticism about the answers that nomological science and church doctrine offer to life's fundamental questions leads him finally both to reject codified roles and espouse a self-reflexive nominalism:

> "I see you are decidedly a reactionary."
>
> "Really, I've never thought about what I am. I am Konstantin Levin, nothing more."[59]

Levin's nominalism is rooted in his knowledge of "life" (as Tolstoy and his narrator would say) unconstrained by inappropriately applied universal laws or principles.[60] Thus in discussing "the peasants" (the collective noun *narod*) with his brother Sergei Ivanovich Koznyshev, Levin is easily brought into self-contradiction, which the narrator upholds as an indication of Levin's actual familiarity with peasants as individuals:

> If Konstantin Levin has been asked whether he loved the peasantry, he would have been quite at a loss to answer. He loved and did not love the peasantry, as he did people in general.

> . . .
>
> To say that he [Levin] knew them [the peasants] would be the same for him as to say that he knew people. He constantly observed and came to know all sorts of people, muzhik-people among them, whom he considered good and interesting people, and continually noticed new traits in them, changed his previous opinions and formed new ones. Sergei Ivanovich did the contrary. Just as he loved and praised country life in contrast to the life he did not love, so he loved the peasantry in contrast to the class of people he did not love, and so he knew the peasantry as something in contrast to people in general. In his methodical mind certain forms of peasant life acquired a clear shape, deduced in part from peasant life itself, but mainly from the contrast. He never changed his opinion about the peasantry or his sympathetic attitude towards them.
>
> In the disagreements that occurred between the brothers during their discussions of the peasantry, Sergei Ivanovich always defeated his brother, precisely because Sergei Ivanovich had definite notions about the peasantry, their character, properties and tastes; whereas Konstantin Levin had no definite and unchanging notions, so that in these arguments Konstantin was always caught contradicting himself.[61]

Levin's lack of "definite and unchanging" principles is accompanied by an ability to empathize with a conversational opponent:

> He had often felt that sometimes during an argument you would understand what your opponent loves, and suddenly come to love the same thing yourself, and agree all at once, and then all reasonings would fall away as superfluous; and sometimes it was the other way round: you would finally say what you yourself love, for the sake of which you are inventing your reasonings, and if you happened to say it well and sincerely, the opponent would suddenly agree and stop arguing. That was the very thing he wanted to say.[62]

In a related passage, where two zemstvo officials are trying to adjudicate between two mutually contradictory rumors about the emperor's position on a certain issue, that ability is given a name, *imagination*: "Levin tried to imagine a situation in which both utterances might have been made, and the conversation on that subject ceased."[63]

Levin's imagination is inversely related to, and ultimately becomes his salvational answer to, his skepticism. When he considers the then fashionable materialist doctrines of behavior Levin finds himself asking not only about their validity, but precisely about the *relationship between those doctrines and their espousers*:

> What amazed and upset him most of all was that the majority of people of his age and circle, who had replaced their former beliefs, as he had, with the same new beliefs as he had, did not see anything wrong with it and were perfectly calm and content. So that, besides the main question [namely, "If I do not accept the answers that Christianity gives to the questions of my life, then which answers do I accept?" and to which science is silent], Levin was tormented by other questions: Are these people sincere [*iskrenni*]? Are they not pretending [*pritvoriaiutsia*]?[64]

We can see Levin's thoughts and actions here as anticipations of two Wittgensteinian responses to metaphysical meaning skepticism. The *first* Wittgensteinian response in Levin's therapeutic solution lies in his inability to imagine a *sense* for the skeptical question, let alone its solution. The therapeutic solution consists in the discovery that the doubt is nonsensical because the logical form of the question is such that it is not clear what logically *could* satisfy it. This kind of dissolution of skepticism runs throughout Wittgenstein's writings, from early to late. In the *Tractatus* he writes:

> 6.51 Skepticism is *not* irrefutable, but obviously nonsensical, when it raises doubts where no question can be asked.
>
> For doubt can exist only where a question exists, a question only where an answer exists, and an answer only where something *can be said*.[65]

Wittgenstein is making an implicit distinction between the feeling or mental state of doubt and what might be called legitimate doubt, a doubt which admits of the *possibility* of expression and hence possible resolution: "If a question can be framed at all, it is also *possible* to answer it" (*Tractatus* 6.5). That is, a legitimate question will admit of a possible answer; the question itself will be part of an articulate conceptual structure that also articulates what an answer *would look like*, were there one. Such an answer may not be finitely decidable (Q: How many grains of sand exist in the universe?) but we understand what an answer satisfying that question would have to look like, because the question "lives" within a language game that makes sense to us (counting discrete physical entities). Wittgenstein, in the passage quoted above, also claims that what can count as an answer is related to what can be said. If it cannot be said, it is *nonsense*, in the Tractarian meaning of the term: a use of language that has no conceptual purchase. Hence, if there is no possible answer to the skeptic's question—if we can't imagine what a possible answer would look like—then the question is nonsense: there is no response to it that could be either true or false because the question makes no sense (Q: how many grains of sand are pious?). In the final year of his life, after he had abandoned the logical metaphysics of the *Tractatus* in favor of language games, Wittgenstein pondered the idealist's skeptical "How do I know the external world exists" and G. E. Moore's practical response, as he waved his hands before his face: "Here is one hand. And here is another." Wittgenstein's comment:

> The idealist's question would be something like: "What right have I to doubt the existence of my hands?" . . . But someone who asks such a question is overlooking the fact that a doubt about existence only works in a language-game. Hence, we should first have to ask: what would this doubt be like?, and we don't understand this straight off.[66]

Robert Fogelin provides this illuminating gloss:

> The difficulty with answering the skeptic's challenge . . . is that the reasons I give will never be any better than the claim that I am trying to defend. It is part of the skeptic's tactics to raise just such questions. But where doubt is wholly unrestricted, nothing can be cited to resolve it. Here claims to know or doubt will be out of place, useless, and thus, according to Wittgenstein, without meaning. We thus arrive at the position that meaningful doubts can be raised, questions asked, answers given, etc., only within the context of a language-game that gives these activities substance. The guile of the skeptic is to ask questions and to force others to give answers to them outside the context of a particular language-game. This, I believe, is Wittgenstein's fundamental response to skepticism.[67]

The "fluidity" (*tekuchest'*), as Lydia Ginzburg describes it,[68] of Levin's character includes his propensity to try to imagine how propositions might make sense. But precisely this ability delivers Levin from his skeptical crisis, for he comes to see that the skeptic's requests for the purpose of life or the meaning of the good, posed as such, are nonsensical, for he cannot imagine what a reasonable answer would even look like, and so he returns the question of meaning to its proper place, the community within which it is given:

> I sought an answer to my question. But the answer to my question could not come from thought, which is incommensurable with the question. The answer was given by life itself, in my knowledge of what is good and what is bad. And I did not acquire that knowledge through anything, it was given to me as it is to everyone, *given* because I could not take it from anywhere.[69]

Levin's skeptical doubt is not solved but *dissolved* by the realization that there is nothing which *could* solve his doubt, that radical skeptical doubt in fact makes no sense, is nonsensical, because it is *unimaginable* what sort of reason or justification could answer it.

The *second* Wittgensteinian response to the skeptic likewise glosses Levin here: to ask for ultimate grounds, final justifications of our language games (e.g., Levin's "what is the purpose of life?" and "what is good?") is to step out of the world we meaningfully share and to try to assume an impossible, nonexistent "sideways on" vantage point upon it *überhaupt*.[70] But, says Wittgenstein, "the *questions* that we raise and our *doubts* depend on the fact that some propositions are exempt from doubt, are like hinges on which those turn."[71] These hinges, our everyday, obvious commonplaces and practices are the "bedrock" beneath which we cannot go, not because they are metaphysically sacrosanct, but simply because they are the basic contingencies that constitute our communal practices. There is no adequate response to a question like "why does a sign-post point *that way* rather than another way?" other than "this is how it is with us."[72] We can question our common background beliefs and practices, but below the level of our shared sense of their necessity, we will find no fixed points.[73] This, I take it, is what Levin means when he says that these things cannot be known through reason, but that they are *given*. One can prepare oneself to accept what is given by endeavoring to still one's will to skepticism, which amounts to stilling one's *will to interpret*. Levin's experience of will-less, immediate understanding of Kitty's joy is paralleled by his learning to work in concert with the peasant mowers by extinguishing his thought and will:

> Levin lost all awareness of time and had no idea whether it was late or early. A change now began to take place in his work which gave him enormous pleasure. In the midst of his work moments came to him when he forgot what he was doing and began to feel light, and in those moments his swath came out as even as [the peasant leader] Titus's. But as soon as he remembered what he was doing and started trying to do better, he at once felt how hard the work was and the swath came out badly. . . .
>
> More and more often these moments of unconsciousness came, when it was possible for him not to think of what he was doing. The scythe cut by itself. These were happy moments. . . .
>
> The longer Levin mowed, the more often he felt those moments of oblivion during which it was no longer his arms that swung the scythe, but the scythe itself that lent motion to his whole body, full of life and conscious of itself, and, as if by magic, without a thought of it, the work got rightly and neatly done on its own. These were the most blissful moments.[74]

Here Levin learns as it were the virtue of allowing his awareness, his conscious thoughts and intentions, his will, to subside; without the self-awareness, self-interpretation, his willful handling of the scythe, the actions of his body merge with those of the peasants. In both cases—that of perceiving Kitty and that of joining the row of mowers—Levin must give up a will to interpret, to infer, and simply accept what is given. Tolstoy perhaps signals Levin's beginning to let go of the skeptical stance entailed by the Cartesian picture by resurrecting and revaluing the "linkage" in images—ruts, tracks, rails (literally "iron roads" in Russian)—hitherto used to trope the Cartesian divide between mind and world:

> Reasoning led him into doubt and kept him from seeing what he should and should not do. Yet when he did not think, but lived, he constantly felt in his soul the presence of an infallible judge who decided which of two possible actions was better and which was worse; and whenever he did not act as he should, he felt it at once.
>
> So he lived, not knowing and not seeing any possibility of knowing what he was and why he was living in the world, tormented by this ignorance to such a degree that he feared suicide, and at the same time firmly laying his own particular definite path [*svoiu osobennuiu, opredelenuiu dorogu*] in life.[75]

7. These Wittgensteinian insights suggest a brief reconsideration of Tolstoy's "spiritual crisis" and his portrayal of it in his autobiographical text, *A Confession* (1881), that is, that it be read as a particular instance of a more general process, namely skeptical doubts about rules and roles and their meaningfulness, as above. In the opening chapter of *A Confession* Tolstoy relates how a man came to lose his faith because, when posed the skeptical question of why he still practiced church rituals, he came to see that

> where he had thought faith to be had long been an empty place [*pustoe mesto*] and that the words he spoke, the signs of the cross and genuflections he made while standing in prayer are in essence meaningless actions [*bessmyslennie deistviia*]. Having recognized their meaninglessness, he could not continue them.[76]

And while Tolstoy offers a theological explanation for faith (faith gives an infinite meaning to the finite existence of man), he also offers an observation regarding "the poor, simple, uneducated people" (*narod*) which resonates with Wittgenstein's thought: "the superstitions of the believers of the laboring people [*narod*] were connected with their lives to such a degree that it was impossible to imagine [*predstavit' sebe*] their lives without these beliefs; they were a necessary condition of this way of life."[77] Tolstoy can give no rational justification for these beliefs nor for their interconnectedness with the life of these people, and for *that* reason he "found it easier to free myself from the temptation of idle theorizing [*prazdnoe umstvovanie*]." This is, in effect, again the therapeutic solution to the skeptical question, recognizing that the question is nonsensical. *A Confession* concludes with a very Wittgensteinian task: to "look and see," to examine each of the church doctrines separately and see whether it is meaningless,[78] or whether it plays a substantive role in his personal and communal life:

> While listening to the church services I paused at each word and whenever I could I gave it meaning. In the liturgy the most significant words for me were: "Love one another in unity." But further on I ignored the words: "We believe in the Father, the Son and the Holy Ghost," because I could not understand them.[79]

> I have no doubt that there is truth in the teachings, but I also have no doubt that there is falsehood in them too, and that I must discover what is true and what is false and separate one from the other. This is what I have set out to do.[80]

In this chapter I have explored how Levin came to grips with the skeptical crisis his creator underwent while writing the novel, and I have emphasized certain "linkages" between characters, plotlines, and lexical forms organized around lines of thought that anticipate Wittgenstein's writings. In particular, I located the phenomenon of will-less, immediate, non-inferential understanding at work in the novel, a phenomenon that arguably contributes essentially to Levin's coming to terms with his skepticism. Tolstoy developed this phenomenon into his sole criterion for distinguishing "genuine" art and the means for instilling religious and ethical values in the recipients of "good" art. It is to this remarkable aesthetic theory that we now turn.

Chapter 3

Tolstoy's Expressivist Aesthetic Theory: *What Is Art?*

> Every great artist carries us away, infects us [*steckt uns an*]. Everything in us which has the same kind of capacity stirs, and as we have an idea [*Vorstellung*] of greatness and a certain disposition for it, we quite easily imagine that the same seed is within us.
>
> —Goethe

> Philosophy can never do more than interpret and explain what is present and at hand; it can never do more than bring to the distinct, abstract knowledge of the faculty of reason the inner nature of the world which expresses itself intelligibly to everyone in the concrete, that is, as feeling.
>
> —Schopenhauer

In the previous chapter we examined how Tolstoy, in the midst of his "spiritual crisis," was developing somewhat inchoately the thought of immediate, involuntary understanding as a response to meaning skepticism, where such a response was also Levin's answer to skeptical doubts about the meaning of life altogether. In this chapter I turn to Tolstoy's subsequent development of this line of thought into a complete aesthetic theory in his treatise *What Is Art?*, which subtends his later writings. Tolstoy's aesthetic theory can be called expressivist, because it holds that an artwork conveys its sense directly, without the requirement for interpretation in the sense of justification or inferential warrant. Thus Tolstoy's *What Is Art?* is the counterpart in aesthetic theory to his anti-Cartesian, anti-interpretivist view of immediate understanding that we explored in *Anna Karenina*.

1. When Tolstoy succumbed to his crisis, he came to see the novels for which he was acclaimed, such as *War and Peace*, as "beautiful lies,"[1] and his subsequent works mark a radical departure in his poetics. His late works—tales

for children, parables, retellings of biblical and saints' lives, in short, what is conventionally called "wisdom literature"—eschews narrative, rhetorical, and literary complexity in favor of minimalist narration, overt sentiment, and moral didacticism. In one late proverb-tale, "Walk in the Light While There is Light" (1893), Tolstoy depicted the kind of reading experience these late works sought to create. The worldly first-century Roman Julius reads an excerpt—reproduced at length by Tolstoy in the tale itself—of the early Christian homiletic *Teaching of the Twelve Apostles*. Immediately following the excerpt the narrator continues:

> Long before he had read the manuscript to the end, something happened to Julius that often occurs to people with a sincere desire for truth who read a book, that is, someone else's thoughts; it happened that he entered with his soul into communion [*obshchenie*] with him who had inspired them [the thoughts]. He continued reading, anticipating what was coming, and not only was agreeing with the thoughts in the book but seemed to be expressing them himself.
>
> What happened to him was that ordinary phenomenon that goes unnoticed by us but which is also a mysterious and important phenomenon in life: that a so-called living person truly becomes alive when he enters into communion, uniting as one with so-called dead persons and living one life with them.
>
> Julius's soul united with him who had written and inspired these thoughts, and after this concourse he looked back on himself, on his life. And he himself, and his whole life appeared to him to be one horrible mistake.[2]

This "allegory of reading" stands out because of all it leaves out: there seems to be no interpretive step, no need for considered reflection on what the words, sentences, narrative might mean, no need to justify one reading against another. There is no risk of error, of misinterpretation, because, apparently, there is no conceptual possibility of divergence either between the author's psychological states and their externalization in the written text, or in turn between the written text and the reader's understanding of it. Thus there is no breach between intended meaning and understanding that threatens to widen into a more radical skepticism about meaning altogether. This account of aesthetic experience, which Tolstoy will define and defend in *What Is Art?*, can be called expressivist: on this account, the artwork immediately expresses or manifests its meaning which, when things go well, is understood immediately by its recipient. That is, in uncomplicated, default cases the meaning is not something separable and independent, to which the text is related contingently as for instance as an intermediary or evidence—precisely what would allow the skeptical wedge to be driven between authorial intentionality, text, and interpretation.

Tolstoy's theory has long been understood as a version of the *expression theory of art*, a tradition that arose with romanticism, in which the concept of expression usurps that of imitation.[3] The theory in general is identified with philosophies of art put forward by R. C. Collingwood, C. J. Ducasse, John Dewey, and others. The central claim of this theory is that an artwork should be understood as an expression of a psychological state, typically but not necessarily that of the artwork's creator. The psychological state may be cognitive (e.g., a belief or concept: in the language of the tradition, an "idea") or non-cognitive (e.g., a feeling, mood, emotion, etc.), and the means of expression may be indirect and hence require interpretation (e.g., a metaphor, symbol, image, or other rhetorical device). In this regard, then, Tolstoy's expressivism is a distinct species of the genus expression theory of art, since his theory apparently holds that the psychological state expressed in an artwork is an emotion, and that the expression is immediate, hence not requiring interpretation *qua* justification.[4] We will return to consider how Tolstoy's aesthetic expressivism, suitably modified in light of the argument of this book, might be defended and thus constitute a viable expression theory of art, in chapter 8. For now, all that my expressivism amounts to is the claim that there is a mode of understanding signs in which the sign directly manifests its meaning content, without the necessary recourse to an act of interpretation: an act where a reason or ground or justification is sought in taking the sign to have the meaning content it does. The event of communion (*obshchenie*)—a freighted concept, to which I shall return later—enabling the conveyance of thought and feeling, unencumbered by artifice or distracted by beauty, underlies the poetics of these late tales, and *What Is Art?* is their theoretical justification. The essay rejects all European aesthetic theories centered around the idea that art is defined as the representation or manifestation of beauty, in favor of an expressivist account of art's affective influence.

While some champions of Tolstoy have declared that his treatise "rejects the entire tradition of Western thought about literature and art," such a judgment implicitly and presumptively equates Western aesthetics—or indeed all aesthetics—with theories of beauty, ignoring alternate (still Western) traditions within and against an aesthetics of beauty.[5] One example of such an alternative tradition would be that inaugurated by Longinus, the sublime.[6] According to Longinus, the sublime is created by "intensity" (*deinosis*) rather than elaborate expression or imagery: he criticizes Aeschylus for language which is "turbid in formulation and confused in images rather than made of intensity."[7] Longinus further defines the sublime as the intensity of an innate "vehement and inspired passion" (8.1; compare 12.5) that inspires both orator and audience. Lastly, whereas rhetoric aims at persuasion and vivid description (1.4, 15.2), the sublime aims to "strike with passion, unhinge" (*ekpladzai*) (12.5, 15.2) the audience, a potentially disturbing consequence we will examine in Tolstoy in chapter 5. Longinian elements, including intensity, passion—"the transport and commotion of the soul" (20.2, ll.22–23)—and a communal ecstatic effect of art also underwrite Tolstoy's admittedly stylistically more modest theory of aesthetic affect. And equally important, these elements have returned in aesthetic theories after Tolstoy that are equally opposed to notions of beauty, representation, and interpretation, and whose genealogy is traced—usually by their detractors—to "Nietzscheanism" or "Dionysianism."[8] Examples might include Lyotard's championing of art's "communicable libido," its ability to release desire, over any misconceived expectation that art is supposed to "communicate the meaning of something to which it stands in a position of lack," or Susan Sontag's programmatic: "In place of a hermeneutics we need an erotics of art."[9] Tolstoy tries to contain such tendencies toward what I shall call a "Nietzschean threat" within his aesthetics. I shall turn to this danger in the next chapter, after we have a clearer idea of Tolstoy's expressivist aesthetic theory, for Tolstoy's views share the elements of the Longinian sublime outlined above, yet diverge from that tradition in locating the communal effect of art not in great thoughts, but in universal communitarian sentiment embedded in everyday life, for "good art" for Tolstoy is "one of the conditions of human life," bestowing "spiritual nourishment" (*dukhovnoe pytanie*) in strict analogy to food providing physical nourishment.[10] Such spiritual nourishment is embodied in art of two kinds: "universal art" conveys "the simplest everyday feelings of life, such as are accessible to everyone in the world," and "religious art" conveys "feelings coming from a religious consciousness of man's position in the world with regard to God and his neighbor."[11] Tolstoy thus maintains the eighteenth-century distinction between thought and sentiment espoused by his two greatest philosophical influences, Rousseau and Schopenhauer: for Tolstoy science communicates thoughts while art communicates feelings; science forges unity among people via rational discourse, art via affective sentiment.

2. Tolstoy presents his positive, normative theory of genuine art in two broad steps.[12] The first step is to define the activity of art as the conveyance of a feeling from author to recipients, by which they are united. The organizing trope of the effect of art as "a means of communion among people"[13] is "infection" (*zarazhenie*), which Tolstoy paronomastically plays off the word for "representation" (*izobrazhenie*). He stipulates:

> *To call up in oneself a feeling once experienced and, having called it up, to convey it by means of movements, lines, colors, sounds, images, expressed in words, so that others experience the same feeling—in this consists the activity of art. Art is that human activity which consists in one man's consciously conveying to others, by certain external signs, the feelings he has experienced, and in others being infected by those feelings and also experiencing them.*[14]

We should allow ourselves, I think, to be taken aback by the image of "infection," occurring as it does in a text written at a time when populations were decimated by consumption, and written by an author who had lost two of his three brothers to the disease.[15] Moreover, the term also perhaps suggested venereal disease; A. N. Wilson observes that Tolstoy's father might have died of syphilis, while during his son's student days in Kazan "three years of sleeping with prostitutes left Tolstoy infected with gonorrhea."[16] (I shall return to this aspect in chapter 5.) Tolstoy's metaphorical use of the term "infection" before his crisis had been confined to its usual negative connotations. For instance, in 1863, as his contribution to the bitter debate between the liberal "men of the forties" (Turgenev, Herzen, etc.) and the radical "men of the sixties" (Chernyshevsky, Dobrolyubov, etc.) that ensued following publication of Turgenev's *Fathers and Children* (1862), Tolstoy wrote the play *An Infected Family* which, like Turgenev's novel, presented a generational conflict inflamed by the "infectious" infiltration by an outsider espousing ideas reminiscent of Chernyshevsky's radical novel *What Is to Be Done?*.

Returning to the treatise, we find that Tolstoy's definition clearly is a *pragmatic* one:[17] the criterion of genuine art is infection of feeling, so whatever factually proves to be infectious of a feeling—to be explored below—will *thereby* qualify as a genuine artwork. Tolstoy does not shy away from the consequence that objects not traditionally considered to be artworks, but which belong to "the entire human activity that conveys feelings," will now be considered artworks:

> The whole of human life is filled with works of art of various kinds, from lullabies, jokes, mimicry, home decoration, clothing, utensils, to church services and solemn processions. All this is the activity of art.[18]

The subsequent properties of art that Tolstoy delineates serve to explain art's infectiousness: the organic unity of form and content,[19] the sincerity of the author (sometimes Tolstoy speaks of the sincerity of the work, or of "sincere [*istinnoe*] art"), the particularity and clarity of the feeling conveyed,[20] and so on. Those works that possess these properties to the highest degree will most fulfill the criterion of universal infectiousness, which is likened, as it was in *Anna Karenina*, to infectious laughter, tears, and yawns: "The tears, the laughter of a Chinese will infect me in just the same way as the tears and laughter of a Russian, as will painting and music, or a work of poetry if it is translated into a language I understand."[21] In fact, here Tolstoy seems to claim that universality of infectiousness is not only a necessary, but a sufficient condition, for genuine art: "Great works of art are great *only* because they are accessible and comprehensible to everyone."[22]

The examples of successful, infectious art that Tolstoy presents, often in gleeful juxtaposition to famous but by his criterion failed works by Beethoven, Balzac, Huysmans, Ibsen, and others, entail certain problems.

Tolstoy's examples include (1) peasant women singing a wedding song that lifts his despondent mood;[23] (2) an anonymous tale in a children's magazine of a mother's love for her children which concludes with a proverb; (3) a genre painting by the English painter Langley "depicting a wandering beggar boy who has apparently been asked in by a woman who feels sorry for him"; (4) and a shamanistic performance by a Siberian hunter-gatherer people, the Vogul, depicting a bow hunter wounding a calf, who clings to its protective mother, while the hunter prepares to strike again, so that "one hears deep sighs and even weeping" in the audience.[24] Certain technical problems suggest themselves. Tolstoy repeatedly claims that the artist's feeling is what is conveyed,[25] but it is possible that the first and fourth examples were not in fact produced by a single artist, or that the process of composition was extended over several people, or indeed even generations. This suggests that there may not need to be a single feeling, a single mental state, as the causal origin of the artwork: rather, the feeling conveyed may itself be a product, rather than producer, of the artwork. Recent work in the expression theory of art has sought to address this problem by postulating a persona manifested by the expressive qualities of the artwork, such that this persona, and not necessarily the factual artist (if there is one), is the locus of the mental state expressed by the artwork.[26]

Tolstoy's theory is liable to a different kind of scrutiny when one observes that all the examples are specifically *gendered* along the lines of a mother-child relation: the peasant women's song celebrates an anticipated wedding and new family, while the other three explicitly portray a motherly figure caring for a child. Figures of motherly protectiveness and nurturing link up with the network of analogies between art and nourishment remarked earlier. In these *mise-en-abîme* examples, the individual artworks as it were themselves depict the overall role that Tolstoy ordains for genuine art, for those in the upper classes who have lost the capacity to be infected "live without the softening, fertilizing effect of art."[27] This network of images reaches its culmination in an extended, Homeric simile in chapter 18, in which genuine art is likened to a fertile wife and mother, while "counterfeit art, like a prostitute" produces "the corruption of man, the insatiability of pleasures, the weakness of man's spiritual force."[28] I shall return to examine the simile in detail in chapter 5.

These examples are all the more problematic because at this stage in Tolstoy's presentation of his theory, which I've called his first step, he explicitly denies that the *content* of the feeling conveyed has any bearing on infectiousness as the criterion of genuine art. In his initial definition of art he writes: "Feelings, the most diverse, very strong and very weak, very significant and very worthless, very bad and very good, if only they infect the reader, the spectator, the listener, constitute the subject of art."[29] And as he nears the conclusion of this first step in his presentation, he repeatedly maintains what could be called the *content-indifferentism* of genuine art:

> *The stronger the infection, the better the art is as art, regardless of its content—that is, independently of the worth of the feelings it conveys.*[30]

> [Sincerity, particularity, clarity of the feeling] are the three conditions the presence of which distinguishes art from artistic counterfeits and at the same time determines the worth of any work of art regardless of its content.[31]

Clearly artworks conveying feelings of misery, horror, loathing, murderous (matricidal, infanticidal, say) rage and so on, could qualify as genuine artworks as easily as the examples of pity, joy, and motherly succor. The criterion of genuine art is for Tolstoy categorically amoral.

3. This brings us to Tolstoy's second step in his exposition, in which he provides criteria for the evaluation of the content of artworks, the specific feelings they convey.[32] Those criteria are explicitly ethical, and form a "linkage" with Levin's conversion during the ring-exchanging ceremony with Kitty in *Anna Karenina*. Levin finds that it is Kitty's attitude towards him and the situation, rather than the words of the prayers, that is meaningful. And on subsequent occasions Levin surprises himself in finding prayers and oaths meaningful not independently of his attitude towards the words, but precisely because of his attitude towards them. For instance, "during the time of his wife's confinement an extraordinary thing had happened to him. He, the unbeliever, had begun to pray, and in the moment of praying he had believed. But that moment had passed, and he was unable to give any place in his life to the state of mind he had been in then." [33] Likewise, when he is swearing allegiance to the Governor in church he is genuinely moved by the experience.[34] Levin utters words and performs rituals, but only on certain occasions does he find them infused with significance; the outward performance is unchanged, but his *attitude* towards the words, their audience, his actions and their effects, is completely different.[35] In the final words of the novel, Levin, having therapeutically stilled his skepticism about the meaning of life by the realization that the doubt was, like the question, nonsensical,[36] concludes that it his precisely his attitude, not his reason, which dissolves the doubt. Outwardly his behavior will appear unchanged, though in actuality all has changed because now imbued with ethical significance by his attitude: "I'll fail in the same way to understand with my reason [*razumom*] why I pray, and yet I will pray—but for my life now, my whole life, regardless of all that may happen to me, every minute of it, is not only not meaningless [*bessmyslenna*], as it was before, but has the indubitable meaning of the good [*nesomnennyi smysl dobra*], which it is in my power to put into it!"[37] Wittgenstein comes to a similar conclusion at the end of the *Tractatus:*

6.41 The sense of the world must lie outside the world. In the world everything is as it is, and everything happens as it does happen: *in* it no value exists—and if it did exist, it would have no value.

If there is any value that does have value, it must lie outside the whole sphere of what happens and is the case. For all that happens and is the case is accidental.

What makes it non-accidental cannot lie *within* the world, since it if did it would itself be accidental.

It must lie outside the world.

. . .

6.43 If the good or bad exercise of the will does alter the world, it can alter only the limits of the world, not the facts–not what can be expressed by means of language.

In short the effect must be that it becomes an altogether different world. It must, so to speak, wax or wane as a whole.

The world of the happy man is a different one from that of the unhappy man.

Values, like the Kantian "good will," are not facts of the world, otherwise they would be contingent, accidental, as are all empirical facts; and Levin too insists that the good, what confers sense upon the world, exists independently of whatever contingently might happen to him within the world. As Robert Fogelin puts it: "Wittgenstein takes essentially the same approach [as Kant] to problems of logic and problems of value. Neither concerns the merely contingent; instead they concern necessary structures within which contingency obtains. In the Kantian sense, both logic (6.13) and ethics (6.421) are *transcendental*."[38]

Tolstoy takes up this thought again when he turns to the task of distinguishing good and bad art in *What Is Art?*:

> The appreciation of the merits of art—that is, of the feelings it conveys—depends on people's understanding of the meaning of life, on what they see as good and evil in life. Good and evil in life are determined by what are called religions.[39]

Tolstoy has a Rousseauistic Enlightenment story at hand, in which mankind advances by developing better—that is, more beneficial to all mankind[40]—feelings and sentiments which constitute an age's "religious consciousness," a potentiality present in all the age's people, but demonstrated in specific leaders who express or manifest this advanced "meaning of life,"[41] religious consciousness as the awareness of good and evil. And, as we saw in Levin's conversion, in *What Is Art?* Tolstoy holds that the good is not determinable by reason or thought, but is transcendental:

> The good is the eternal, the highest aim of our life. No matter how we understand the good, our life is nothing else than a striving towards the good—that is, towards God.
>
> The good is indeed a fundamental understanding [*poniatie*],[42] which metaphysically constitutes the essence of our consciousness, an understanding undefinable by reason.
>
> The good is that which no one can define, but which defines everything else.[43]

If we read this passage over the shoulder of Wittgenstein, we find a powerful theory. The meaning of life, the good, is a certain ethical attitude that pervades one's consciousness, that is, it is not something in the world, but *how* one views the world, hence it transcendentally defines everything in the world. This attitude is thus a feeling, not susceptible to reason or thought, inexpressible in the language of natural science. The improvement of mankind thus depends *not* on rationality or reason, but rather on feeling, which is disseminated by genuine, that is, infectious artworks. Thus "it is this religious consciousness that determines the worth of the feelings conveyed by art," "good art, conveying good feelings, and bad art, conveying wicked feelings."[44]

Tolstoy understands the religious consciousness of his age to be the Christian principles portrayed in the Gospels: "the consciousness of the fact that our good, material and spiritual, individual and general, temporal and eternal, consists in the brotherly life of all people, in our union of love with each other."[45] The purpose of this religious consciousness is to unite all people, and according to Tolstoy there are only two kinds of feelings capable of such influence, and therefore there may be only two types of good art: *religious art*, "which conveys feelings from a religious consciousness of man's position in the world with regard to God and his neighbor," and *universal art*, "which conveys the simplest everyday feelings of life, such as are accessible to everyone in the world. Only these two kinds of art can be considered good art in our time."[46]

By its own logic and rhetorical organization, *What Is Art?* concludes with chapter 19, a passionate manifesto announcing the impending art of the future, when art will become "a means of transferring Christian religious consciousness from the realm of mind and reason to the realm of feeling, thereby bring people closer, in practice, in life itself, to the perfection and unity indicated to them by religious consciousness."[47] That Tolstoy, after working on the treatise for fifteen years, nonetheless felt compelled to add a final chapter in an altogether different voice, is a topic for chapter 5.

4. Now that we have presented the rudiments of Tolstoy's theory with some helpful elaboration from Wittgenstein, let us turn to a critical examination of Tolstoy's views. An initial worry is whether all instances of the infection of "feeling" via an artwork are liable to immediate, non-inferential understanding, for recall that this is Tolstoy's main point in the treatise. He has taken the cases of immediate "communication" of feeling in *Anna Karenina* and developed them into a full-blown normative theory of art. A likely worry to be broached in our age of "the hermeneutics of suspicion" is whether artworks necessarily require interpretation to be understood. And if that is so, then meaning skepticism reappears, for how can one be sure one has the proper, intended meaning (feeling), or that there even *is* a proper intended meaning (feeling)?

Wittgenstein returned to this line of inquiry throughout his writings, from his notebooks leading to the *Tractatus* up through the *Philosophical Investigations* and his later writings.[48] Interpretation, justified inference, and the skeptical questions it can spawn presuppose a distinction between some sort of uninterpreted given on the one hand, and the interpretation or understanding of that given after the act of interpretation, on the other.[49] Wittgenstein again and again explores experiences where such a distinction is not present. Wittgenstein's paradigmatic example of this phenomenon is our reaction to a face:

> "We *see* emotion."—As opposed to what?—We do not see facial contortions and make inferences from them (like a doctor framing a diagnosis) to joy, grief, boredom. We describe a face immediately as sad, radiant, bored, even when we are unable to give any other description of the features.—Grief, one would like to say, is personified in the face.
>
> This belongs to the concept of emotion.[50]

Here Wittgenstein is suggesting that perceptual experiences of emotion regularly occur without the step of interpretation or inference, experiences where understanding is immediate and where there is no separation between a given (sense impression, sense datum, "raw sense data," etc.) and its interpretation. It is not the case that we see a particular face and then interpret its expression as being joyful or sad: rather we see directly a happy or a sad face. The grammar of "a face having an expression" leads us astray; rather, according to Wittgenstein, we should use the verb "express" *transitively* in such cases—the face *expresses* joy or sadness—because the face and its expression are not two separable elements requiring a mediating interpretation, but rather one experience of immediate understanding.[51] "My attitude towards him is an attitude towards a soul. I am not of the *opinion* [or belief] that he has a soul"[52]–where an opinion would require justification–because "the face is the soul of the body."[53]

What Wittgenstein is denying here is a version of the Cartesian divide, here between *intransitive* expressive qualities on the one hand, and a *transitive* expression of a psychological state on the other or, as Alan Tormey puts it, between a "ϕ expression" and an "expression of ϕ." In the example that has become canonical in the literature, a basset hound may have a "sad expression" but its face does not "express sadness," since the basset hound is not perpetually sad. However, the relation between expression and psychological state expressed *may* be noncontingent in the case of human behavior, typically in discourse about the "natural" expressions of such states. Tormey writes:

> Wherever the relation *is* noncontingent, description of the behavior as an expression cannot be given independently of the description of the condition that is expressed. Part of what we mean by "desire" is the disposition to act in particular ways, and such actions are expressions of the desire. Hence part of what we mean by "desire" is the disposition to initiate appropriately expressive behavior. Clearly then if this is the case, the relation between a desire and its behavioral expression is noncontingent, and any description of the behavior which presents it *as* an expression is, to that extent, a function of the description of the desire. Thus a description of behavior as expressive of a particular desire is also a partial description of the desire.
>
> This should help to explain, finally, why actions *express*, rather than *signify*, intentions and desires. The concept of sign is inadequate to describe a relation, such as that between intention and action or desire and action in which the terms are noncontingently connected. "Expression" is the only logically adequate term that we possess for indicating a complex in which object-directed action and a noncontingently related condition of the agent are present.[54]

And J. L. Austin has made a similar argument regarding the noncontingent relation between certain behavior and the emotion of anger of which it is the expression or manifestation:

> There is a peculiar and intimate relationship between the emotion and the natural manner of venting it, with which, having been angry ourselves, we are acquainted. The ways in which anger is normally manifested are *natural* to anger just as there are tones *naturally* expressive of various emotions (indignation, &c.). There is not normally taken to be such a thing as "being angry" apart from any impulse, however vague, to vent the anger in the natural way.[55]

Tormey and Austin thus argue for the normatively necessary relation between human expressions and the psychological states, including emotions, that they express. Because of this normatively necessary relation, inferential reasoning from "ϕ expression" to "expression of ϕ" is *not* warranted: rather, in normal cases we *see*, non-inferentially, the emotion (manifested, expressed) *in* one's behavior, in one's face. This is an epistemic corollary to the logic of the term "expression" as opposed to "sign."

Now one might counter that physiognomy and behavior is one thing, literary or aesthetic understanding by way of signs is another. But Wittgenstein demurs: there is not a single or essential (metaphysical) nature of "understanding"—"For we are under the illusion that what is sublime, what is essential, about our investigation consists in its grasping *one* comprehensive essence"—but rather a variety of phenomena and experiences, including immediate noninterpretive understanding. Shortly after the passage cited above he considers precisely this rejoinder:

> What happens is not that this symbol cannot be further interpreted, but: I do no interpreting [*Ich deute nicht*]. I do not interpret, because I feel at home [*heimisch*] in the present picture. When I interpret, I step from one level of thought to another.[56]

Wittgenstein's demurral comes *not* from denying the possibility of endless interpretation, *différance*, and the like: it is not a denial of what Derrida calls the "metaphysics of the sign." Rather, Wittgenstein observes that very often we do not set off on unending interpretive quests, because there is no desire—or no skeptical itch—to do so. The passage, from late writings published posthumously as *Zettel*, harkens back to a distinction Wittgenstein made decades earlier in the *Tractatus* between signs and symbols by way of diagnosing a fundamental confusion in our understanding of logic and language:

> 3.32 A sign is what can be perceived of a symbol.
>
> 3.321 So one and the same sign (written or spoken, etc.) can be common to two different symbols—in which case they will signify in different ways.
>
> 3.322 Our use of the same sign to signify two different objects can never indicate a common characteristic of the two, if we use it with two different *modes of signification*. For the sign, of course, is arbitrary. So we could choose two different signs instead, and then what would be left in common on the signifying side?
>
> . . .
>
> 3.326 In order to recognize a symbol by its sign we must observe how it is used with a sense.

We have here a version of the "signpost" problem discussed in chapter 1. The mere physical mark or sound is the "dead" sign; only its embeddedness in a signifying practice or custom, where it is "used with a sense," renders it "alive," as a symbol with a particular meaning and logical form. Mere signs are "arbitrary," and hence can in principle be used in any mode of symbolization and therefore "we cannot give a sign the wrong sense" (5.4732). That is, the mere sign, isolated or abstracted from all modes of signification,[57] bears *no* normative relation, no standard of correctness, and hence has no meaning. We fall into philosophical confusion when we maintain the idea of meaningfulness, and inquire what such an isolated sign means when it is stripped of precisely that which confers meaning upon it: the mode of signification that renders it a symbol. As Denis McManus writes: "we generate the illusion by disconnecting words from their customary use while at the same time keeping that use at the back of our minds. In other words, we treat these words simultaneously as signs and as symbols."[58] This is an alternatively worded diagnosis of the Derridean arguments examined in chapter 1.

In the passage quoted above from *Zettel*, Wittgenstein speaks of one's being at home with a symbol, that is, familiar with the mode of signification, the customary use, the practice, and implies that that familiarity must be disrupted before the urge to interpret, to step from one level of thought (thinking *in* the given mode of signification, say) to another (thinking *about* possible modes of signification, perhaps). Wittgenstein is making an observation about our *will*, not the structure and play of the sign or the necessity of interpretation. And it is this observation that links Wittgenstein to Tolstoy's *What Is Art?*, about which he is surely speaking in these two passages from *Culture and Value:*

> Tolstoy: the meaning (importance) of something lies in its being something everyone can understand. That is both true & false. What makes the object hard to understand—if it's significant, important—is not that you have to be instructed in abstruse matters in order to understand it, but the antithesis between understanding the object & what most people *want* [*wollen*] to see. Because of this precisely what is most obvious may be what is most difficult to understand. It is not a difficulty of the intellect [*des Verstandes*] but one for the will [*des Willens*] that has to be overcome.

> There is *much* that could be learned from Tolstoy's false theorizing that the work of art conveys "a feeling."—And you really might call it, if not the expression of a feeling, an expression of feeling, of a felt expression. And you might say too that people who understand it to that extent "resonate" with it, respond to it. You might say: The work of art does not seek to convey *something else*, just itself. As, if I pay

> someone a visit, I don't wish simply to produce such & such feelings in him, but above all to pay him a visit, & naturally I also want to be well received.[59]

Common to these two observations by Wittgenstein is his emphasis upon suspending the deleterious effects of the will in order to understand a "thing" or a "felt expression." That is, when a recipient has the appropriate *ethical attitude*, that is, when one is undisturbed by one's will, *then* "you might say: the work of art does not aim to convey *something else*, just itself." For Levin in *Anna Karenina*, for Tolstoy in *What Is Art?*, as for Wittgenstein, immediate, non-interpretive understanding occurs because the *will* to interpret has been stilled, no longer obstructing our immediate recognition of what is obvious in our everyday lives. Tolstoy's expressivist aesthetics would then be an analogue of this experience in the realm of art.

Returning to *What Is Art?*, we find that here too Tolstoy espouses a similar view, namely that interpretation is superfluous, indeed inimical, in aesthetic experience. Such immediate, will-less understanding, the merging (*sliianie*) of author and reader of "true" (*istinnoe*) artworks occurs without the need for interpretation:

> If the work of art is good as art, then the feeling expressed by the artist is conveyed to others, regardless of whether the work is moral or immoral. If it is conveyed to others, they experience it, and experience it, moreover, each in his own way, and all interpretation is superfluous. If the work does not infect others, then no interpretation is going to make it infectious. Artistic works cannot be interpreted. If it had been possible for the artist to explain in words what he wished to say, he would have said it in words. But he has said it with his art, because it was impossible to convey the feeling he experienced in any other way. The interpretation of a work of art in words proves only that the interpreter is incapable of being infected by art. That is indeed so, and strange as it may seem, it is the people least capable of being infected by art who have always been critics.[60]

We shall return to this passage in chapter 5 in another regard, but here we note the coincidence of Tolstoy and Wittgenstein regarding the immediate understanding of feeling that can occur in aesthetic experience.

6. A second worry is less easy to dispel. In the previous chapter we attended to the lexical distinction between "to infect" and "to communicate itself" in *Anna Karenina*: although both verbs indicate immediate, involuntary expression, the former indicates a physiological, causal relation resulting in outward mimicry, as in "infectious laughter" or "infectious yawning," whereas the latter seems to indicate an expression of meaning content that includes a

normative relation, that is, what is communicated may be misunderstood or inadequately understood.[61]

Interestingly, the same distinction lexically marked in *Anna Karenina* returns during the unfolding argument of *What Is Art?*, but here the distinction is not marked between the two verbs "to infect" and "to communicate itself": rather, it *inhabits* the meaning of "infection" (*zarazhenie*) and "infectious feelings" as they are used throughout the treatise and indicates a potential central tension, if not paradox, within Tolstoy's aesthetic theory.[62] In fact, the semantic field "to communicate itself" (*soobshchat'sia*) and its nominal relation "communion" (*obshchenie*)[63]—examined earlier in Tolstoy's late tale "Walk in the Light While There is Light"—is largely supplanted by the semantic field of infection in *What Is Art?*. In chapter 5 of *What Is Art?* Tolstoy provides examples of "feeling" (*chuvstvo*) that seem to run the spectrum from physiological stimulus to complex, acculturated, and propositionally articulated mental states:

> The simplest example: a man laughs, and another feels merry; he weeps, and the man who hears this weeping feels sad; a man is excited, annoyed, and another looking at him gets into the same state. With his movements, the sounds of his voice, a man displays cheerfulness, determination, or, on the contrary, dejection, calm—and this mood [*nastroenie*] is transmitted [*peredaetsia*] to others. A man suffers, expressing his suffering in moans and convulsions—and this suffering is communicated to others; a man displays his feeling of admiration, awe, fear, respect for certain objects, persons, phenomena—and other people become infected, experience the same feelings of admiration, awe, fear, respect for the same objects, persons or phenomena.
>
> On this capacity of people to be infected by the feelings of other people, the activity of art is based.[64]

By this enumeration it becomes clear just how broad the scope of Tolstoy's notion of "feeling" actually is, extending from *sensations*, such as pain, to cognitively articulated *emotions*, such as fear or admiration.[65] Just what an emotion is, and what qualifies as an emotion, is an ongoing pursuit among philosophers and psychologists; I will present my own view of the matter in greater detail in chapter 6, but here it is necessary to indicate the general terrain by way of some fundamental distinctions. An emotion cannot be simply equivalent to a *sensation* or *feeling*, since there are feelings—like an itch, heartburn, a tickle, a hunger pang—that clearly are not emotions. Likewise an emotion cannot be simply equivalent to a type of *behavior* or a *behavioral disposition*, for at least two reasons. First, behavior is not as fine-grained as emotions (there do not seem to be discrete forms of behavior individuating regret, remorse, guilt, etc.). Second, behavior may be expressive of emotion, but need not be (e.g., my solicitousness of your well-being may be expressive of my affection for you, or may simply reflect my sense of duty). And emotion is not simply equivalent to *physiological responses*, because the latter do not correspond one-to-one to the former (my face may redden due to embarrassment, or due to indigestion).

The most important criterion used in the philosophical tradition to distinguish emotions on the one hand from feelings, sensations, or physiological responses on the other, is that emotions have *intentionality*. A sensation like pain or hunger is traditionally understood as a physically caused occurrent mental state, whereas an emotion may be an occurrent mental state or a mental disposition (that can manifest itself in mental states),[66] but in either case "emotions, unlike sensations, are essentially directed to objects. It is possible to be hungry without being hungry for anything in particular, as it is not possible to be ashamed without being ashamed of anything in particular."[67] According to Anthony Kenny, who rehabilitates a scholastic distinction, emotions can be categorized according to their formal, that is, intentional object.[68] He defines formal object as follows: "The formal object of ϕing is the object under that description which *must* apply to it if it is to be possible to ϕ it. If only what is P can be ϕed, then 'thing which is P' gives the formal object of ϕing."[69] For example, and with some simplification, the formal object of *fear* is "thing which is dangerous." The tradition further distinguishes between emotions, which have formal or intentional objects, and *moods*, which either have no such objects or have vague or diffused objects.[70]

Several consequences of this theory are noteworthy. First, the description of a formal object of an emotion must contain reference to a cognitive state, that is, something similar or equivalent to a belief. This *cognitivist* view of emotions goes back to Aristotle, who defined anger as "a desire accompanied by pain, for a conspicuous revenge for [*dia*] a conspicuous slight at the hands of men who have no call to slight oneself or one's friends" (*Rhetoric* 1378a30–32), and who defined fear as "a pain or disturbance due to imagining some destructive or painful evil in the future" (*Rhetoric* 1382a20–22), before making further qualifications: the imagined pain must be great, its onset imminent, and so on. If I am afraid, then it follows that I fear some object that I believe to be dangerous to me, regardless of the truth of my belief. Thus there is a cognitive aspect or dimension to emotions, and moreover, a normative cognitive standard implicit in emotions: if I tell you that I fear the chirping of cicadas, it is incumbent upon me to explain some feature or property of that chirping which is dangerous; otherwise my fear is unreasonable, irrational, or inappropriate. There is a great deal of controversy regarding how exactly the cognitive dimension of emotion should be conceived. Thus *cognitivist* or *judgment* theories characterize emotions in terms of their associated propositional attitudes, explicit beliefs, and so on, and therefore hold that emotions are subject to the same, or closely related, normative rational constraints as beliefs.[71] *Appraisal* theorists by contrast hold that not all emotions need involve propositional attitudes or explicit beliefs:

they may be non-propositional in content, unconscious, and irrational.[72] Common to both views, however, is the claim that emotions involve some *evaluative* dimension, and therefore are at least in principle subject to normative assessment of appropriateness, if not full-blown rationality. Because sensations do not have formal objects, or at the very least because they lack such an evaluative dimension, they are not susceptible to this *normative* constraint. Second, the formal object of an emotion may have different logical forms. For instance, I may fear a property (canine aggressivity), an object (my neighbor's dog), or a state of affairs expressed as a proposition (that my neighbor's dog did not get its rabies test). Moreover, while some formal objects refer to the natural world (as in the previous example), others are deeply embedded in our second nature: cultural objects and practices. Thus I may be ashamed of the color of my tie, or that I misused my salad fork at a state dinner. Here the cognitive aspect involves beliefs not (only) about the natural world, but about norms, etiquette, expectations, rules, and so on. Third, the *cause* and the *object* of an emotion may not be identical. For instance, if I hear scratching at my door, the cause of my fear is the scratching, but the object of my fear is my (imagining of my) neighbor's dog.

These distinctions between sensation and emotion have consequences for our understanding of Tolstoy's theory of infection. At one end of the spectrum, we may involuntarily wince in correspondence with another's wincing in pain, and feel discomfort. But how shall we know whether our sensation of discomfort is pain, or irritation, or annoyance, and so on? Here Tolstoy's theory seems close to that of William James, who held that emotions are feelings specifically caused by changes in one's physiological condition: "we feel sorry because we cry, angry because we strike, afraid because we tremble, and [it is] not that we cry, strike, or tremble, because we are sorry, angry, or fearful, as the case may be."[73] Richard Wollheim has sought to reappraise James's theory, but finds that it must incorporate some kind of cognitivism: "when feeling does tell us something about emotion, it does so, not unaided, but against the background of ancillary or contextual belief. This being so, we might expect, in the absence of such belief, to be ignorant of what the emotion is, or, for that matter, what the feeling is like."[74] And, as we'll see in chapter 8, Jenefer Robinson's sophisticated theory of emotional expression in art likewise requires what she calls "cognitive monitoring" of initial physiological changes that occur in aesthetic experience. So even the cases of physiological, causally induced mimicry such as laughing, crying, yawning, must presuppose ancillary and contextual beliefs in order for the feeling to be determinate: you laugh and I laugh, but are you laughing at something because it is hilarious, or whimsical, or preposterous, or absurd, or are you laughing out of joy, or exasperation? Only my beliefs about your beliefs and desires will provide the normative constraints necessary to delimit the emotion by in part supposing its intentional object: what the emotion is in part derives from what it is *about*. And such cognitive-evaluative considerations obviously are essential to explaining complex, culturally mediated emotions bearing specific formal objects such as fear of/that, awe before, respect for, admiration of, pride, remorse, and so on. Indeed, one commentator concludes: "In short, 'feeling,' as it is used in *What Is Art?* may include all human experience, for it is not an entity or a list, however long, of entities, but rather the subjective mode of regarding any entity. Thus Tolstoy's concept of feeling is extremely broad."[75] Tolstoy's concept of feeling in fact cuts across the distinction between sensations that bear no necessary relation to a formal object and are usually explained *causally* (e.g., itching, pain, etc.) and emotions that do essentially bear a relation to a formal object, and hence essentially involve a cognitive dimension (belief, judgment, evaluation, etc.) constrained by *normative* standards of adequacy or appropriateness.[76]

Tolstoy's assimilation of art to affect—and, as we will see in chapter 5, above all musical affect—in his model of infection thus involves a problem. For infectious affect, understood as a *causal* or *dispositional* relation, does not allow for the possibility of misunderstanding. But if by affect is understood emotion, and if emotion involves a cognitive-evaluative dimension, then such emotions, since they involve a formal object, or propositional content, or at the very least an evaluative appraisal, bear *meaning*. But meaning, in turn, bears a *normative* relation: knowing the meaning or use of an expression requires that one be able to distinguish between correct and incorrect uses of that expression; as we saw in chapter 1: that is constitutively part of what it means to understand an expression at all. Indeed, the broad scope of "feeling" in *What Is Art?* ignores the very difference between dispositional affective reactions that are merely causal effects—sensations, physiological reactions—on the one hand, and emotions involving beliefs or judgments or evaluative appraisals containing cognitive content, that is, meaning content which presupposes a normative relation of correctness, on the other. The assimilation of meaning content, with its inherent normative relation, to the causal-dispositional model of infection becomes most problematical in the case of music.

Chapter 4

Schopenhauer's Shadow

> For rhythm and harmony penetrate deeply into the mind and have a most powerful effect on it.
>
> —Plato

> All nuances of cheerfulness and serenity, the sallies, moods and jubilations of the soul, the degrees of anxiety, misery, mourning, lament, sorrow, grief, longing, etc., and lastly of awe, worship, love, etc., become the peculiar sphere of musical expression.
>
> —G. W. F. Hegel

> The passions enjoy themselves by dint of music.
>
> —Nietzsche

1. I have noted in passing Tolstoy's occupation with the writings of Schopenhauer during his crisis and thereafter. Although the younger Tolstoy was inspired by Fichte and Schelling,[1] Tolstoy's diaries and letters indicate that while he was working out his aesthetics in *What Is Art?* and composing *Kreutzer Sonata* he was wrestling with Schopenhauer's philosophy, and that he read all of the philosopher's major works: *The World as Will and Representation, Parerga and Paralipomena*, and *The Two Fundamental Problems of Ethics*, the latter work comprised of the *Prize Essay on the Freedom of the Will* and the *Prize Essay on the Basis of Morality*. In 1869 Tolstoy wrote to the poet and translator of Schopenhauer into Russian, Afanasii Fet:

> Do you know what this summer has been for me? A continuous ecstasy over Schopenhauer and a series of mental pleasures such as I have never before experienced. I ordered all his works and have read and am reading them (as well as Kant's). And certainly no student in his course has learned and discovered so much as I have during this summer. I do not know whether I shall ever change my opinion, but at present I am certain that Schopenhauer is the greatest genius among men. You said he somehow wrote something about philosophical

> matters. How something? This is all the world in an unbelievably clear and beautiful reflection. I began to translate him . . . Reading him I just cannot understand how his name can remain unknown. There is only one explanation, namely, that—as so often repeated by himself—there are none but idiots in this world.[2]

While in 1869 he thus wrote to Fet that "I am certain that Schopenhauer is the greatest genius among men,"[3] on August 16, 1889, he noted in his diary that his philosophy is all "fluff and nonsense."[4] While scholars have traced the influence of Schopenhauer's thoughts on free will and causal determinism in the epilogues of *War and Peace*,[5] it appears that little attention has been devoted to the possible presence of Schopenhauer's moral philosophy in *What Is Art?* and its trope of "infection." But I shall argue that a consideration of Schopenhauer's thoughts on ethics and aesthetics, which Tolstoy quite likely knew, entails what I shall call a "Nietzschean threat" for Tolstoy's aesthetic theory. But in order to understand the possible significance of Schopenhauer's moral and aesthetic theories for Tolstoy, we must first outline the philosopher's general metaphysics and epistemology from which his specific theories of ethics and art issue.

2. Schopenhauer works from a Kantian position regarding the transcendental ideality of space and time, that is, that they are conditions of human (phenomenal) experience but not necessarily of objective (noumenal) reality or "the thing-in-itself." Since space and time, and the principle of causality relating them, are transcendental forms of intuition and categories of the understanding respectively, they likewise condition the appearance of a plurality of individuals as well; thus Schopenhauer calls the transcendental ideality of space, time, and causality the *principium individuationis*. Individuation—including individual wills and desires—is a characteristic of phenomenal experience, not of the thing-in-itself. The epistemic subject experiences reality as individuated objects that are perceived and known as *representations*: mental images that result from sensory input conditioned by the transcendental forms of intuition and the categories of the understanding. Because subjects of knowledge condition the possible structure of objects of knowledge, as phenomena perceived as representations and interrelated causally, we can have intersubjectively confirmable experiences of phenomenal reality, although we cannot know the nature of noumenal reality via outer sense. Schopenhauer departs from Kantian metaphysics and epistemology, however, by reasoning *a contrario* regarding the thing-in-itself, noumenal reality, and claiming that we have an awareness of it via inner sense:

> On the path of *objective knowledge*, thus starting from the *representation*, we shall never get beyond the representation, i.e., the

> phenomenon. We shall therefore remain at the outside of things; we shall never be able to penetrate into their inner nature, and investigate what they are in themselves, in other words, what they may be by themselves. So far I agree with Kant. But now, as the counterpoise to this truth, I have stressed that other truth that we are not merely the *knowing subject*, but that *we ourselves* are also among those realities or entities we require to know, that *we ourselves are the thing-in-itself*. Consequently, a way *from within* stands open to us to that real inner nature of things to which we cannot penetrate *from without*. It is, so to speak, a subterranean passage, a secret alliance, which, as if by treachery, places us all at once in the fortress that could not be taken by attack from without. Precisely as such, the *thing-in-itself* can come into consciousness only quite directly, namely by *it itself being conscious of itself*; to try to know it objectively is to desire something contradictory.[6]

Whereas one can perceive one's body and its mechanistic movements as simply representations of yet another individuated phenomenon, one can *also* be aware of the inner nature of one's own body by means of intentional action and the experience of pleasure and pain. This inner nature, according to Schopenhauer, in this way is revealed to be *will* (*Wille*). Thus one's body is given to one in two distinct ways: by perception as representation, conditioned by the *principium individuationis*, and immediately, self-consciously as will. Thus an intentional action is at once both a bodily movement subject to causal explanation, and an act of will of which the agent is immediately aware in self-consciousness. In intentional action the agent is aware of herself not as representation, but as thing-in-itself, as "will."[7] Schopenhauer then generalizes from the agent's will as the inner sense of intentional action to conclude that the will is the inner nature, the in-itself, of phenomena generally, the single striving, movement, force in all of nature, or as he expresses it: the world of representations is the objectivity of the will, the will experienced as an object of representation.[8] The will can be expressed and experienced at various grades or levels of objectification corresponding to how distinct and complete the representation is, and Schopenhauer associates the various grades of objectification of the will with Platonic Ideas: unchanging forms of representation not subject to spatiotemporal existence, and hence ontologically closer to the inner nature of reality. When one adopts a will-less, contemplative attitude and perceives the object represented to one divorced from its spatiotemporal attributes and devoid of any causal relations in which it stands to other objects, one becomes aware of the Idea embodied by that object. The perceiving subject loses his individuality and becomes a pure, will-less knowing subject of knowledge, no longer distinct from the universal object of knowledge:

> The transition that is possible . . . from the common knowledge of particular things to knowledge of the Idea takes place suddenly, since knowledge tears itself free from the service of the will precisely by the subject's ceasing to be merely individual, and being now a pure will-less subject of knowledge. Such a subject of knowledge no longer follows relations in accordance with the principle of sufficient reason; on the contrary, it rests in fixed contemplation of the object presented to it out of its connexion with another other, and rises into this. . . . We *lose* ourselves entirely in the object . . . we forget our individuality, our will, and continue to exist only as pure subject, as clear mirror of the object, so that it is as though the object alone existed, without anyone to perceive it, and thus we are no longer able to separate the perceiver from the perception, but the two have become one, since the entire consciousness is filled and occupied by a single image of perception. If, therefore, the object has to such an extent passed out of all relation to something outside it, and the subject has passed out of all relation to the will, what is thus known is no longer the individual thing as such, but the *Idea*, the eternal form, the immediate objectivity of the will at this grade.[9]

Schopenhauer holds aesthetic experience to be this privileged state of will-less, dispassionate contemplation of the object *qua* Platonic Idea.[10] Within this metaphysical and epistemological framework Schopenhauer developed intriguing and compelling theories of the nature of moral actions and the aesthetic experience of music, both grounded in a will-less awareness of feeling.

3. Schopenhauer's views on ethics recur throughout book 4 of *The World as Will and Representation* (*Die Welt als Wille und Vorstellung*, 1819) but are presented with greater clarity and concentration in his *On the Basis of Morality* (*Über die Grundlage der Moral*, 1839), the sole entry to a prize essay competition administered by the Royal Danish Society of Scientific Studies, which nonetheless saw fit to pass over the submission. In the essay Schopenhauer rejects Kant's deontological moral theory because it fails to convincingly account for the empirical roots of morality, most importantly that of motivation for moral action. Schopenhauer had stressed the role of egoism—the tendency to use one's own will exclusively in self-regarding actions—in explaining human motivation, and so the possibility and recognized existence of ethical—genuinely other-regarding—action presented him with a problem: to show how egoism is overcome in ethical action. He does so by invoking the empirically observed common phenomenon of compassion (*Mitleid*), arguing that the immediate empathetic participation (*Teilnahme*) in another's suffering—so that one experiences another's suffering literally as one's own—moves one to act morally by overcoming one's egoistic will. The central passage, occurring in §16 of the essay, merits quotation at length:

> Thus, how is it possible at all for *another's* weal and woe [*das Wohl und Wehe*] to become directly [*unmittelbar*]—that is, completely as otherwise only my own weal and woe would move my will—my motive, and this sometimes to such a degree that I more or less subordinate to them my own weal and woe, normally the sole source of my motives? Obviously only through that other man's becoming *the ultimate object* [*Zweck*] of my will in the same way as I myself otherwise am, and hence through my directly desiring [*will*] *his* weal and not *his* woe just as immediately [*unmittelbar*] as I ordinarily do only *my own*. But this necessarily presupposes that, in the case of his *woe* as such, I suffer directly [*geradezu mitleide*] with him. I feel *his* woe just as I ordinarily feel only my own; and, likewise, I directly [*unmittelbar*] desire his weal in the same way I otherwise desire only my own. But this requires that I am in some way *identified with him* [*mit ihm identificirt sei*], in other words, that this entire *difference* between me and everyone else, which is the very basis of my egoism, is eliminated [or sublated, *aufgehoben*], to a certain extent at least. Now, since I do not exist *inside the other man's skin*, then only by means of the *knowledge* [*Erkenntnis*] I have of him, that is, of the presentation [*Vorstellung*] of him in my head, can I identify myself with him to such an extent that my practical action [*That*] declares that difference abolished [*aufgehoben*]. However, the process here analyzed is not one that is dreamed or fancifully imagined [*aus der Luft gegriffener*]; on the contrary, it is perfectly real and indeed by no means infrequent. It is the everyday phenomenon of *compassion* [*Mitleid*], of the immediate [*unmittelbar*] *participation* [or sympathy, *Theilnahme*], independent of all ulterior considerations, primarily in the *suffering* [*Leiden*] of another, and thus in the prevention or elimination [*Aufhebung*] of it. For all satisfaction and all well-being and happiness consist in this. It is simply and solely this compassion that is the real basis of all *voluntary* justice and *genuine* love of humanity [*Menschenliebe*]. Only insofar as an action has sprung from compassion does it have moral value; and every action resulting from any other motives has none. As soon as this compassion is aroused, the weal and woe of another are immediately [*unmittelbar*] next to my heart in exactly the same way, although not always in the same degree, as otherwise only my own are. Hence the difference between him and me is now no longer absolute.[11]

Although the German "*Mitleid*" is commonly translated as "sympathy" or "compassion," Schopenhauer's psychological concept differs importantly from both sympathy and empathy (which entered English as the translation of the German "*Einfühlung*").[12] While disagreement among psychologists and philosophers remains, among several thinkers empathy is often taken to be some sort of relation of type-identity of feeling between two people: one person participially imagines (imagines *being* that person) the thoughts, feelings, and emotions of another, and thereby shares mental states of the same sort. Sympathy, on the other hand, is the emotional capacity to recognize the feelings of another, but need not be the experiencing of the same emotions. If I sympathize with your suffering a migraine headache, I have feelings of sympathy toward you, but do not suffer the pain of a migraine headache myself.[13]

Schopenhauer's concept of *Mitleid*, however, diverges from the common understanding of empathy as well, for in his view, the emotional identification with, and immediate empathetic participation in, the other occurs as it were not above but below the operations of imagination and conscious will. Against competing theories that suppose that one *imagines* the pains of another as though they were one's own, Schopenhauer counters:

> This is by no means the case; on the contrary, at every moment we remain clearly conscious that *he* is the sufferer, not *we*; and it is precisely in *his* person, not in ours, that we feel the suffering, to our grief and sorrow. We suffer *with* him and hence *in* him [*Wir leiden mit ihm, also in ihm*]; we feel his pain as *his*, and do not imagine that it is ours.[14]

Schopenhauer does not ground the phenomenon of compassion in a cognitive operation, such as observing the other's suffering and imagining it were my own, by analogical inference (that is, assuming that the other's mind is like mine, hence his experiences will be relevantly similar to mine). Instead he claims that there is an immediate, non-inferential feeling or sensation of his pain. It would thus appear that here, in the ethical realm, we are meeting the same model of immediate, involuntary understanding that we saw in *Anna Karenina* and *What Is Art?*.

So far in his explication, Schopenhauer has provided an empirical, psychological, explanation for ethical action, by the "natural compassion that is inborn and indestructible in everyone . . . [and is] the sole source of *non-egoistic actions*."[15] But in the final section of his treatise, entitled "On the Metaphysical Explanation of the Primary Ethical Phenomenon," Schopenhauer argues that the psychological "foundation of ethics" in fact rests on a transcendental grounding, whereby the *principium individuationis* that constitutes the phenomenal world of representations is contrasted with the underlying thing-in-itself, the universal and monistic will. Therefore, the experience of compassion in fact offers proof of and insight into the underlying metaphysical unity of all nature:

> Accordingly, if plurality and separateness belong only to the *phenomenon*, and if it is one and the same essence that manifests itself

> in all living things, then that conception that abolishes [*aufheben*] the difference between ego and non-ego is not erroneous; but on the contrary, the opposite conception must be. We find also this latter conception is described by the Hindus as *Māyā*, i.e., illusion [*Schein*], deception, phantasm, mirage. It is the former view which we found to be the basis of the phenomenon of compassion; in fact, compassion is the proper expression of that view. Accordingly, it would be the metaphysical basis of ethics and consist in *one* individual's again recognizing in *another* his own self, his own true inner nature.[16]

> The good character . . . lives in an external world that is homogeneous with his own true being. The others are not a non-ego for him, but an "I once more." His fundamental relation to everyone is, therefore, friendly; he feels himself intimately akin [*verwandt*] to all beings, immediately [*unmittelbar*] takes part [*Theil nimmt*] in their weal and woe, and confidently assumes the same sympathy [*Theilnahme*] in them.[17]

Recall our discussion of Levin's epiphany in *Anna Karenina*, and Tolstoy's claim in *What Is Art?* that "the good is indeed a fundamental understanding, which metaphysically constitutes the essence of our consciousness, an understanding undefinable by reason . . . but which defines everything else,"[18] which I likened to Wittgenstein's claim in the *Tractatus* that value, like logic, is transcendental, conditioning the possibility of any representation and knowledge of phenomenal experience. What is common to Schopenhauer, Tolstoy, and the Tractarian Wittgenstein is here the idea that transcendentally, representation, and the incumbent need for interpretation, is an illusory and misleading addendum to a fundamental immediate common understanding requiring no interpretation. This metaphysical, rather than psychological or physiological, explanation at least suggests a way to understand the continuity of Tolstoy's examples of immediate understanding, of which ethical and aesthetic experience appear to be two species.

4. But what the German metaphysician gave Tolstoy with one hand he took back with the other, for Schopenhauer's aesthetic theory precisely identified a tension between causal affect and normative meaning content, a distinction that, we saw in the previous chapter, Tolstoy's broad extension of "feelings" fails to acknowledge. The continuum between the universal physiological responses *qua* sensations and the complex, propositionally articulated and possibly acculturated feelings *qua* emotions ("The tears, the laughter of a Chinese will infect me in just the same way as the tears and laughter of a Russian, as will painting and music, or a work of poetry if it is translated into a language I understand")[19] does face a threat of rupture from another direction. Recall that in *What Is Art?* Tolstoy claimed that:

> If the work of art is good as art, then the feeling expressed by the artist is conveyed to others, regardless of whether the work is moral or immoral. If it is conveyed to others, they experience it, and experience it, moreover, each in his own way, and all interpretation is superfluous.[20]

The *content indifferentism*—including the *moral indifferentism*—of infectious art implies what I shall call the "Nietzschean threat" to Tolstoy's project. Its primary locus is music. In §§5–6 and §§16–20 of the *The Birth of Tragedy out of the Spirit of Music* (*Geburt der Tragödie aus dem Geist der Musik*, 1871) Nietzsche explicitly draws on Schopenhauer's aesthetics of music in formulating the Dionysian "art-drive" (*Kunsttrieb*). In fact, in §1 Schopenhauer's *principium individuationis*, a.k.a. the "veil of Māyā," the illusion of a plurality of phenomena due to our exercise of the principle of sufficient reason, serves as the criterion for Nietzsche's first exposition of the two art-drives: the Apolline aesthetics of beauty, plastic and imagistic arts, disinterested contemplation, with its existential analogue in sleep and dream, and the Dionysiac aesthetics of rapture, the musical arts, communal absorption, with its existential analogue in ecstasy and intoxication (*Rausch*). In §§5–6 Nietzsche presents a metaphysical interpretation of pre-tragic melic poetry (represented by the poet Archilochus) that is in essence Schopenhauerian: "the lyric poet, a Dionysiac artist, has become entirely at one with the primordial unity, with its pain and contradiction, and he produces a copy [*Abbild*] of this primordial unity as music, which has been described elsewhere, quite rightly, as a repetition of the world and a second copy of it."[21] This thought is then radicalized: the poet is liberated from his individual will to become merely a *medium* through which the ground of being makes its appearance (§5), which reaches its logical telos in communal music bereft of individual creative will altogether, that is, the folk song: "Indeed it ought to be possible to demonstrate historically that every period which was rich in the production of folk songs was agitated by Dionysiac currents, since these are always to be regarded as the precondition of folk song and as the hidden ground from which it springs" (§6).[22] And in §16, after quoting extensively from §36 of *The World as Will and Representation*, Nietzsche returns to Schopenhauer's metaphysics of music to vindicate the Dionysian element in tragedy. Music, unlike the other arts, does *not* represent phenomena, but rather directly conveys the metaphysical essence underlying those phenomena: "according to Schopenhauer, we understand music, the language of the Will, directly," hence "only the spirit of music allows us to understand why we feel joy at the destruction of the individual. For individual instances of such destruction merely illustrate the eternal phenomenon of Dionysiac art, which expresses the omnipotent Will behind the *principium individuationis*, as it were, life going on eternally beyond all appearance and despite all destruction."[23]

Nietzsche's analysis of the effects of music harkens back to §52 of *The World as Will and Representation*, where Schopenhauer writes that music "is such a great and exceedingly fine art, its effect on man's innermost nature is so powerful," before offering this account of its aesthetic effect:

> As our world is nothing but the phenomenon or appearance of the Ideas in plurality through entrance into the *principium individuationis* (the form of knowledge possible to the individual as such), music, since it passes over the Ideas, is also quite independent of the phenomenal world, positively ignores it, and, to a certain extent, could still exist even if there were no world at all, which cannot be said of the other arts. Thus music is as *immediate* an objectification and copy of the whole *will* as the world itself is, indeed as the Ideas are, the multiplied phenomenon of which constitutes the world of individual things. Therefore music is by no means like the other arts, namely a copy of the Ideas, but a *copy of the will itself*, the objectivity of which are the Ideas. For this reason the effect of music is so very much more powerful and penetrating than is that of the other arts, for these others speak only of the shadow, but music of the essence.[24]

Thus music "expresses the metaphysical to everything physical in the world, the thing-in-itself to every phenomenon. Accordingly, we could just as well call the world embodied music as embodied will."[25] The singular metaphysical significance of music, its direct presentation of the will, explains why it "is so powerful, and is so completely and profoundly understood by man in his innermost being as an entirely universal language"; why it is "instantly understood by everyone . . . [with] direct understanding."[26] Because music is non-representational, appealing to neither actual objects (referents) or abstract entities (Platonic Ideas), it is non-inferentially, immediately, and universally understood, and provides unique intuitive insight into the noumenal essence underlying the illusion of phenomena transcendentally conditioned by our cognitive faculties of sensibility and understanding. Music therefore is the *aesthetic* counterpart to *ethical* compassion (*Mitleid*), which also is direct understanding of the essential monism underlying the phenomenal existence of individual wills; though Schopenhauer would cavil that this fundamental level of metaphysics is prior to the distinction between ethics and aesthetics. And precisely that lack of differentiation between ethical effect and aesthetic affect represents a problem for Tolstoy.

5. The problem emerges concretely in Schopenhauer's further description in §52 of *The World as Will and Representation* of the nature of music's influence:

> Music does not express this or that particular and definite pleasure, this or that affliction, pain, sorrow, horror, gaiety, merriment, or peace of mind, but joy, pain, sorrow, horror, gaiety, merriment, peace of mind *themselves*, to a certain extent in the abstract, their essential nature, without any accessories, and so also without the motives for them. . . . Everywhere music expresses only the quintessence of life and of its events, never these themselves, and therefore their differences do not always influence it. It is just this universality that belongs uniquely to music, together with the most precise distinctness, that gives it that high value as the panacea of all our sorrows.
>
> . . .
>
> The inexpressible depth of all music, by virtue of which it floats past us as a paradise quite familiar and yet eternally remote, and is so easy to understand and yet so inexplicable, is due to the fact that it reproduces all the emotions of our innermost being, but entirely without reality and remote from its pain.[27]

In order to understand Schopenhauer's claim that music expresses emotions "without the motives for them," we need to understand at least the rudiments of his theory of action and moral psychology. In contrast with volitional theories, according to which my act of will or volition constitutes a distinct mental state which then causes (or can cause) my action, a bodily movement, Schopenhauer holds what can be called a "dual-aspect" theory of the will, according to which my act of will is identical to my action, that is, my bodily movement. Whereas the volitional theory maintains that there are two events causally connected—the mental act of will on the one hand, and the resultant action, the movement of one's body on the other hand—a dual-aspect theory claims that there is only one event known by two different means: internally by immediate, non-observational knowledge (I typically know what I'm doing, or about to do, without having to observe myself), and externally by observation of bodily movement.[28] The physical movement and the willing in this view are simply two aspects of a single event.[29] Thus in Schopenhauer's view, volitional accounts erroneously infer from the duality of aspects (that is, two different description-types of a single event) to a duality of events causally mediated, whereas in fact there is only one event known in two different ways. It follows from this view, however, that acts of will cannot be the cause of physical movement. Something else must cause the single event that is known immediately to self-consciousness as will and known observationally as bodily movement.

Schopenhauer works towards explicating the cause of willing by first claiming that self-consciousness contains exclusively and exhaustively its own willing; that is, the self is known only through immediate awareness of its own willing. Self-consciousness contains not only discrete *acts* of the will, but also what he calls *manifestations of willing*, which include "all desiring, striving, wishing, longing, yearning, hoping, loving, rejoicing, exulting, and the like, as well as the feeling of unwillingness or repugnance, detesting, fleeing, fearing, being angry, hating, mourning, suffering, in short, all affects and passions."[30] Notice that, like the examples of "feeling" given by Tolstoy in *What Is Art?*, these "manifestations of willing" run from sensations (suffering) to moods (unwillingness) and emotions (anger), through to complex, syntactically articulated propositional attitude verbs (hoping *for*, rejoicing *that* or *in*, wishing *for*, fleeing *from*, etc.). Schopenhauer explains the transition from manifestations of willing to an act of will by specifying how the subject comes to relate these manifestations to objects and states of affairs in the world:

> When a human being *wills*, he wills something; his act of will is always directed to an object, and is conceivable only in reference to such. Now what is meant by willing something? This means that the act of will, which is itself in the first instance only an object of self-consciousness, arises on the occasion of something that belongs to the consciousness of *other things* and thus is an object of the faculty of cognition. In this connection such an object is called a *motive* and is at the same time the material of the act of will, in that the latter is directed to it, that is to say, aims at some change in it, and thus reacts to it; its [the act of will's] whole essence consists in this *reaction*.[31]

According to Schopenhauer, while self-consciousness contains exclusively and exhaustively its own willing (that is, the self is known only through immediate awareness of its own willing), it is only by means of the faculty of cognition (*Erkenntnis*) that the external world is known by the subject, in that "other things" are representations (*Vorstellungen*) of objective states of affairs for the subject.[32] The cognitive representation of a state of affairs is what Schopenhauer means by "motive," and motives are the causes of acts of the will: "Motivation is merely causality which passes through cognition [*Erkenntnis*]: the intellect is the medium of motives, because it is the highest grade of receptivity."[33] "*Motivation is causality seen from within.*"[34] So motives—representations of objective states of affairs, including imaginatively or purposively conceived futural states of affairs—exert a causal influence upon the will,[35] and willing is the effect of the motive, a reaction to it.

There is a final piece of Schopenhauer's deterministic picture, for two people in similar circumstances, with similar motives (cognitive representations of objective states of affairs) can will and act differently, including ethically differently. In his early work *World as Will and Representation*, Schopenhauer attributes the cause to the unfathomable nature of the metaphysical will as expressed in a particular individual, and itself an inexplicable force that reacts to the specific motives acting upon it:

> Motives do not determine a man's character, but only the phenomenon or appearance of that character, that is, the deeds and actions, the external form of the course of his life, not its inner significance and content. These proceed from the character which is the immediate phenomenon of the will and is therefore groundless. That one man is wicked and another good does not depend on motives and external influences such as teaching and preaching; and in this sense the thing is absolutely inexplicable. But whether a wicked man shows his wickedness in petty injustices, cowardly tricks, and low villainy, practiced by him in the narrow sphere of his surroundings, or as a conqueror oppresses nations, throws a world into misery and distress, and sheds the blood of millions, this is the outward form of this phenomenon or appearance, that which is inessential to it, and it depends on the circumstances in which fate has placed him, on the surroundings, on external influences, on motives. But his decision on these motives can never be explained from them; it proceeds from the will, whose phenomenon this man is.[36]

In his late text on the freedom of the will, Schopenhauer addresses the same issue by elaborating on the notion of a person's *character*, which causally interacts with the motives to determine the person's willing and acting:

> Now just as this is the case with causes in the narrowest sense and with stimuli, so too is it equally the case with *motives*; for in essence motivation is not different from causality, but is only a form of it, namely causality that passes through the medium of cognition. Therefore here too the cause calls forth only the manifestation of a force that cannot be reduced and consequently cannot be explained any further. The force in question, which is called *will*, is known to us not merely from without as are the other forces of nature, but also from within and immediately by virtue of self-consciousness. Only on the assumption that such a will is present and is of a definite quality in a particular case are the causes directed to it, here called motives, efficacious. This particularly and individually determined quality of the will, by virtue of which the will's reaction to the same motives is different in each human being, constitutes what we call his *character*, and indeed his *empirical* [as opposed to Kantian intelligible] *character*, since it is known not *a priori* but only through experience. It determines first of all the mode of operation of the different kinds of motives on the given human being. For it underlies all the effects that are called forth by the motives, just as the universal forces of nature underlie the effects that are produced by causes in the narrowest sense, and the vital force underlies the effects of stimuli. Like the forces of nature, this character is also original, unalterable, and

> inexplicable. In animals it is different in every species; in the human being it is different in every individual.[37]

We now have a sufficiently refined picture of Schopenhauer's theory with which to explain his understanding of the influence of music.[38] Music offers emotions, "manifestations of willing," without however, the corresponding motives, the cognitive representations of the objects and states of affairs that would, presumably, be appropriate or commensurate with those emotions, as their intentional objects.[39] Moreover, since motivation is causality through the medium of cognition, without motives acts of the will would not be object-directed, would not be willings *of* anything. As Schopenhauer says, music "speaks not of things, but simply of weal and woe as being for the *will* the sole realities."[40] How these powerful "manifestations of willing" would causally interact with the person's will, therefore, would depend entirely on whatever *other* motives are acting on the listener at the time in conjunction with that person's empirical character. And it is the person's character that constitutes the basis for judging the moral worth of that person's actions:

> It is owing to this truth [that once deceived by a person we no longer trust them] that, when we wish to estimate the moral worth of an action, we first try to reach certainty as to its motive; yet our praise or blame is later directed not to the motive, but to the character that allowed itself to be determined thereby, which is the second factor of this deed and the only one inherent in the human being.[41]

Thus, according to Schopenhauer, music is "the most powerful of all the arts" for it conveys powerful emotions "without the motives for them," whereby the missing motives would presumably include the reasons, purposes, justifications *for* those emotions: precisely the articulated representations and attendant cognitive judgments we examined in our analysis of fear in chapter 3. "From its own resources, music is certainly able to express every movement of the will, every feeling; but through the addition of the words, we receive also their objects, the motives that give rise to that feeling."[42] Without these cognitive contextualizations, the conveyed "manifestations of willing" will interact with the fundamental ethical character of the listener and whatever motives, cognitive representations, he or she is entertaining at the time. Thus Schopenhauer writes: "Because music does not, like all other arts, exhibit the *Ideas* or grades of the will's objectification, but directly the *will itself*, we can also explain that it acts directly on the will, i.e., the feelings, passions, and emotions of the hearer, so that it quickly raises these or even alters them." This is the "Nietzschean threat" inherent in Schopenhauer's theory.[43] Tolstoy presents an intimation of that threat in a short scene in *Anna Karenina*, in which Levin attends a concert that includes in its program a contemporary "fantasia" entitled *King Lear on the Heath*. Levin's disorientation is described:

> But the longer he listened to the *King Lear* fantasia, the further he felt from any possibility of forming some definite opinion for himself. The musical expression of feeling was ceaselessly beginning, as if gathering itself up, but it fell apart at once into fragments of new beginnings of musical expressions and sometimes into extremely complex sounds, connected by nothing other than the mere whim of the composer. But these fragments of musical expressions, good ones on occasion, were unpleasant because they were totally unexpected and in no way prepared for. Gaiety, sadness, despair, tenderness and triumph appeared without justification, like a madman's feelings. And, just as with a madman, these feelings passed unexpectedly.[44]

It is only when his companion, Pestsov, reminds him of the text upon which the fantasia is based ("You can't follow without it") that Levin reads the program notes, which include the relevant Shakespearean verses in Russian translation, and thereby contextualizes the apparently disjointed series of emotions triggered in him by the music. For without the characters and narrative, there is, as the narrator above states, no "justification" for the cascade of emotions, which without that normative contextualization are "like a madman's feelings."[45]

6. In *What Is Art?* Tolstoy apparently grasps Schopenhauer's metaphysics of music, characterizing it in his discussion of Wagner and Beethoven as the "mystical theory that music is the expression of the will—not particular expression of the will at various stages of objectivization, but of its very essence."[46] Yet he cannot dismiss it so easily, for Schopenhauer's thought inhabits passages of this essay *implicitly* as well. For instance, I would suggest that Tolstoy acknowledges the influence of music noted by Schopenhauer above early in *What Is Art?* when he insists that the term "beautiful" (*krasivyi*) as understood by a "Russian man of the people [*narod*]" is limited to visual aesthetic phenomena, whereas "good" (*dobryi*, *khoroshii*) extends from ethics (many actions can be characterized in ethical terms) to non-visual, that is, non-representational, aesthetic phenomena, principally music:

> In Russian an action [*postupok*] can be kind and good, or not-kind [*nedobryi*] and not-good [*nekhoroshii*]; music can be pleasant [*priiatnaia*] and good [*khoroshaia*] or unpleasant and not-good, but never beautiful nor not-beautiful.
>
> A man, horse, view, a movement [*dvizhenie*] may be beautiful, but of actions [*postupki*], thoughts, character, music, we may say they are good, if we like them very much, or not good, if we do not like them; we can say "beautiful" only of what is pleasing to our sight.[47]

The fundamental difference between a movement (*dvizhenie*) and an action (*postupok*) is the presence of the agent's intentionality, his *will*,[48] and we have just seen how, according to Schopenhauer, an agent's acts of will are in part determined by his character, which in turn is the basis for his moral appraisal by others. Why Tolstoy should place music alone of the arts in the same category as action, a category often characterizable in ethical terms, receives its best answer, I suggest, by considering Schopenhauer's theory of music. Like action, music must be contextualized into a semantic framework inherently ethical, because otherwise its affect is "without motive," and that represents what I have called the "Nietzschean threat" lurking within Tolstoy's theory of infection. In the next chapter I shall explore how Tolstoy examined that threat in the medium of a literary text.

Chapter 5

Tolstoy's *Kreutzer Sonata* and Consequences

> The sublime as semblance has its own absurdity and contributes to the neutralization of truth; this is the accusation of art in Tolstoy's *Kreutzer Sonata.*
>
> —T. W. Adorno

Tolstoy confronts what I have called the "Nietzschean threat" obliquely in the novella *The Kreutzer Sonata*, which he wrote concomitantly with *What Is Art?*. In this chapter I offer a reading of the novella specifically from the vantage point of the problematic I have been tracing out, and I draw once again on Wittgenstein's thoughts about the ethical attitude and will, in order to interpret the protagonist, Pozdnyshev, as a dramatic realization of the threat I developed in my reading of Schopenhauer. Tolstoy, I shall argue, tried to answer that threat in the final chapter of *What Is Art?*, but that answer is liable to a definitive criticism inspired by Wittgenstein.

1. The problematic of music, and the presence of Beethoven's sonata, in fact entered the novella relatively late in its genesis. The original, rather Dostoevskyan, plot was composed of Pozdnyshev's confession of the murder of his wife after finding explicit evidence of her betrayal, with ideological reflections addressing women's growing sexual liberation and Strindbergian anxieties about paternity (the story ends with Pozdnyshev leaving the train compartment with a young girl who may or may not be his daughter); only in later redactions did Tolstoy advert to music.[1] The canonical story of the novella's development refers to an evening recital of the Beethoven sonata that so impressed Tolstoy that he proposed to the artist Repin, also in attendance, that they each compose artworks inspired by the sonata; Tolstoy's story would be read publicly accompanied by Repin's painting on stage.[2] Against this *biographical-genetic* interpretation I suggest a *discursive-genetic* explanation. Tolstoy was working on *What is Art?* and *Kreutzer Sonata* simultaneously: indeed, his diary entries alternate between the works literally day by day.[3] Hence my suggestion is that in *Kreutzer Sonata* Tolstoy developed in the literary medium a problem that arose for him while working on his aesthetic philosophy in *What Is Art?*. That

problem is the divorce between the ethical and aesthetic in immediate understanding, the modality of understanding which, according to Schopenhauer, is characteristic of both ethical and aesthetic consciousness.

Earlier redactions of the art essay—all of which define art as infectiousness, with analogies to yawning and hypnotism—reveal Tolstoy concerned with music's unique status, among the arts, as defined by its lack of representational content, its potential to evoke distinct feelings, and its transience of influence precluding the listener from understanding, explaining, or justifying the feelings evoked. For instance, in "On What Is Called Art" ("O tom, chto nazyvaetsia iskusstvom," ca. 1896), he writes:

> And in no other art form have people traveled so far in artificiality [*iskusstvennost'*] as in music . . . The reason for this is that other artforms may still somehow be explained [*raz'iasnit'*], but with music this is impossible. It is literally an immediate thing [*Ona priamo neposredstvennoe delo*]. And therefore, if a painting is senseless [*bessmyslenna*] or incorrect, any viewer will judge it and explain its deficiencies. It is the same situation with poetry. Any person can say that this character, situation is expressed unnaturally or untruthfully; only with music, almost with lyric poetry, it is impossible to deliberate and debate [*rassuzhdat'*], it is impossible to say why it is good or not good.
>
> For this reason music (like lyric poetry), having fallen upon the false path of arts of our time . . . entered into those terrible debris of senselessness [*bessmyslitsy*] in which today it is located.
>
> Music is an art that acts directly upon the feelings, and that is why it would seem that in order to be an art, it should act upon the feelings. Besides this, music is a transient art. The work is played and finished; you cannot at will continue your impression, as you can with a painting or a book. And that is why it would seem that a musical work, in order to be an art, must act on the feelings. And what then? The majority of musical works in imitation of senseless works of Beethoven are essentially a collection of sounds having interest for those who have studied the fugue and counterpoint, but not evoking any feeling in the usual listener; and musicians not only are not embarrassed by this, but quietly assert that this proceeds from the fact that the listener *does not understand music*.[4]

Because of these specific features of music as a form of art, Tolstoy concludes that unlike discursive thought and verbal art, music is simply not accessible to the question of intelligibility: to ask what a piece of music means is like asking how much the color green weighs, it is simply nonsensical. Rather, the logically appropriate question is whether a piece of music does or does not infect listeners, whether they assimilate or appropriate it or not:

> I began, as I said earlier, with music, with that very art form that immediately always acts upon the feelings and in which it seems it is impossible to talk about not understanding [*neponimanie*]. But in the meantime least of all with music can one use the word "to understand," and this seems to have led to the idea that one has to understand music. But what does it mean to understand music? Apparently the word—understand—is here being used as a metaphor, in a figurative sense. It is impossible to either understand or not understand music. And this expression, apparently, only means that one can assimilate [*usvaivat'*] music, that is, receive from it that which it gives, or not receive it, just as, with a thought stated verbally, it can either be understood or not understood. Thought can be explicated and made clear by means of words. Music cannot be explicated and made clear, and therefore it is impossible to say in the literal sense [*v priamom smysle*] that music can be understood. Music can only infect or not infect.[5]

Finally, in the recollections of his conversations with Tolstoy about music, A. B. Gol'denveizer emphasizes precisely the same point, namely that music alone among the arts is non-representational, and draws the useful distinction between referent (*predmet*) and contents (*soderzhanie*):

> If we exclude "program" music and music with words (this is no longer pure musical art, but rather the blending in one artwork of elements of various artforms), then a characteristic feature of music is its "lack of referent" ["*bezpredmetnost'*"]. "Lack of referent," that is, the absence of *concrete* objects of representation [*konkretnyx ob"ektov izobrazheniia*], is often confused with the absence of *contents* [*soderzhaniia*], and music is turned into merely a play of sounds. But this is profoundly untrue: no other artform besides music conveys [*peredaet*] with such force of influence and with such immediacy [*neposredstvennost'*] intellectual and emotional contents, experienced by the composer and expressed by him in sounds. . . . The "contents" of a musical work most clearly and forcefully of all is transmitted by the musical work itself, and has no need for any kind of "interlinear notes" ["*podstrochniki*"].[6]

And in this context he notes: "Of the various attempts to explain music philosophically, it seemed to Lev Nikolaevich that the most important was the original views upon music of Schopenhauer, although he [Tolstoy] did not think that he [Schopenhauer] really explained its essence."[7]

What is the problem with Schopenhauer's philosophy of music for Tolstoy? Precisely its lack of a referent, its nonsensicality; in a word, music evokes or conveys affect without contextualizing discursive or narrative justification, as we saw in the previous chapter. Schopenhauer writes:

> [Music] never expresses the phenomenon, but only the inner nature, the in-itself, of every phenomenon, the will itself. Therefore music does not express this or that particular and definite pleasure, this or that affliction, pain, sorrow, horror, gaiety, merriment, peace of mind, but joy, pain, sorrow, horror, gaiety, peace of mind *themselves*, to a certain extent in the abstract, their essential nature, without any accessories, and so also *without the motives for them*.[8]

Music is thus for Tolstoy the extreme case of the *content-indifferentism* of aesthetic affect: that an artwork may successfully transmit (infect) its "definite feeling" to its audience, but that that feeling will interact with each recipient's will and character, which in turn may be virtuous or vicious. Music (other than communal forms like folk songs) is the extreme version of this because, in Tolstoy's understanding of Schopenhauer, it conveys affective contents ("manifestations of willing," in Schopenhauer's phrase) without the normatively structured motives that would be appropriate for them; the result is powerful affective forces set free in the recipient to interact with whatever *other* motives and *his* character might be. This then is a sharpened formulation of the "Nietzschean threat" discussed in the previous chapter.

2. In *The Kreutzer Sonata*, the figure of Pozdnyshev embodies this Nietzschean danger, even when we take into account that he is narrating his own encounter with the presto movement of Beethoven's sonata, which he calls "a fearful thing." For he explicitly generalizes his observation to claims like "music in general's a fearful thing" and "yet this fearful medium is available to anyone who cares to make use of it."[9] Pozdnyshev describes the effect of music in similes of immediate cause and effect seemingly borrowed directly from *What Is Art?*:

> Music makes me forget myself, my true condition, it carries me off into another state of being, one that isn't my own: under the influence of music I have the illusion of feeling things I don't really feel, of understanding things I don't understand, being able to do things I'm not able to do. I explain this by the circumstance that the effect produced by music is similar to that produced by yawning or laughter: I may not be sleepy, but I yawn if I see someone else yawning; I may have no reason for laughing, but I laugh if I see someone else laughing.[10]

The continuity between feeling and action ("feeling things I don't really feel" to "being able to do things I'm not able to do") suggests the Schopenhauerian expanded conception of will as both manifestations of willing (emotions, feelings, moods, sensations) and acts of will (actions) that we examined in chapter 4. Moreover, Pozdnyshev likewise uses the same verb—*slivat'sia*—as in *What Is Art?* to describe the "merging" of recipient and artist through the conveyed feeling: "Music carries me instantly and directly into the state of consciousness that was experienced by its composer. My soul merges [*slivaetsia*] with his, and together with him I'm transported from one state of consciousness into another."[11] Correspondingly in *What Is Art?* we read a revised definition of "infection" as

> the perceiver merges [*slivaetsia*] with the artist to such a degree that it seems to him that the perceived object had been made, not by someone else, but by himself, and that everything expressed by the object is exactly what he has long been wanting to express. The effect of the true work of art is to abolish in the consciousness of the perceiver the distinction between himself and the artist, and not only between himself and the artist, but also between himself and all who perceive the same work of art. It is this liberation of the person from his isolation from others, from his loneliness, this merging [*sliianie*] of the person with others, that constitutes the chief attractive force and property of art.[12]

That is, the universal infectiousness of art abrogates the *principium individuationis* equally loathed by Schopenhauer, Nietzsche, *and* Tolstoy. But whereas Nietzsche draws the conclusion from Schopenhauer's metaphysics of music that art is indifferent to morality, a conclusion that Tolstoy accepts in his analytic division between what constitutes genuine art (infectiousness of *any* distinct feeling) and what constitutes good, worthy art (genuine art that infects morally *good* feelings), he cannot abide by this conclusion, and so introduces the further step in his argument that only virtuous feelings—those of "the good" and religious feeling—are most universal and most uniting of mankind, hence most infectious, hence belong to true or most perfect works of art (*What Is Art?*, chapter 16).

Yet the obvious counterexample to Tolstoy's claim is—following Schopenhauer and Nietzsche—music, which is considered the most universal of arts. And in fact Tolstoy implicitly concedes the point by differentiating two kinds of feelings that can unite universally: those of religious (Christian) sentiment that are embodied in "religious art' " and simple, everyday feelings accessible to everyone, such as merriment, tenderness, and so on that are embodied in "universal art." Further, according to Tolstoy, religious art manifests itself mainly in verbal art, while universal art manifests itself mainly in music.[13] When Tolstoy comes to ask what contemporary music might fulfill this condition of being universal art, he faults modern compositions *not* directly for their immoral content but for their *lack of content* and exclusive emphasis on technique: "Owing to a poverty of content, of feeling, the melodies of modern composers are strikingly vapid."[14] Tolstoy, echoing Pozdnyshev virtually verbatim, concludes that "in music, apart from marches and dances by various composers, which approximate to the demands of universal art, one can point only to the folk songs of various peoples."[15]

In fact Pozdnyshev—though with a difference, as we shall see—provides some of the missing steps in *What Is Art?* on this point. Music infects the listener with the feelings felt or recollected by the composer when she or he wrote the piece. But for the composer those feelings were part of a more or less rational, that is, consistent and coherent set of beliefs and desires (i.e., Schopenhauerian motives and the composer's underlying character) that render those feelings meaningful, and in principle liable both to normative standards (of consistency, coherence, appropriateness, etc.) and associated action (acts of will). But the listener, according to Pozdnyshev, receives these feelings without that context for understanding them, let alone evaluating them:

> And that's why that kind of music's just an irritant—because it doesn't lead anywhere. A military band plays a march, say: the soldiers march in step, and the music's done its work. An orchestra plays a dance tune, I dance, and the music's done its work. A Mass is sung, I take communion, and once again the music's done its work. But that other kind of music's just an irritation, an excitement, and the action the excitement's supposed to lead to simply isn't there! That's why it's such a fearful thing, why it sometimes has such a horrible effect.
>
> . . .
>
> Such pieces [as the "Kreutzer Sonata"] should be played only on certain special, solemn, significant occasions when certain solemn actions have to be performed, actions that correspond to the nature of the music. It should be played, and as it's played those actions which it's inspired with its significance should be performed. Otherwise the generation of all that feeling and energy, which are quite inappropriate to either the place or the occasion, and which aren't allowed any outlet, can't have anything but a harmful effect. On me, at any rate, that piece had the most shattering effect; I had the illusion that I was discovering entirely new emotions, new possibilities I'd known nothing of before then.[16]

Why is the effect so "shattering" on Pozdnyshev? If we understand this, we will understand better the relationship between *The Kreutzer Sonata* and *What Is Art?*. In fact, by his description of the immediate effect of the Beethoven sonata—"my awareness of this new state of consciousness filled me with joy"—one might be led to think the effect salutary. But we need, in a first step, to consider Pozdnyshev's experience of music against the background of all we know about him, and then, in a second step, view our considerations against the background of Tolstoy's assertions in *What Is Art?*.

3. The tension between the *causal* (or "physiological") and *normative* (or "moral") orders which we saw inhabiting Tolstoy's understanding of aesthetic "infection" in *Anna Karenina* and *What Is Art?* is operative in *Kreutzer Sonata* as well. One could characterize Pozdnyshev's general, self-exculpatory discursive strategy as that of materializing, or desublimating, the normative, by which I mean that moral concepts and categories are unmasked through materialist, physiological explanations. The greatest target of course is romantic notions of love, which he redescribes in purely physiological vocabulary of cause and effect. For him, love is lust: "every man experiences what you call love each time he meets a pretty woman,"[17] and debauchery promotes (male) health.[18] Moreover, the ideology of romantic love is a ruse played by both partners: "she knows that our man's lying when he goes on about lofty emotions—all he wants is her body . . . what we live in is a sort of licensed brothel. . . . As a rule, we may say that while short-term prostitutes are generally looked down upon, long-term prostitutes are treated with respect."[19] This general argumentation reaches an emphasis of sorts in chapter 5, when Pozdnyshev describes his courting of a landowner's daughter that evokes the immediate understanding between Levin and Kitty in *Anna Karenina*: "it seemed to me that she understood everything, all I was thinking and feeling, and that all my thoughts and feelings were of the most exalted kind."[20] And, like Levin in the novel and Tolstoy himself, after they become engaged he gives her his diary—the diary of a seducer.[21] Pozdnyshev implies that at the time he too believed the ideology but now—at the time of narration—he unmasks his own earlier beliefs as mere physical attraction: "Yes, I was a dirty pig [*uzhasnaia svin'ia*], and I thought I was an angel."[22] These revised self-attributions indicate how reliant we are on Pozdnyshev's narration and how unreliable he is as a narrator.[23] For the argument at hand it is important to observe that he performs the same materialization on other normative concepts, including music, "the most refined form of sexual lust."[24] Love is not the expression of noble sentiments, but is redescribed physiologically as the release or "safety valve" (*spasitel'nyi klapan*) of pent-up energy. Pozdnyshev's discourse is laced with what could be called *hydraulic* imagery. For instance, sex provides the safety valve for accumulated energy:

> Every day each of us eats perhaps two pounds of meat, game and all kinds of stimulating food and drink. Where does it all go? On sensual [*chustvennye*] excesses. If we really do use it up in that way, the safety valve is opened and everything is all right. If, on the other hand, we close the safety valve, as I did mine from time to time, there immediately results a state of physical arousal which, channeled through the prism of our artificial way of life, expresses itself as the purest form of love, sometimes even as a platonic infatuation. I, too, fell in love that way, like everyone else.[25]

Moreover, sex represents for Pozdnyshev the single greatest impediment to mankind collectively attaining higher moral goals, because "carnal love has become a safety valve" dissipating those idealist energies.[26] Sex as safety valve both promotes physical health and hampers moral progress. And, Pozdnyshev describes his jealousy in similar imagery: "I was like an upturned bottle from which the water won't flow because it's too full."[27] And lastly, as we saw above, Pozdnyshev conceives of the causal effect of the contemporary decontextualized music such as Beethoven's sonata according to exactly the same hydraulic model: it arouses energies without providing a (contextualized) "outlet."

For Pozdnyshev, thus, sex and art are both matters of physiology: cause and effect, desire and pleasure, safety valves and outlets. Pozdnyshev in short functions as an extreme spokesperson for those Tolstoy in *What Is Art?* calls "aesthetic physiologists," for whom art is "a form of play in which man releases a surplus of stored-up energy," rather than a "means of human communion" by conveying feeling.[28] Moreover, music is especially suited to such a physiological conception of aesthetic response:

> The substitution of effects for aesthetic feeling is especially noticeable in musical art—an art peculiar in its direct physiological impact on the nerves. Instead of using melody to convey the feelings experienced by the composer, the new musician accumulates and interweaves sounds, and by alternately intensifying and weakening them, produces a physiological effect on the public, which can be measured by an apparatus specially designed for that purpose. And the public mistakes this physiological effect for the effect of art.[29]

And in excoriating Wagner's operas, Tolstoy in *What Is Art?*—like Pozdnyshev in chapter 23 of *Kreutzer Sonata*—likens the effect of such music to that of hypnosis, "drinking wine or smoking opium."[30] Such effects, including "that certain vague and almost morbid excitement from the works of Beethoven's late period," are then juxtaposed by Tolstoy to the conveyance of a "definite feeling," with "impressions received from Italian, Norwegian and Russian folksongs, from Hungarian *czardas*, and other such simple, clear, strong things."[31]

4. In Pozdnyshev, Tolstoy presents a mouthpiece of the aesthetic physiologists, but he does much more: he presents a detailed portrait of what someone who exists maximally—if not exclusively—within the causal order might look like, namely a person wholly given up to the impingements the world exerts upon him, a man who *wills* his causal dependencies. He is a virtual chain-smoker, "inhaling greedily,"[32] a drinker of tea so strong it is "really like beer,"[33] possibly an opium addict,[34] definitely a self-confessed fornicator (*bludnik*), where "being a fornicator is a physical condition similar to that

of a morphine addict, an alcoholic or a smoker of opium."[35] Pozdnyshev defines himself, and virtually his entire gender, by their chosen, that is, *willed*, dependencies on physical stimulation: "men can't survive without it. . . . Tell a man he needs vodka, tobacco and opium, and all those things will become necessities for him."[36] Richard Gustafson rightly emphasizes Pozdnyshev's addictions, but to my mind overemphasizes them all as "intoxications,"[37] missing thereby the greatest of Pozdnyshev's dependencies: jealousy.[38] Tolstoy takes some care insinuating this into Pozdnyshev's narrative. His first mention of jealousy in fact reveals that it has bedeviled him even before he was married: "the torments of jealousy *reawoke* in me: they continued to plague me throughout the whole of my married life";[39] and later in his story he refers to "similar attacks of jealousy I'd had previously."[40] Whereas his first mention of the "beast" (*zver'*) refers to the purported mutual attraction between Trukhachevsky and his wife (whom in turn he will call "bitch" [*suka*]),[41] thereafter Pozdnyshev uses the term exclusively to refer to his own jealousy. "The rabid beast of jealousy began to snarl in its kennel, trying to get out, but I was afraid of that beast, and I hastily locked it up inside me";[42] "I was like a wild animal in a cage: at one moment I'd leap up and go to the window, at another I'd pace stumblingly up and down, willing the train to go faster";[43] "I gave free rein to my hatred—I became a beast, a savage and cunning beast";[44] had he forgiven her then the next day "the beast of jealousy would have taken possession of my heart for ever and torn it to shreds."[45] Pozdnyshev describes his state of mind just before he sets to murdering his wife as: "I entered that state a wild animal knows, or the state that's experienced by a man who is under the influence of physical excitement at a time of danger, and who acts precisely, unhurriedly, but without ever wasting a moment, and with only one end in view."[46] And twice in describing the murder itself he speaks of a "rabid frenzy" (*beshenstvo*) possessing him.[47] In short here too Pozdnyshev at least portrays himself as determined by causes somehow different from himself. In one lapse he reverts to a *musical* metaphor to describe the involuted causal agency which he strangely both concedes and denies: to his wife's frantic appeals he comments "the reply had to be in keeping with the state of mind *into which I'd brought myself* [*privel sebia*] which was inexorably rising to a *crescendo* and which could not but continue to rise. Rabid frenzy too has its laws."[48] Pozdnyshev is both agent and victim of the causal laws—be they those of music or frenzied rage—at work upon him. In his uncontrollable sounds and gesticulations, his addictions, his jealousy and even his desperate need for a listener, Pozdnyshev manifests his dependence upon and solicitation of the world's impingements upon him, his will to causal dependency. Indeed, Pozdnyshev tells his acquired confidant that during his return journey from his country estate to confront his wife and her suspected lover, the rhythm of the train so affected him that under its influence he imagined again her adultery: "It was as though some devil was inventing the most abominable notions and suggesting them to me against my will" but then adds, "I'd pace stumblingly up and down, willing the train to go faster; but the carriage just went on shaking and vibrating all its seats and windows, exactly as ours is doing now," and indeed, as Pozdnyshev recounts his story in the train carriage that he had *voluntarily* boarded he becomes—again—more and more agitated.[49] The same willed dependence operates at the narratological level: Pozdnyshev's unreliability as a narrator is coupled with his desperate need *for* an addressee, a confessor, and he arguably distends and retards, foreshadows and builds suspense for the traveling companions that constitute his audience in order to hold them enthralled. And Tolstoy keeps the nameless frame-narrator as *transparent* as possible so that we perceive that need clearly. Indeed, the narrator who met Pozdnyshev and is now recounting the latter's story never tells us, the narrator's audience, of his reactions to Pozdnyshev's tale.[50]

5. How are we to understand Pozdnyshev's as it were willful dependence on the world? I think once again Wittgenstein can be of assistance. In the *Tractatus* he maintains that ethics, like logic, is transcendental. In her commentary Cora Diamond has remarked:

> Just as logic is not, for Wittgenstein, a particular subject, with its own body of truths, but penetrates all thought, so ethics has no particular subject matter; rather, an ethical spirit, an attitude to the world and life, can penetrate any thought or talk. Wittgenstein . . . speaks of two different as it were attitudes to the world as a whole; he refers to them as that of the happy and that of the unhappy. The happy and the unhappy as it were inhabit different worlds.

She suggests that "the ethical spirit is tied to living in acceptance that what happens, happens, that one's willing this rather than that is merely another thing that happens and that one is in a sense 'powerless.' "[51] Now one might suppose that Pozdnyshev fulfills that condition, albeit in a strained sense, because he appears to be so dependent on the impingements of the world; but he *wants and seeks out* those impingements, and this betrays his immeasurable willful grasp *upon* the world, which becomes resentment and jealousy when, as it must, the world fails to answer his will, the conditions he lays down for it.[52] I think Pozdnyshev means something like this when he admits that his wife is "a mystery, just as she's always been, just as she'll always be. I don't know her. I only know her as an animal"[53] and, ultimately:

> What was really so horrible was that I felt I have a complete and unalienable right to [his wife's] body, as if it were my own, yet at the same time I wasn't the master of this body, that it didn't belong to me, that she could do anything with it whatever she pleased, and that what she wanted to do with it wasn't what I wanted.[54]

Wittgenstein, on Cora Diamond's account, holds that an "evil will" is not empirical in the sense that it is essentially determined *as* evil by *what* it wills in particular; rather an evil will is one that has the attitude to the world of issuing conditions upon it and when frustrated, bearing it resentment.[55] This would accord with what Schopenhauer held, as we saw in the previous chapter: which particular actions issue from a vicious character depends on what particular motives act upon that character. Because, on this account, evil and an evil character are not a relation in the world of persons, objects, states of affairs, and so on, but rather an attitude towards the world, Wittgenstein states in the *Tractatus*:

> 6.421 It is clear that ethics cannot be put into words.
> Ethics is transcendental.
> (Ethics and aesthetics are one and the same.)

I think Tolstoy in *What Is Art?*, like Levin after his conversion, is getting at something very similar when he states that

> the good is indeed a fundamental concept, which metaphysically [This echoes Schopenhauer; Wittgenstein would say "transcendentally"] constitutes the essence of our consciousness ["our attitude to the world"], a concept undefinable by reason ["cannot be put into words"].
>
> The good is that which no one can define, but which defines everything else.[56]

Likewise Tolstoy implicitly claims that aesthetics, like ethics and logic for Wittgenstein, is not restricted to beautiful objects in the world, but rather pervades one's attitude to and involvement in the world, when Tolstoy expands the meaning of genuine art as "the entire human activity that conveys feelings: so that art in the broad sense pervades our entire life."[57] Furthermore, Tolstoy can be seen to be identifying aesthetics and ethics in what could be called their "attitude toward the world" when he grounds a person's infection by art in that person's specific character, understood in terms Schopenhauer and Wittgenstein would affirm: "the appreciation of the works of art—that is, of the feelings it conveys—depends on people's understanding of the meaning of life, on what they see as good and evil in life."[58] And we recall that in reporting the hypnotic effects of the sonata, and of music in general, Pozdnyshev was careful to qualify "*for me, at any rate*."[59]

Pozdnyshev is just such an evil will in Wittgenstein's account, and the astute reader will perceive this, hear it from within, as it were, his story. Tolstoy, I suggest, intimates as much within the second epigraph to the novella: "But he said unto them, All men cannot receive this saying, save they to whom it is given" (Matt. 19:11). Quite similarly, in a letter to his friend and publisher, Wittgenstein wrote that he regarded the *Tractatus* as a work of ethics, but that this most important part of his work cannot be expressed discursively:

> But now I am counting on you. And there it may be of some help to you if I write you a few words about my book: since—I am quite sure of that—you won't get very much at all out of reading it. For, you won't understand it; its subject matter will appear entirely foreign to you. But in reality it isn't foreign to you, for the sense of the book is an ethical one. I once wanted to include a sentence in the preface which doesn't in fact appear there now. But I am writing it to you now because it might serve you as a key: For I wanted to write that my work consists of two parts: the one you have in front of you and all that I have *not* written. And just that second part is the important one. Because the ethical is delimited by my book at it were from within; and I am convinced that *strictly* it can *only* be delimited like that. In short, I believed: Everything that *many* are *blathering* about today, I settled by being silent about it. And that's why this book, unless I am very mistaken, says much that you yourself want to say, but perhaps won't see that it is said in it. I would now recommend that you read the *preface* and the *conclusion*, since these express the sense most immediately.[60]

The meaning of life understood as an *ethical* attitude cannot be "said" because it is not something in or of the world, but rather an attitude towards the world as such. Wittgenstein returned to this thought in a lecture on ethics he gave in 1929:

> I see now that these nonsensical expressions ["judgments of absolute value" like the meaning of life, being absolutely safe, etc.] were not nonsensical because I had not yet found the correct expressions, but that their nonsensicality was their very essence. For all I wanted to do with them was just *to go beyond* the world and that is to say beyond significant language.[61]

If ethical statements, statements of "absolute" value, are nonsensical, then the direct presentation of an ethical spirit or an ethical character will not be understood: such an attitude to the world cannot be "said," but only "shown." Consider these passages from chapter 7 of Tolstoy's *The Gospel in Brief* (1881), a work that Wittgenstein carried on his person for over a year:

> At another time, Jesus was speaking with the orthodox, and said to them: "There can be no proofs of the truth of my teaching, as there cannot be of the illumination of light. My teaching is the real light,

> by which people tell what is good and what is bad, and therefore it is impossible to prove my teaching; which itself proves everything. Whoever shall follow me shall not be in darkness, but shall have life. Life and enlightenment, which are one and the same."
>
> And Jesus said to them: "If your father were one with me, you would love me, because I came forth from that Father. For I was not born of myself. You are not children of the one Father with me, therefore you do not understand my word; my understanding of life does not find place with you."
>
> And yet a third time Jesus taught the people, he said: "Men surrender themselves to my teaching, not because I myself prove it. It is impossible to prove the truth. The truth itself proves the rest. But men surrender to my teaching, because there is no other than it; it is known by men, and promises life."[62]

Pozdnyshev's narrative, I suggest, functions analogously to Wittgenstein's description of the *Tractatus* in his letter to his publisher. Gary Saul Morson plausibly reads the novella as a sophisticated conjuration and subsequent condemnation of the pre-conversion Tolstoy by the post-conversion Tolstoy, but solely for *aesthetic* reasons: "Tolstoy wants us to reject Tolstoy as Tolstoy rejected Tolstoy. It follows that we can understand fictions like *The Kreutzer Sonata* best if we treat them as anti-fictions. *The Kreutzer Sonata* is a brilliantly contrived aesthetic masterpiece that teaches us to despise such contrivance and mastery—and that is its duplicitous strategy." But it is not Tolstoy's narrative art that is duplicitous, but rather Pozdnyshev's addiction to narrative—and to any listener—that is duplicitous. By keeping the frame-narrator as invisible as possible Tolstoy allows Pozdnyshev as it were to speak directly to the reader as needed addressee, but both the direct speech and the described mannerisms of Pozdnyshev "show" what cannot be said: the attitude of an evil character, in Wittgenstein's sense.[63]

6. Morson is correct, however, to detect a gesture of self-abjuration in *The Kreutzer Sonata*, of Tolstoy's condemning (an earlier) Tolstoy, but this self-condemnation—another "linkage"—is effectuated between *The Kreutzer Sonata* and *What Is Art?*. The latter work, we recall, argues that beauty "come[s] down to a certain sort of pleasure that we receive, meaning that we recognize as beauty that which pleases us."[64] Aesthetic theories of the beautiful—such as the "art for art's sake movement" to which the young Tolstoy himself once subscribed—are rejected by the older Tolstoy because such theories see art as a "means of pleasure" rather than "one of the conditions of human life" and "spiritual nourishment."[65] The most extended—indeed, Homeric—simile in *What Is Art?* elaborates upon this contrast in distinctly

sexual imagery at the conclusion of chapter 18, beginning: "Terrible as it may be to say it, what has happened to the art of our circle and time is the same as happens with a woman who sells her feminine attractions, destined for motherhood, for the pleasure of those who are tempted by such pleasures." "The art of our time and circle," he asserts, "has become a whore," using the feminine form (*bludnitsa*) of the word Pozdnyshev uses to describe himself: "fornicator" (*bludnik*).[66] My schematic understanding of the simile, which is developed by Tolstoy over the next several paragraphs, is as follows:

Genuine Art	**Tenor**	**Vehicle**
Effect	new feeling	new life
Result of action (= conception)	artwork	child
Agent	soul of artist	mother/wife
Cause	stored-up feeling	love (not lust)

Counterfeit Art	**Tenor**	**Vehicle**
Effect	pleasure	[sexual addiction, disease]
Result of action	counterfeit art	[pleasure]
Agent	artisan	whore
Cause	money	money

The values placed in brackets are not explicitly stated by Tolstoy, though they can be inferred from the general semantics of the simile. They also, it may be said, evoke the earlier life of Tolstoy himself, in Kazan and St. Petersburg, during which time he, according to A. N. Wilson, contracted and received treatment for a venereal disease.

There is some indication that Pozdnyshev, for whom music is "that most refined form of sensual lust," is a syphilitic. Here too he is unreliable. Early on when castigating the ideology of "sex as healthy" he acknowledges the existence and promulgation of a medical cure—"The danger of infection? But that, too, is taken care of. Our solicitous government takes pains to see to it."[67] But later, when he launches into a tirade against "the moral rot of materialism," he contradicts himself: "and all that's quite apart from the fact that if they were to follow the doctors' instructions regarding the infection they say is rife everywhere and in everything, people would have to seek not union but disunion; according to the doctors' version of things, everyone ought to keep apart from one another and never take the spray-syringe of phenol acid (which they've found doesn't have any effect anyway) out of their mouths."[68] Moreover, it is precisely the conflict between her "moral obligations of a mother" and "her obligations as a wife" that make Pozdnyshev's wife the object of his rabid jealousy.

Here then, perhaps, we have a "linkage" connecting autobiographical elements from Tolstoy's youth, reworked into an extended simile used to define "counterfeit" art in contradistinction from "genuine" art, then literalized in the character and plotline of Pozdnyshev. The young gallant author, adherent to the art for art's sake movement in his veneration of beauty as the instrument of aesthetic pleasure and his veneration of women as the instruments of physical pleasure, is rejected by the older Tolstoy, who teases out the parallels in his treatise on aesthetics and his novella on jealousy. Grounding both the rejected aesthetics of beauty and rejected ethics of willful dependency is a notion of ethical character that reaches back to Schopenhauer and forward to Wittgenstein.

7. But this story of conversion, confession, and self-abjuration, which we have traced from *Anna Karenina* to the normative aesthetic theory of *What Is Art?*, leads to a significant problem for Tolstoy, for—as he makes clear in the later chapters of *What Is Art?*—he wants genuine artworks to trigger such conversions in others, to *instill* and *foster* moral sensibility, religious values, and universal feelings. Because music can be morally inert while still causing a powerful feeling "without motive," the normative meaning content of the feeling conveyed will be determined by the recipient's good or evil will, his ethical attitude, which contextualizes the feeling. Thus, Schopenhauer's view implies that the effect of music, and perhaps other art forms, is determined by rather than determining of the ethical outlook of the recipient. And we recall that in reporting the "fearful . . . [and] horrible effect" of music in general, Pozdnyshev was careful to qualify "for me, at any rate." If an evil attitude or will can thwart the will-less immediate understanding that Tolstoy advocates in *What Is Art?*, he may feel the metaphysical pull to somehow *guarantee* the universal transmission of those values he wants art to instill in people.

What Is Art? does not end with chapter 19, the passionate manifesto announcing the coming genuine and morally good art of the future; instead there is a final chapter, bearing the title "Conclusion" (it is the only chapter of the book to have a chapter heading). At its outset Tolstoy tells of working on the treatise for fifteen years, laying it aside in frustration and returning to it repeatedly. The implication is that only with this chapter was Tolstoy able to bring his treatise to a satisfying conclusion, but if that is true, such satisfaction is achieved only by placing the entire argument of the previous nineteen chapters in a greater framework, for in this final chapter Tolstoy expands his enlightenment story of progressive religious consciousness and art to include the role of science in the modern world, because "art has always been closely dependent" upon science.[69] Whereas earlier in the treatise Tolstoy had claimed that morally good art depends on and disseminates the contents of the most advanced religious consciousness of the time, he now incorporates science as a mediating link:

> True science studies and introduces into human consciousness the truths and the knowledge which are regarded as most important by the people of a certain period and society. Art transfers these truths from the realm of knowledge to the realm of feeling.
>
> . . .
>
> The degree of importance both of the feelings conveyed by art and of the knowledge conveyed by science is determined for people by the religious consciousness of the given time and society—that is, the general understanding among people of that time and society of the purpose of their life.[70]

The model Tolstoy presents now seems to be the following. Religious consciousness, that is, beliefs about the purpose or meaning of life, fundamental values ("the good") and so on, still provides the criterion of importance, but now to two "spiritual activities,"[71] science and art. Therefore, for Tolstoy science, like art in earlier chapters, will be evaluated according to how well it follows the religious consciousness of the age. Unsurprisingly, Tolstoy has as little sympathy for the science of his day as he does for its art. He divides contemporary science into two areas. The first area, what we might call social science (history, political economy, theology, philosophy) "is occupied predominantly with proving that the existing order of life is the very one which ought to exist" and hence cannot advance the moral improvement of society. The second area, what he calls "experimental science," or what would today be called pure science, is rejected because its practitioners "have invented a theory of science for science's sake, exactly like the theory of art for art's sake" which he had excoriated in earlier chapters.[72] By the criterion of religious consciousness, therefore, both these areas of science are false or counterfeit because, like false art, they do not work for the benefit of people. "True science" would "become a harmonious, organic whole with a definite and reasonable purpose, understandable to all people—namely the introducing into people's consciousness of the truths that come from the religious consciousness of our time."[73] Tolstoy's claim, I take it, is that true science would convey in discursive thought, as a kind of applied social science, knowledge about society and the natural world necessary for implementing the values of religious consciousness and universal brotherhood.

According to Tolstoy's model, the feelings which art conveys themselves depend on the science of the day and therefore, if the science is false or counterfeit, so too will be the feelings. The first area of science—social sciences legitimating the retrograde status quo—"calls up backward feelings which have been outlived by mankind, feelings which in our time are bad and exclusive," while the other area—pure science—"occupied with the study of subjects that by their very essence have no relation to human life, cannot serve as the basis of art."[74] The dependency relation between art and science diagnosed by Tolstoy in chapter 20 is a substantial departure from his earlier chapters, in which discursive thought—knowledge and speech (*rech'*)—apparently operated independently of feelings and art:

> Art, together with speech, is a means of communication, and therefore also of progress—that is, of mankind's movement forward towards perfection. . . . And just as in the evolution of knowledge—that is, the forcing out and supplanting of mistaken and unnecessary knowledge by truer and more necessary knowledge—so the evolution of feelings takes place by means of art, replacing lower feelings, less kind and less needed for the good of humanity, by kinder feelings, more needed for that good.[75]

One possible explanation for Tolstoy's reconceiving the relationship between discursive thought and emotion is Schopenhauer's theory of motives and willing: ethical character is expressed by its causal interaction with emotions ("manifestations of willing") and motives (cognitive representations of the world). If science constitutes the discursive body of cognitive representations of the world, then it would follow that it would influence the causal interaction of conveyed feelings and the character of an artwork's recipient. And therefore Tolstoy needs not only morally good artworks for his aesthetic education of mankind, but the right science as well.

8. However, since the science of his time is on the "false path" (*na lozhnom puti*), "the art of our time, in order to be art, must bypass science and make its own path" (*prokladyvat' sebe put'*), echoing the image of Levin's nominalistic revelation in *Anna Karenina*.[76] Drawing an analogy with the role of church art, he reasons: "If through art there could be conveyed the customs [*obychai*] of treating religious objects in a certain way, . . . then this same art can evoke other customs, more closely corresponding to the religious consciousness of our time."[77] That is, Tolstoy now advocates the *creation* of new customs, practices, habits, through art: new contexts of significance within which words and actions acquire normative content and meaning, as we saw in chapter 1. Rather than the infection of a distinct feeling alone, which runs the risk of the Nietzschean threat, art's task now is to *train* its recipients in new practices and customs, "not in reasoning but in life itself":

> Art should make it so that the feelings of brotherhood and love of one's neighbor, now accessible only to the best people of society, become habitual feelings, an instinct for everyone. By calling up the

> feelings of brotherhood and love in people under imaginary conditions, religious art will accustom people to experiencing the same feelings in reality under the same conditions; it will lay in people's souls the *rails* [*reil'sy*] along which the life behavior of people brought up by art will *naturally* [*estestvenno*] run.[78]

In one compacted sentence, on the verge of self-contradiction, he ushers back in precisely the image—and the significations it has for him—that on my reading he had endeavored so earnestly to prescind from his understanding of ethics and aesthetics.[79] Against the whims of causality art will lay down the normative "rails" along which people's behavior will henceforward run "naturally." Art will lay the rails of communal understanding along which collective consciousness will find its semblance of "natural" community. Only this way can infection ultimately be guaranteed.

Fifty years later Wittgenstein perhaps borrowed Tolstoy's image to capture the idealization of meaning Platonism, of the rule of the application of a concept seen as rails extending into infinity: "Well, we might imagine rails instead of a rule. And infinitely long rails correspond to the unlimited application of a rule."[80] Wittgenstein here captures precisely the problem that confronted Tolstoy, and Wittgenstein's choice of metaphor, I suggest, indicates that he recognized Tolstoy's failed solution. One of the tensions within Wittgenstein's argument lies in whether knowing a concept necessarily entails having an intentional content of each and every of its applications, of knowing presently all cases in which the concept's application would be correct, which he calls "rails extending into the future." The pressure that leads to the fantasy of rails extending into the future is the skeptical question of how one can be certain that one does in fact possess the concept in question, that one does understand its normative reach, that is, all its possible contexts of correct usage. The analogous question in Tolstoy's treatise is how we can be sure we are the community we assume ourselves to be, such that we all will recognize, respond to, and participate in the customs and practices that constitute our communal consciousness, our being a community at all. In his *Philosophical Investigations* Wittgenstein calls such a fantasy of infinite rails a "crossing of different pictures of determination" (§191)—the confounding of a normative with a causal relation. Wittgenstein's rejection of the infinite rails as a fantasy of metaphysical Platonism translates into a rejection of Tolstoy's attempt to make art the promissory placeholder of a communal understanding that is at best always a contingent and ongoing but absolutely empirical *achievement*.

We have seen how Tolstoy's proposed answer to the "Nietzschean threat" he perceived in Schopenhauer's philosophy—how an expressivist aesthetics can convey distinct feelings—amounts to his slipping back into a form of meaning Platonism, and confounding two orders of relations: the causal and the normative.[81] In the next three chapters I will suggest modifications to Tolstoy's theory, in the context of contemporary debates surrounding the philosophy of emotions, the nature of moral emotions, and aesthetic expression. In this way I will show how a more sophisticated and yet more modest version of Tolstoy's theory, suitably reconstructed, is worthy of consideration today. If Wittgenstein's argument for immediate, non-interpretative understanding and against Derridean interpretivism makes sense, then the revisions to Tolstoy's theory of art elaborated in the next chapters will amount to an argument against the universal validity of deconstructive literary theory. At the very least it will fall to advocates of that theory to defend it against the arguments and interpretations presented in this book.

Chapter 6

Reconstructing Tolstoy I: The Nature of Emotions

> The human body is the best picture of the human soul.
>
> —Wittgenstein

We have seen that Tolstoy falls back into a metaphysical picture of meaning Platonism, specifically regarding the normativity of emotions, in order to guarantee the success of his moral-aesthetic program in the face of the "Nietzschean threat" of decontextualized affect posed by Schopenhauer's theory of the emotional effects of music. And we have seen how the implicit tension between a causal relation of "infectious" emotions and an intentional relation of emotions, which in turn permits normativity, underwrites that threat. Hence an adequate theory of emotions must precede the question of how Tolstoy's theory might be suitably modified in order to make it viable as a theory of aesthetic expression. In what follows I sketch out just such a theory dialectically, by in this chapter showing how it can resolve a tension between the causal and intentional relations that emerges within current debates in the philosophy of emotions in general and, in the next chapter, from a second tension that emerges in the discussion surrounding specifically moral emotions and virtue theory. Both tensions arise from the Cartesianism that was identified in chapter 1. We shall see that a proper account of moral emotions resolves these tensions and sets the stage for a constructive account of how artworks express and elicit emotions from audiences. This specific theory of aesthetic expression will be shown in chapter 8 to answer the same tension between causal and normative relations that bedevil rival accounts of the expression of emotion in art, even in the "hard case" of absolute music. Thus I will show how Tolstoy's theory, suitably modified, offers a viable expressivist alternative to the interpretivist aesthetic theories developed from Derridean principles.

My account will take its cues from the constraints on a theory of moral emotions that have emerged in the previous chapters of this study. A successful account of moral emotions must meet the following conditions of adequacy. First, ontologically an emotion—including a moral emotion—must exhibit not only a causal relation, but also an intentional relation underlying normativity; that is, an account of emotion must include some kind of correctness condition by which an emotional response can be fitting, appropriate, warranted, rational, or justified. The account of emotions provided in this chapter fulfills this first condition. Second, also ontologically, an account should acknowledge that Tolstoy speaks of two classes of morally important emotions: universal feelings, and religious feelings, where it appears that universal feelings are morally relevant sentiments common to human nature, while religious feelings are in some sense culturally established and individuated moral emotions. Third, epistemologically, moral emotions must provide some cognitive access to morally salient features of the world, such that this knowledge is immediate or non-inferential. The account of moral emotions and sensibility theory provided in the next chapter fulfills these second and third conditions. Fourth, aesthetically, it must be possible for artworks to elicit, inculcate, and develop moral emotions in their recipients. The account of aesthetic expression provided in chapter 8 fulfills this fourth and final condition. Thus these constraints orient the discussion and elaboration of the account provided in the following chapters.

The dialectic of the following chapters proceeds through the construction and resolution of a series of dilemmas in the specific philosophical topics relevant to thinking with Tolstoy and Wittgenstein about moral emotions and their possible expression and transmission in art. First I construe the causal-intentional tension in contemporary debates in the philosophy of emotion in the form of a dilemma between non-cognitivist or "feeling" theories of emotion on the one hand, and cognitivist or "judgment" theories of emotion on the other. Then, turning to morality in chapter 7, I locate a second but related dilemma in contemporary meta-ethics between moral judgment as a kind of belief on the one hand, and as a kind of desire on the other. These dilemmas arise from tacit Cartesian presuppositions that, once identified and set aside, permit alternative characterizations to come into view. Characterizing central moral emotions as sui generis states inseparably composed of conative and cognitive, and often physiological, phenomenological and behavioral-dispositional aspects, resolves these dilemmas. Third, turning to the epistemology of moral emotions, I construct a dilemma between objective and subjective theories of moral awareness and show how a "sensibility theory," which rests on key analogies and disanalogies with perceptual knowledge, best resolves the dilemma. Fourth and finally, I offer an explanatory gloss on Tolstoy's categories of "universal" and "religious" feelings in the context of contemporary thinking about emotions and their development into moral emotions through acculturation that sets the stage for chapter 8. In that chapter, I consider aesthetic expression, and more specifically how an artwork can elicit in its audience a determinate emotion. The result will be a robust reconstructive account of how Tolstoy's expressivism, suitably modified, constitutes a viable theory in light of today's debates surrounding moral emotions and aesthetic expression.

We should begin, however, with a hefty caveat regarding virtually *any* theory of emotion, namely that the concept EMOTION does not lend itself to necessary and sufficient conditions, but rather seems to function as a family resemblance concept, "a complicated network of similarities overlapping and crisscrossing: sometimes overall similarities, sometimes similarities in detail."[1] Thus our everyday concept of EMOTION extends from objectless moods (elation, depression, anxiety), through noncognitive, intentionless, involuntary reflexes (the startle response has been defended as an emotion),[2] to cognitive, propositionally articulated, voluntary emotions (vengeful ambition for something because of someone, say); emotions that involve specific bodily states (e.g., one's hairs bristle with fear) and those that don't (e.g., nostalgia). Some emotions are conceived as occurrent *states* of short duration (e.g., explosive rage), others as dispositional *traits* that can manifest occurrent states (e.g., the emotional trait of jealousy); some emotions seem to combine both occurrent states and dispositional traits in a complex, temporally extended and stagewise segmented *process*, as in the stages of grief that may extend over years or decades.[3] Choice of criteria determines categorization, but that choice is contested, so that often determinate definitions amount to stipulations.[4] Keeping in mind that our topic will eventually narrow to central moral emotions and their transmission or inculcation through art, we shall draw on those examples in elaborating our reconstruction.[5] While thus acknowledging that there are emotions on the periphery of any theory, the tradition of thinking about emotions has reliably delineated several aspects or dimensions of an emotion. First, often an emotion has a distinctive *phenomenology* or what-it-is-likeness: anger feels a certain way, distinct from how guilt or joy feels. Second, such phenomenal characteristics can include the perception of distinct *physiological* changes, only some of which may be perceptible to the person; anger is accompanied by a "boiling of the blood," Aristotle famously says:[6] one's pulse perceptibly quickens, one's capillaries imperceptibly open. One might feel oneself flush red with shame or guilt, and so on. Third, most emotions have *intentionality*: they are directed at or toward an object (real, imagined, or remembered).[7] One is frightened *of* the dog, or *of* the prospect of a downturn in the market; one is angry *at* the person who jumps the line, and so on. Fourth, often emotions involve a *behavioral* disposition, or an "action readiness" tendency: a disposition to act a certain way.[8] Thus when frightened one adopts a "fight, freeze or flight" attitude, and when ashamed one hangs one's head, and so on. Lastly emotions tend to involve a cognitive dimension: an *evaluation* or *appraisal*, or perhaps even a *belief* of some kind. One is indignant at a person because one believes that she has wronged one (or another) in some way; one is frightened of an object because one in some sense appraises it as dangerous. More generally, we seem to be able to easily categorize emotions as *valenced*, that is, positive or negative in regard to their intentional objects, and usually we view the emotions as correspondingly either pleasant or unpleasant.[9]

1. Recall that in *Anna Karenina*, and later in *What Is Art?*, Tolstoy introduces the term "to infect" with examples of what is now called emotional contagion: one person laughs, and another person begins to laugh, and so on.[10] These examples suggest that Tolstoy conceives of emotion in physiological terms, such that sensing another person's laughing as it were causally triggers a physiological response in oneself. This tradition in emotion theory—often called the *non-cognitive* or *feeling theory* of emotion—reaches back to William James and Curt Lange, Tolstoy's contemporaries, and forward to current neuroscientific studies and their partisan appropriation as "affect theory" by some scholars in cultural studies, social and political theory. Therefore, considering the James-Lange theory of emotion, its current versions and their shortcomings will prepare us for considering an equally one-sided response—the so-called *cognitivist theory* of emotion—before our dialectic leads us to a more promising conception of emotion in our reconstruction.

The James-Lange theory holds that emotions are feelings of patterned variations in one's body: muscular, vascular, epidermal, respiratory, etc. changes, but also facial expressions and behavioral dispositions.[11] In his influential article "What Is an Emotion?" (1884), William James argues that the bodily changes that one is tempted to call the "expression" of an emotion in fact are the primary constituent of the emotion:

> Our natural way of thinking about these standard emotions is that the mental perception of some fact excites the mental affection called the emotion, and that this latter state of mind gives rise to the bodily expression. My thesis on the contrary is that *the bodily changes follow directly the* PERCEPTION *of the exciting fact, and that our feeling of the same changes as they occur* IS *the emotion*. Common sense says, we lose our fortune, are sorry and weep; we meet a bear, are frightened and run; we are insulted by a rival, are angry and strike. The hypothesis here to be defended says that this order of sequence is incorrect, that the one mental state is not immediately induced by the other, that the bodily manifestations must first be interposed between, and that the more rational statement is that we feel sorry because we tremble, and not that we cry, strike or tremble, because we are sorry, angry or fearful, as the case may be. Without the bodily states following on the perception, the latter would be purely cognitive in form, pale, colorless, destitute of emotional warmth. We might then see the bear, and judge it best to run, receive the insult and deem it right to strike, but we would not actually *feel* afraid or angry.[12]

That is, the emotion was not originally a cognitive act—say, perceptual construal, appraisal, or judgment—that then affected the body, but was originally a bodily, physiological state that was subsequently perceived or *felt* as an emotion. Emotions are feelings, according to this theory, not cognitions.

Although at the outset of the article James specifies that "the only emotions I propose expressly to consider here are those that have a distinct bodily expression," he generalizes his claim to the effect that "a purely disembodied human emotion is a nonentity," that is, that by definition all emotions are bodily changes:

> The more closely I scrutinize my states, the more persuaded I become, that *whatever* moods, affections and passions I have are in very truth constituted by, and made up of those bodily changes we ordinarily call their expression or consequence; and the more it seems to me that if I were to become corporeally anaesthetic, I should be excluded from the life of the affectations, hard and tender alike, and drag out an existence of merely cognitive or intellectual form.[13]

The passage above presents James's central argument for his claim that emotions are perceived physiological changes, the so-called "abstraction argument": imagine undergoing a powerful emotion, and then subtract from it every somatic sensation associated with that emotion; the result will not be a state one would associate with that emotion; therefore emotions are felt changes in the body. At the conclusion of the article James reconsiders the "purely cerebral" emotions—moral, aesthetic and intellectual feelings—and now, given his physiological constitution theory, concludes that such emotions are not emotions at all:

> Unless in them there actually be coupled with the intellectual feeling a bodily reverberation of some kind, unless we actually laugh at the neatness of the mechanical device, thrill at the justice of the act, or tingle at the perfection of the musical form, our mental condition is more allied to a judgment of *right* than to anything else. And such a judgment is to be classed among awarenesses of truth: it is a *cognitive* act.[14]

Thus on the James-Lange view, emotions are passive feelings of bodily changes and are completely divorced from any cognitive acts of mind.[15] By virtue of the abstraction argument, James's theory is a "feeling" theory of emotion, for it holds that emotions are constituted completely of phenomenological felt perceptions of physiological changes.

2. Pursuing one line of criticism of the James-Lange theory will lead to a reconstructed notion of emotion that better serves the theory that I am developing from Tolstoy and Wittgenstein. The line of criticism I have in mind is the observation that the feeling theory fails to attribute any *intentionality* to emotions: on this theory emotions are not "about" or "directed toward" anything; rather, they are internal perceptions of causal-dispositional effects

of the body. But, as we saw in chapter 3, many of the examples of emotion that Tolstoy provides in *What Is Art?*, and many emotions in general, are at least partly comprised of intentional states, are directed toward, or are about, something. Emotions such as admiration, fear, regret, love, and hate are typically directed at certain objects, or classes of objects (real, imagined, or remembered), whereas moods—elation, depression, and so on—are objectless (or have everything as their object) and sensations—itchiness, pain, and so on—have causes, not intentional objects. If emotions, unlike moods and sensations, have intentional objects or properties, the James-Lange theory appears unable to account for this dimension of emotions.

A possible response would be to claim that the cause of the Jamesian emotion is what the emotion is about, and thus the intentionality relation of emotions is vindicated. But while there are certainly cases where the *cause* and the *object* of an emotion coincide (e.g., I was frightened by the snake in the garden), this coincidence is empirical and contingent, not conceptual and necessary. For example, suppose I mistake a garden hose for a snake; then the cause of my fright is the garden hose, but the object of my fright is the imagined snake. Wittgenstein makes clear the distinction we should uphold: "We should distinguish between the object of fear and the cause of fear. Thus a face which inspires fear or delight (the object of fear or delight), is not on that account its cause, but—one might say—its target."[16] Anthony Kenny draws the lesson from this passage and further examples that a person's emotions seem to involve that person's knowledge or beliefs:

> The distinction between the cause and the object of an emotion is thus most easily made out by reference to the knowledge or beliefs of the subject. Faced with any sentence describing the occurrence of an emotion, of the form "A φed because *p*," we must ask whether it is a necessary condition of the truth of this sentence that A should know or believe that *p*. If so, then the sentence contains an allusion to the object of the emotion; if not, to its cause.[17]

Kenny and others have further distinguished between the various different kinds of intentional object an emotion-type may possess: in the case of fear, for example, an *apparent* object (this snake, imaginary or real), a *formal* object (the property of dangerousness), and perhaps a *deep* object (the first particular object that elicited fear from me, and that serves, consciously or unconsciously, as the *paradigm* or *precedent* for the emotion-type).[18] Moreover, philosophers note that the formal object of an emotion's intentional relation is also required in order to individuate some emotions whose phenomenological and physiological dimensions are either identical or very similar. Thus anger and indignation may exhibit the same felt qualities, but will be distinguished based on the nature of the formal object, since indignation seems to be directed at violations of moral norms only, whereas anger's formal object is broader.[19]

Lastly, the intentional relation of an emotion is also a *normative* relation, that is, the formal object of an emotion provides *correctness* or *justification* conditions for the emotion. My fear of the garden hose perceived to be a snake is mistaken and unjustified: my fear response can correctly or incorrectly fit the corresponding evaluative properties in the world—in this case, dangerousness. This suggests that emotions have a mind-to-world direction of fit, like beliefs, and that their correctness condition implies that there is a kind of objectivity possessed by the evaluative properties to which they respond. I shall return to this point in sections 2 and 3 of chapter 7.

Given the intentionality relation inherent in central emotions, we can appraise the shortcomings of Tolstoy's initial examples of infectious laughter and crying. For what the conceptual analysis of emotion by Kenny reveals is that such "emotional contagion" or unconscious mimicry, while perhaps being physiologically type-identical (the same bodily or somatic states) between infector and infectee, does not amount to the transfer of emotion, because the response in the recipient is not directed toward anything, the intentional relation is not instantiated. Likewise, we can return to Schopenhauer's theory of music and see the danger inherent within the emotional power of music is that such transfer of emotion does not include the intentionality of that emotion, which renders it susceptible to recontextualization, that is, to its being directed toward new intentional objects and motives. Annette Baier unwittingly echoes Schopenhauer when she writes of music's inducing "degenerate emotions":

> But if emotions, to be emotions rather than moods, must have apparent objects, and behind them deep objects, then what music produces in us may not count as anything but degenerate emotions. For when music makes us rejoice, there is nothing in particular about which we are rejoicing (except the music itself), when it brings tears to our eyes, it is not grief at some mentionable loss, when it arouses courage and martial spirit, it is not the will to face any particular enemy or threat that we feel. . . .
>
> . . . Normally what dimly evokes the deep objects [of emotions] are apparent objects, the current loved one or disgusting one. What they may do is arouse the "precipitate of a reminiscence" [Freud's definition of emotion] by a shortcut—not via a current object, but by a more direct revival of the memory of past loved ones or lost ones, or of the *general* common features of such ones (the formal object), without needing or providing us with any current focus of that emotion. Musical emotions differ from ordinary emotions, that is, in going straight to the depths of emotions. . . . A version of the intentionality of emotions that makes place both for current apparent objects, and for formal and deep objects (and so for a dim memory of all the previously current apparent objects linked with a given deep

> object) allows us to recognize in the emotions music arouses both a certain vagueness about its objects and a definite directedness.[20]

Baier's conjecture regarding musical emotions thus both confirms the supposition that emotions have intentional objects while also providing an account of how "musical emotions" seem to lack an apparent intentional object while yet affecting listeners differently, depending on their characters in the sense of specific "precipitates of a reminiscence." Thus Baier's account offers a distinctly Freudian construal of Schopenhauer's picture of musical emotions.

3. A successor of the James-Lange view of emotion can be seen in the contemporary "turn to affect," which inherits the shortcomings of its nineteenth-century ancestor.[21] Drawing on work from cognitive and neuroscience, "affect theorists" posit subliminal, autonomic affective responses to one's environment, occurring below the level of consciousness, cognition, and judgment, from which two opposed "schools" can be distinguished. What can be called Left Affectism views the potential for affective response below the level of conscious judgment as an emancipatory, creative possibility for escaping ideology, language, and psychoanalysis.[22] Right Affectism, on the other hand, views affective response, called "basic emotions" or "primitive emotions," as evolutionarily selected and constituting a universal, transcultural and hard-wired uniformity.[23] On this view emotions are causally triggered neurophysiological events whose manifestations typically include facial expressions, distinct bodily movements, and physiological changes.[24] Both schools issue from the neuroscience of "affect programs" and its tenet that affective responses are solely related causally to their triggering stimuli, that is, independently of intentional states such as belief and desire. Thus Paul Griffiths holds that basic emotions are "sources of motivation not integrated into the system of beliefs or desires. The characteristic properties of the affect program system states, their informational encapsulation and their involuntary triggering, necessitate the introduction of a concept of mental state separate from the concepts of belief and desire."[25] On this view, basic emotions such as fear, disgust, joy, sadness, surprise, and so on are causally triggered and in turn manifest autonomic, physiological responses (skin conductance, hormone levels, heart rate, etc.), characteristic facial expressions and behavioral dispositions (e.g., the "fight, freeze, or flight" response in the case of fear). These affective program states and responses occur automatically and more quickly than conscious cognition, and therefore constitute a bodily "substrate" for emotions.[26] One virtue of this view is that, because it holds that emotions do not necessarily involve thought or evaluation, it can easily countenance the commonsensical belief that non-human animals and human infants, which lack propositionally articulated thought and linguistic facility, nonetheless possess these "basic" emotions, understood to be inherited instincts or innate dispositions.

As Ruth Leys has recently shown, the turn to affect, in both its Right and Left orientations, holds that "affect is independent of signification and meaning":

> Although at first sight the [Right Affectism] work of Tomkins—or Ekman, or Damasio—might appear to be too reductive for the purposes of those [Left Affectism] cultural theorists indebted to Deleuzean ideas about affect, there is in fact a deep coherence between the views of both groups. That coherence concerns precisely the separation presumed to obtain between the affect system on the one hand and intention or meaning or cognition on the other. For both the new affect theorists and the neuroscientists from whom they variously borrow—and transcending differences of philosophical background, approach, and orientation—affect is a matter of autonomic responses that are held to occur below the threshold of consciousness and cognition and to be rooted in the body. What the new affect theorists and the neuroscientists share is a commitment to the idea that there is a gap between the subject's affects and its cognition or appraisal of the affective situation or object, such that cognition or thinking comes "too late" for reasons, beliefs, intentions, and meanings to play the role in action and behavior usually accorded to them. The result is that action and behavior are held to be determined by affective dispositions that are independent of consciousness and the mind's control.[27]

How do brain/body states interact with traditionally mental events, processes, and states such as beliefs, desires, decisions, and so on, that bear an intentional relation to objects or situations? We can take Antonio Damasio's work on affect as a case in point, since recent commentators on Tolstoy's *What Is Art?* have adopted his theory and hence offered an "affectivist" reading of Tolstoy's aesthetic theory.[28] According to Damasio, in order to maintain homeostatic self-regulation of the living organism, the brain generates "maps" of bodily states, and these mappings in turn generate higher-level cognitive activities such as beliefs and desires. Thus, for instance, enzyme and hormone levels in the digestive system would trigger a "hunger" map that will generate sensations of hunger, desire for food, and strategic beliefs for obtaining food. Moreover, Damasio holds that while some somatic mappings are biologically fixed, others are somewhat flexible, so that specific body states can trigger conditioned or learned mappings, which as "gut reactions" constitute impulses toward or against given behavior. He writes: "In short, *somatic markers are a special instance of feelings generated from secondary emotions.* Those emotions and feelings *have been connected, by learning, to predicted future outcomes of certain scenarios.* When a somatic marker is juxtaposed to a particular future outcome the combination functions as an alarm bell. When a positive somatic marker is juxtaposed instead it becomes a beacon of incentive."[29] The somatic markers thus causally either reinforce or weaken specific behavioral dispositions, and in this way "guide" action. The literary scholar Douglas Robinson summarizes Damasio's theory as preface to his understanding of Tolstoyan infection along these lines: through repeated instances of similar homeostatic response we "build a self-regulatory regime around somatically triggered impulses, around 'somatic markers' that channel stored (learned, conditioned) behavioral patterns, through feelings into guided thought and action. This is the core of Damasio's somatic theory of human behavior: the guidance of thought and action through learned or conditioned bodily signals."[30]

Damasio illustrates this general thesis about subpersonal bodily states being subsequently mapped onto emotions and conscious thoughts and desires by recounting the story of a patient who, when electrically stimulated in a certain part of her brain, laughed uncontrollably:

> The laughter was quite genuine, so much so that the observers described it as contagious. It came entirely out of the blue—the patient was not being shown or told anything funny, and was not entertaining any thought that might lead to laughter. And yet, there it was, entirely unmotivated but realistic laughter. Remarkably . . . the laughter was followed "by a sensation of merriment or mirth" in spite of its unmotivated nature. Just as interestingly, the cause of the laughter was attributed to whichever object the patient was concentrating on at the time of the stimulation. For example, if the patient was being shown a picture of a horse, she would say, "The horse is funny." On occasion the investigators themselves were deemed to be an emotionally competent stimulus as when she concluded: "You guys are just so funny . . . standing around."[31]

Damasio concludes from such experiments that "emotion-related thoughts only came *after* the emotion [bodily] began."[32] Thus Damasio adheres to the Jamesian-Lange feeling theory of emotion.

Damasio further hypothesizes that the brain can *simulate* its own body mappings via what he calls the "as-if body loop" mechanism: "mirror neurons" represent the behavior one sees in another, and thereby trigger the body-mapping function, such that the emotions and conscious mental states associated with that behavior are themselves triggered.[33] The behavior that is mirrored may be seen, or narratively heard or read; in any case, the empathetic reaction proceeds via one's body imitating the other, and subsequently consciously becoming aware of the associated emotion, thoughts, and desires. Robinson calls this "somatic mimeticism," and maps Damasio onto Tolstoy to arrive at Robinson's own interpretation of the "infectiousness" of art:

> Tolstoy's infection theory is objectivistic, quasiscientistic, based on the assumption that a feeling exists in one body like a disease and somehow makes the jump across the intervening space to another body, where it burrows in and infects its new host. Damasio's empathy theory is constructivistic, based on the assumption that the new host is the active party in the transaction, that we are constantly reaching out to our world creatively and mimetically, seeking out stimuli, which we then convert into something internally meaningful. It doesn't really matter where we find such stimuli—in novels and poems and plays, in critical works, in oral narrations, in the embodied speaking of our friends, in the pattern of a tapestry or a table arrangement, in the sounds of cars in a city street, in the swaying of trees or the crash of thunder—we convert it all, constructively, constitutively, into our own somatic material, as we need it. Another boundary blurred by the somatic theory is that between the spoken and written word; we can distinguish them, obviously, but only by mapping a more analytical layer of understanding onto our somatic mimeses.[34]

In this way, Robinson understands Tolstoy as a proto-Jamesian affect theorist *avant la lettre*. While affect theory may coincide with Tolstoy's view on the emotional influence of art, that does not make the view *true*, for there are several telling criticisms of affect theory and its neuroscientific underpinnings, which in turn cast doubt upon the probity of the related reading of Tolstoy's aesthetic theory.

4. For the purposes of the present study, the chief criticism of Damasio-style theories is that they conflate causal and normative relations, what Wittgenstein called the "crossing of different pictures" regarding the normativity of meaning as a super-rigid machine, as we saw in chapter 5.[35] A reliable causal relation is not sufficient for meaning, or intentionality, and a fortiori for normativity, since meaning *qua* intentionality is a normative relation. This mistake was brought out by Kripke in his critique of causal-dispositional theories of meaning, and is clearly committed by Damasio when he attributes normative psychological predicates (thinking, deciding, choosing, guiding) to causal mechanisms.[36] The most sophisticated philosophical defense of the James-Lange or "feeling" theory of emotions to date is by Jesse Prinz, who offers what he terms an "embodied appraisal theory of the emotions" that takes as its point of departure the James-Lange claim that emotions are feelings or perceptions of bodily (or somatic) changes.[37]

Folk psychology (that is, how we talk about emotions) holds that emotions are not merely causally induced somatic responses to the environment, but that they moreover are meaningful, and subject to rational assessments of correctness or appropriateness: my being afraid of a normal mouse is unwarranted, or inappropriate, and, provided reasons for believing the mouse to be harmless, I should withhold my endorsement of my emotional response. If I am angry at a colleague for a perceived offense, I should when queried be able to provide a reason—that is, a justification or warrant—for my anger. My emotional responses, at least in many central cases, are responses to reasons, not simply causes. Prinz attempts to accommodate this aspect of emotions—their meaningfulness, their intentionality and normativity—by drawing on contemporary theories of mental representation that hold that a mental state can represent by virtue of its causal relationship to the world. According to informational semantics (Fred Dretske), psychosemantics (Jerry Fodor), and biological semantics (Ruth Millikan) some type of mental state or episode is reliably caused by a state in the world, and if the capacity to have such mental states came about because they are reliably caused in that way, then we may conclude that the mental state or episode represents or indicates that state of the world. These various naturalistic theories claim to reduce the intentionality and normativity of mental states to nomological or teleological causal relations. Relying on these theories of representation, Prinz holds that if a particular somatic perception reliably occurs under certain circumstances and was learned or evolved for that purpose, then that perception represents, or is about, that situation. So for example, confronted with a dangerous situation, one's body undergoes certain vascular, muscular, circulatory, and respiratory changes that evolved in order to prepare the body for fighting, freezing, or fleeing. Following Damasio, Prinz claims that one's mind has the ability to recognize this pattern of changes perceptually, and to use that pattern to inform decisions about what to do next. Thus the perception of the pattern of somatic changes is a representation of, is *about*, danger. Following the work of Richard Lazarus, Prinz calls such fundamental organism-environment relationships that bear on well-being, such as danger, loss, offense, and so on, "core relational themes." On his "embodied appraisal theory" then, core relational themes are represented by perceptions of patterned somatic changes. The James-Lange "feeling" theory is vindicated because, drawing on the causal theories of representation, causally induced somatic responses can be shown to be about core relational themes. The intentionality of emotions has been saved without recourse to reasons and concepts that the cognitivist theories of emotion deploy.

But each of the causal theories of representation that Prinz invokes has been shown either to presuppose intentionality and normativity or else fail to demarcate semantic relations correctly. For instance, the utterance of the word "cow" plausibly indicates (reliably causally co-varies with) the presence of a cow, but it also indicates the presence of a horse on a dark night, or a 3D plastic print of a cow, or a hallucination of a cow, or the projection of a cow-image onto one's retina, and thus if we take causal indication to be equivalent to meaning, then "cow" means a potentially infinite disjunction of such causal elicitors of the expression "cow" or concept COW in thought.[38] Moreover, taking reliable causal co-variance to equate to meaning proliferates meaning beyond established practices: the presence of cows reliably causally co-varies with the presence of flies, but cows do not mean flies, or vice versa.[39] Naturalized semantic theories either fail to account adequately for the normativity of meaning, for the fact that the use of an expression or concept can be incorrect, or unwarranted, or they implicitly rely on semantic notions they purportedly aim to explain.[40] In his criticism of Prinz, John Deigh points out that the perceived feelings of bodily alterations are said to "represent" or "carry information"—that is, bear an intentional relation—about the world, but this is a mere *façon de parler*, for the feelings are related merely to the proximate cause of them, *whatever* that may be. Deigh illustrates his point with an example of fear at a possible assailant:

> Nothing in this relation of representation, however, implies that these feelings [of fear] are directed at or toward any object in the world, real or imagined. Nothing in the relation implies that they orient you toward the threat you are facing. In particular, even though the assailant is the object about which the feelings carry information in the sense of "information" borrowed from the theory of perception, nothing in the relation implies that the feelings are directed toward him. For their carrying information about him just means that he, being dangerous, is a reliable cause of such feelings, and his being a reliable cause of the feelings implies nothing about the feelings being directed at or toward him. Obviously nothing changes if the information they carry about the object is erroneous, if for instance you mistook a deliveryman with a cell phone for an assailant wielding a knife. We have no more reason to regard the feelings in this case to be directed at or toward their cause than we had in the case of correct information. The feelings, in either case, represent danger exactly as a sound made by an alarm that is part of a home security system represents a home invasion. Just as the alarm's sound is not directed at or toward whoever sets off the alarm, so the feelings are not directed at or toward the assailant or anyone, like the deliveryman, mistaken for one.[41]

That is, in this model the feelings of fear merely register the causal impact of an object—any object—that reliably triggers that registering reaction. The concept of error or mistake has no purchase here, and if we aver that the causal mechanism is functioning correctly just in cases that it registers actual dangers, then we have smuggled in our correctness condition in the notion of proper or correct functioning. Thus Prinz summarizes his embodied appraisal theory as follows:

> In sum, we can explain how emotions represent concerns without supposing that emotions are, contain, or essentially involve

> judgments. This conclusion falls out of Dretske's theory of representation and others like it. Emotions represent things such as losses and dangers because they are set up to be set off by such things. They represent these things even if they have no constituent concepts or ideas. Like the beep of a smoke detector, emotions can represent without describing.[42]

But the smoke detector is a loaded example. It detects, registers, bears an intentional relation towards smoke because it was designed ("set up") to do so. Its intentionality is derived from the intentionality of its design, the purpose for which it was designed.[43] Moreover, that such causal reliabilism does not explain normativity is shown by the fact that we can take the smoke detector to be so, to be directed at smoke, only by tacitly assuming that the mechanism is functioning *correctly*: we impute the correctness condition to the causal mechanism when we make that assumption, and then claim that the mechanism itself fulfills the normative relation of correctness. Feelings on Prinz's model, like Damasio's, can at best describe a causal relation or association between object, feeling, and response, but they cannot explain how a feeling on this model justifies or warrants the response, because the feeling stands in no normative intentional relation to either the "correct" object or the "correct" response. By resting his theory of emotions on the unfulfilled promise of such causal theories of representation, Prinz's somatic theory of emotion for all its sophistication fails to adequately address the causal-normative problem that Wittgenstein laid bare.

The causal-normative tension also underlies Leys's charge that the neo-Jamesian account of Damasio, Prinz, and others is a form of implicit *Cartesianism*. First, she notes that several *empirical* criticisms have been raised regarding the experimental setups and evidence adduced in support of Damasio's somatic marker hypothesis and more generally in support of neuroscientific conclusions that attribute traditionally conscious and intentional psychological activities like deciding, willing, and thinking to unconscious, implicit, causal affective states and processes.[44] Second, and more importantly for the present chapter, several *conceptual* criticisms have been lodged against neuroscience's attributing psychological—that is, intentional—properties and relations to the body or parts of the body (e.g., the brain) which amounts to a kind of "crypto-Cartesianism." In other words, this line of criticism by Leys and others charges these neuroscientists and theorists, despite their espoused Spinozaist anti-dualism, with tacitly assuming a Cartesian dualism between mind and body/brain, between intentionally directed mental state and causally operative bodily state:

> Indeed, it is only by adopting a highly idealized or metaphysical picture of the mind as completely separate from the body and brain to which it freely directs its intentions and decisions that they can reach

> the skeptical conclusions they do . . . The mistake they make is to idealize the mind by defining it as a purely disembodied consciousness and then, when the artificial requirements of the experimental setup appear to indicate that consciousness of the willing or intention comes "too late" in the causal chain to account for the movements under study, to conclude in dualist fashion that intentionality has no place in the initiation of such movements and that therefore it must be the brain which does all the thinking and feeling and moving for us. (All the "willing," so to speak.)[45]

That is, these thinkers—be they Left or Right Affectivists—surreptitiously import intentionality and normativity into their descriptions of the causal operations of bodily states (including those of the brain, amygdala, autonomic nervous system, etc.). So, for instance, Damasio claims that "our brains can often decide well, in seconds, or minutes, depending on the time frame we set as appropriate for the goal we want to achieve, and if they can do so, they must do the marvelous job with more than just pure reason."[46] Paradoxically, then, in assigning higher-order cognitive functions like decision-making to the body/brain, these theories reinstate the Cartesian dualism between a spatiotemporal, causal-mechanical body and an extensionless, physically transcendent, disembodied mind. And in chapter 1 we have seen how Cartesianism underwrites one version of the dilemma between causal and normative relations.

5. The standard response to the failure of feeling theories of emotion to account for the intentional and normative relation is simply to jump the Cartesian divide, as it were, and assimilate emotions to the model of belief, as an evaluation or propositional judgment. While "pure" theories of this sort claim that emotions are nothing but judgments, most *cognitivist theories* of emotion hold that emotions essentially involve a cognitive state of judgment, thought, or appraisal, and thus hold that emotions are not mere feelings or other non-cognitive states.[47] Cognitivist theories reach back to Aristotle's *Rhetoric*, in which he defines several emotions with reference to their having an inherent judgment about or toward something: anger "may be defined as a desire accompanied by pain, for a conspicuous revenge for [*dia*] a conspicuous slight at the hands of men who have no call to slight oneself or one's friends" (1378a30-32); fear "may be defined as a pain or disturbance due to imagining some destructive or painful evil in the future" (1382a21–22); indignation "is pain caused by the sight of undeserved good fortune" (1387a9); envy "is pain at the sight of such good fortune . . . we feel it towards our equals; not with the idea of getting something for ourselves, but because the other people have it. We shall feel it if we have, or think we have, equals; and by 'equals' I mean equals in birth, relationship, age, disposition, distinction, or wealth" (1387b23–26).[48] In this general cognitivist view,

emotions are felt responses to, or otherwise include, some kind of normatively assessable representation of one's environment.[49] For example, one's experiencing fear essentially involves one's judging or evaluating that one is being threatened by something dangerous. So I fear the dog because of its sharp teeth, growling, and stance. Hence these theories easily accommodate the normative, intentional relation of emotions that the feeling theories could not, for beliefs are directed at and ratified by the world (mind-to-world direction of fit) and bear a correctness relation to their objects. So my unwarranted or unjustified fear at the garden hose is a cognitive (rather than purely affective) state essentially involving my mistaken belief or appraisal that there is a dangerous snake under foot.[50] A more moderate cognitivist approach holds that the beliefs involved are not epistemic beliefs regarding facts of the world, but rather evaluative or axiological beliefs or construals that apprehend the world evaluatively. So my fear of the dog is an appropriate response to the evaluative property or value of dangerousness that I as it were perceive in the dog. Thus emotions can be individuated by means of the particular evaluative property to which they respond (the dangerous for fear, the admirable for admiration, the contemptible for contempt, etc.), and these evaluative properties constitute the formal objects of emotions, providing them with correctness and justification conditions.

6. There are two central objections to the cognitivist theory of emotions, and they amount to the compound claim that an evaluative belief, judgment, or construal is neither necessary nor sufficient for an emotion. The first part of the objection is that emotions do not necessarily imply evaluative beliefs. There are cases where one has an emotional response *despite* having a belief that does *not* warrant, or even contradicts, the emotion. Thus, one example provided by Kant to illustrate the dynamic sublime is that we will be gripped by fear when standing on a precipice even though we know that we are safely and fixedly on firm ground.[51] Likewise many people have a "fear of flying" despite their conscious acknowledgment that flying is statistically quite safe.[52] On the cognitivist view, it seems that we have contradictory propositional beliefs, but in these situations, phenomenologically, it does not seem to the subjects that they are merely holding contradictory beliefs; rather, it seems that the bodily or phenomenological or behavioral-dispositional response is of a different kind than the calm, reflective belief that undermines the reason for the affective response.[53] Even more strongly, if evaluative beliefs are a component of emotions, it would seem that having an emotion necessarily requires having the relevant evaluative concepts that are deployed in the evaluative beliefs. But we generally think that non-human animals and human infants exhibit emotional responses without having the relevant conceptual repertoire. So it seems that in cases of non-human animals and human infants concept possession and cognitive belief are not necessary for emotions, as the cognitivist theory would seem to imply.[54] (We shall attempt to answer this

objection in section 4 of chapter 7, when we consider a developmental theory of emotional acquisition and education).

Conversely (the second part of the objection), and running James's "abstraction argument" as it were in reverse, it seems possible to have the relevant kind of evaluative belief without having the corresponding affective state: in some cases the beliefs can leave us emotionally unmoved. The cognitivist view seems to ignore the fact that in many cases emotions have specific physiological reactions, action readiness tendencies, and a typical phenomenology, a certain way they feel. This would suggest that having an evaluative belief, judgment or construal is not sufficient for having the corresponding emotional response.

We have therefore arrived at a dilemma of sorts in our survey of traditional theories of emotion. On the one hand, in assimilating emotions to *bodily*, affective states, feeling theories capture the phenomenology, physiology, and action readiness dimensions of emotions, but because of their reliance on a causal relation between inciting state of affairs and responding emotion, these theories fail to do justice to the intentionality—and correctness and justification conditions—of many emotions. On the other hand, in assimilating emotions to *mental*, epistemic, or doxastic states, cognitivist theories of emotion capture the intentionality relation, and correctness and justification conditions of emotions, but fail to do justice to the phenomenology, physiology, and action readiness dimensions of emotions, and seem to over-intellectualize emotions so that they are unavailable to non-human animals and human infants. This dilemma issues from the crypto-Cartesianism, the rigid divide between mental and bodily states, identified above.

The Wittgensteinian alternative to this crypto-Cartesianism is to embrace a holistic understanding of psychological concepts, including emotion concepts, as including mental representations, phenomenological and physiological qualities, and behavioral dispositions. Peter Hacker, who has energetically deployed this Wittgensteinian picture against neuroscientific affect theory, quotes the *Philosophical Investigations*: "It comes to this: only of a living human being and what resembles (behaves like) a living human being can one say: it has sensations; it sees; is blind; hears; is deaf; is conscious or unconscious."[55] This is the alternative to Cartesianism because "[it] was a characteristic feature of Cartesian dualism to ascribe psychological predicates to the mind, and only derivatively to the human being . . . But the predicates which dualists ascribe to the immaterial mind, the third generation of brain neuroscientists [e.g., LeDoux, Damasio, etc.] applied unreflectively to the brain instead."[56] The Wittgensteinian alternative holds that psychological predicates should be applied to the whole human being, and not merely to *either* side of the Cartesian divide: for example, it is only the whole human being who can be said to be in pain, *neither* (casually-mechanically, materially) her hand, or her afferent nerves, or her subcortical pathways, *nor* (normatively, immaterially) her mind, the insulated introspectable theater of her self-awareness. The continuum of mental and physical, of sensations, beliefs, thoughts, intentions, desires on the one side, and action readiness, behavioral dispositions, and action on the other constitutes the holistic domain of psychological predicate ascriptions.[57] That is, in this view at least central emotions such as fear, anger, guilt, pride, and so on should be conceived as sui generis states intrinsically involving a cognitive dimension (which includes intentionality and hence a normativity relation), a conative dimension (which includes specific desires and aversions), often a distinctive phenomenology (what it feels like), action readiness tendencies, and distinctive physiological changes (facial expressions, events in the autonomic nervous system, etc.). This conception of emotion contrasts with what Peter Goldie laments as "add-on" theories, whereby one state (typically either the cognitive/conative dimensions or the affective, that is, the bodily dimensions) is taken to be the essence of an emotion and the other dimensions are merely aggregated contingently to distinguish the emotional state from a non-emotional state.[58] Instead, in this view all dimensions relate intrinsically and essentially to the emotion, so that an emotion cannot be analyzed or reduced to fundamentally merely a specific kind of belief, desire, or affective state.

We have seen that Tolstoy's insight, in anticipation of Wittgenstein, is to countenance the possibility of an episode of understanding that does not epistemologically rely on an act of inference. A causal theory of the representational function of mental states would provide an account of such an episode if it were construed as merely the immediate elicitation of an affective state, but we have just seen that the most prevalent causal theory of emotions, the James-Lange theory and its contemporary versions by Damasio and Prinz, fails to account for the intentionality and normativity that characterizes the cognitive dimension—whether specified as belief, judgment, construal, or appraisal—of emotional mental states: the gulf between a naturalistic, causal order and an intentional, normative order seems unbridgeable. And one might characterize this impasse as yet another version, or consequence, of an implicit Cartesianism: the mind, home to intentionality and normativity, falls short of the natural world, conceived as the home of the causal order. And we have seen that Wittgenstein offers an alternative view, on which psychological predicates, including emotion ascriptions, are to be applied holistically, to both the body and mind of creatures we acknowledge to be enough like us as to warrant such ascriptions. When we turn to the sphere of morality proper, we shall find that this insight affords a resolution of yet another dilemma that arises from a tacit Cartesianism.

Chapter 7

Reconstructing Tolstoy II: The Morality of Emotions

> How am I filled with pity *for this man?* How does it come out what the object of my pity is? (Pity, one might say, is a form of conviction that someone else is in pain.)
>
> —Wittgenstein

In the previous chapter I showed how a conception of central emotions as sui generis states, irreducibly involving cognitive, conative, and affective (physiological, phenomenological, action readiness) aspects can resolve the dilemma between causal and intentional relations that arises in current debates on emotion. If we turn to *morality*, we find a related version of the dilemma outlined earlier, and in this chapter I argue for a similar conception of specifically *moral* emotions, whereby I define moral emotions as non-controversially as possible, as emotions that arise, and respond to, morally relevant situations.[1] I then present a further, distinctively epistemological dilemma in meta-ethics, that between moral objectivity and moral subjectivity, and show that it can be resolved by adopting a *sensibility theory*, which rests on certain analogies between moral-emotional responsiveness and the perception of secondary qualities like colors, and which is consistent with Tolstoy's picture of the immediate, non-inferential understanding of emotions in aesthetic experience. Lastly, considering a recent version of sensibility theory, *neo-sentimentalism*, equips us to explain Tolstoy's distinction between "universal feelings" and "religious feelings" and how they might be related in Tolstoy's picture of aesthetic-moral education.

1. What Michael Smith has termed "the moral problem" is a certain dilemma that arises from the standard picture of human psychology, which has come to be called "the Humean picture of motivation." On the standard picture, there are two main kinds of psychological state:

> On the one hand there are beliefs, states that purport to represent the way the world is. Since our beliefs purport to represent the world, they are assessable in terms of truth and falsehood, depending on

> whether or not they succeed in representing the way the world is [that is, the direction of fit is mind-to-world]. And on the other hand there are desires, states that represent how the world is to be. Desires are unlike beliefs in that they do not even purport to represent the way the world is [that is, the direction of fit is world-to-mind, as one tries to change the world to accord with one's desires]. These are therefore not assessable in terms of truth and falsehood. Hume concludes that belief and desire are therefore distinct existences: that is, that we can always pull belief and desire apart, at least modally. For any belief and desire pair that we imagine, we can always imagine someone having the desire but lacking the belief, and vice versa.[2]

So according to the standard picture there are two kinds of psychological state—beliefs and desires—that are completely distinct from each other. And these two psychological states seem to map onto two completely distinct features of morality as understood by our ordinary moral practice. On the one hand, we seem to think that moral questions have correct answers that are made correct by objective moral facts; hence we engage in moral argument and reasoning. Smith calls this the "objectivity of moral judgment." On the other hand, we also think that moral judgment has practical implications, that if we judge that an action A is morally required, that in itself gives us a motivation to do A; that is, moral judgment (and practical judgment in general) seems to exhibit *motivational internalism*: making a moral judgment seems to be internally related to having a reason, a motive, to do the corresponding action.[3] Smith calls this the "practicality of moral judgment." The "moral problem" is that the objectivity feature suggests that moral judgment is a form of belief, a *cognitive* state, while the practicality feature suggests that moral judgment is a form of desire, a *conative* state. Smith summarizes, claiming this is the "central organizing problem in contemporary meta-ethics":

> But the problem is that ordinary moral practice suggests that moral judgments have two features that pull in quite opposite directions from each other. The objectivity of moral judgment suggests that there are moral facts, wholly determined by circumstances, and that our moral judgments express our beliefs about what these facts are. This enables us to make good sense of moral argument, and the like, but it leaves it entirely mysterious how or why having a moral view is supposed to have special links with what we are motivated to do. And the practicality of moral judgment suggests just the opposite, that our moral judgments express our desires. While this enables us to make good sense of the link between having a moral view and being motivated, it leaves it entirely mysterious what a moral argument is supposed to be an argument about; the sense in which morality is supposed to be objective.[4]

That is, if moral judgment tracks moral facts and states of affairs, it would be a kind of belief, and would be motivationally inert. If moral judgment exhibits motivational internalism, it would seem to be a kind of desire, and would lose all claim to evaluative objectivity. This is the dilemma between cognitivism and non-cognitivism in meta-ethics, and it parallels the dilemma between cognitivist and non-cognitivist (or "feeling") theories of emotions. Smith despairs that "what is required to make sense of a moral judgment is a strange sort of fact about the universe: a fact whose recognition necessarily impacts upon our desires," for that sort of fact would avoid the dilemma between cognitivism and non-cognitivism in meta-ethics, as it would avoid the parallel dilemma in theories of emotions.[5]

But we have seen that a conception of emotions as intrinsically involving cognitive, conative, and affective dimensions delivers just the strange sort of fact Smith is looking for, and if we define specifically *moral* emotions as emotional responses to morally salient situations, we can resolve the meta-ethical dilemma (the "moral problem"), because emotions include the cognitive judgment or appraisal or construal required by the "objectivity of moral judgment" and the conative dimension—say, action readiness as a kind of motivational internalism—required by the "practicality of moral judgment." Emotional responsiveness to the evaluative features of a situation, action, or person's character is at once both a cognitive way of perceiving features of the world and a conative way of caring about and being moved by them. As Linda Zagzebski aptly describes it, "to appreciate is not just to understand, but to *feel the* force of that which is appreciated."[6] Because the appreciation of a morally salient situation is an expression of a moral emotion, and emotions are intrinsically motivating, moral-emotional responsiveness is both a cognitive state and a conative state that is intrinsically motivating.[7] That is, on this theory a moral emotion is "a unitary psychic state that is both cognitive and affective, where the cognitive and affective aspects are not separable states. . . . When I see something as rude, I feel offended *at* the offensive features of the situation, and those features cannot be fully described independently of their quality as intentional objects [rather than merely triggering causes] of the feeling of offense."[8] Because my sense of being offended is directed at the offending features, it bears an intentional relation to those features as its intentional object, and that intentional relation entails the correctness condition, the possibility of being mistaken, and the logical space for adducing reasons as justification for my feeling. And because my sense of being offended is also an affective state, it is intrinsically motivating, that is, it gives rise to action readiness tendencies. In this view, emotions are states that affectively perceive their intentional objects as falling under "thick concepts" that inseparably include descriptive and evaluative aspects.[9] Zagzebski summarizes her view that "emotion is a kind of value perception that feels a characteristic way" as follows:

> Since my [moral] judgment expresses an emotion, it expresses an intrinsically motivating state. And since the judgment also asserts that some person, object, or state of affairs falls under the thick concept [like RUDE or PITIFUL] that applies to the intentional object of that emotion, it is propositional in form, is about the intentional object of the emotion, and I am in the cognitive state of taking the intentional object to fall under the thick concept. If it does fall under that concept, the judgment is true; if not, it is false. Hence judgments like "That is rude" or "She is pitiful" are both cognitive and intrinsically motivating when these judgments are expressions of emotions.[10]

Because emotions are unitary psychological states essentially containing cognitive, conative and affective aspects, it is not possible to see a situation as rude without being in the emotional state of feeling offended, and one expresses that emotion by asserting a proposition like "That is rude."

2. This conception of moral emotional responsiveness as a metaphorical kind of perception of value goes back to Aristotle's characterization of the *phronimos*, the person of practical wisdom and virtue, as the person who is skilled in perceiving immediately—without inference or invocation of explicit rules or principles—what is to be done in a particular situation with "the eye of the soul,"[11] and it is this account that best fulfills Tolstoy's epistemological criterion of immediate, non-inferential understanding. Here too the construction of a dilemma—this time between moral objectivity and moral subjectivity—can dialectically reveal the virtues of the preferred account, called *sensibility theory*, which rests on a distinctive understanding of the analogy between moral-emotional response and the perception of Lockean secondary properties such as colors.[12] On the one hand, moral responses to situations are not to be conceived along the lines of the perception of primary qualities (physical properties like shape). Such an analogy with primary qualities would easily explain moral objectivity in terms of a strong *realism* about values, since in this view a value, just like the shape of an object, is independent of how we perceive it. But this realist view renders the perception of value into a mysterious sixth sense of ethical intuitionism, so that the "primary-quality model turns the epistemology of value into mere mystification."[13] On the other hand, colors are not merely projections of our subjective states, like hallucinations, which would be an *anti-realist* view regarding color and, by analogy, value. Rather, according to Locke, colors are real but essentially relational, since they are powers to cause sensations in us. Likewise, the analogy suggests, our emotional responses are not wholly internal and subjective, but are reliably elicited by situations we confront. So our emotional responses, just as our color responses, are not merely erroneous projections of our inner sentiments upon the world.[14] Rather, sensibility theory takes the analogy of value to secondary quality to entail an *internal realism*: there are facts of

the matter regarding values, but they are mind-dependent facts.[15] That is, sensibility theory explicates the analogy with the perception of color along the following lines. For an object to be green is for it to be disposed to present a green appearance to normal human beings under suitable conditions. However, the greenness of the object is not reducible to the microphysical properties that elicit such an appearance; on the contrary, this view takes colors to depend essentially on their appearances. The dispositions or powers to elicit color responses in humans are on the one hand located in the world, but on the other they are constituted and individuated by the subjective states they elicit in humans. Hence colors are taken to be "response-dependent" properties.[16] To ascribe greenness to an object is to ascribe the property of eliciting a green appearance in normal humans under suitable conditions.[17] Likewise, to ascribe cruelty to a person's action is to ascribe to the action the property of eliciting in normal humans under suitable conditions a response of moral disapproval of the action ("that is cruel") and a moral-emotional response: the perception of the cruel action disposes an observer to feel moral indignation or outrage at the agent and compassion or sympathy with the victim of such action. As David Wiggins writes: "we grasp the sense of a [value predicate] by acquiring a sensibility all parties to which respond in a particular way to certain particular features in what they notice in any given act, person, or situation."[18]

This internal-realist picture of evaluative properties, on the analogy with secondary qualities, permits the possibility of error and mistake (something looks green, but in fact is not [the lighting conditions are not standard]; something appears to be cruel, but in fact is not [it's a game]), and so includes a *correctness condition*. Just as colors exhibit a degree of independence from subjective responses (a degree that allows for error or ignorance, without the mind-independence being as absolute as it is with primary qualities), so too evaluative properties demonstrate a degree of independence: one can be wrong about judging an action cruel or kind. The correctness condition is given substance in the account of colors by spelling out the constituents of "standard conditions" (e.g., no lights with colored filters attached) and "normal humans" (e.g., not color-blind).[19]

The establishment of a correctness condition moves the account from one of a causal relation of response-elicitation to include a *normative* relation: values do not merely dispose us, as a matter of fact, to respond with moral feelings, but *ought* to elicit those responses. This step therefore brings up the first disanalogy with perception, for colors can be conceived as dispositions to elicit certain subjective experiences without any essential normative relation. Thus McDowell writes: "The disanalogy . . . is that a virtue (say) is conceived to be not merely such as to elicit the appropriate 'attitude' (as a color is merely such as to cause the appropriate experiences), but rather such as to *merit* it."[20] The virtuous person's moral perception of a situation, in this view, includes the person's appreciating, or appraising the situation, and hence is a cognitive state, a state involving an intentional object (in this case, the evaluative properties of the situation at hand) that is seen as morally salient.[21] Moreover, in our everyday moral practice we disagree with each other regarding the evaluations of actions, persons, and situations (real or literary), offering reasons and counter-reasons to justify our moral-emotional response. We try to get each other to "see things this way," to perceive the moral salience of a situation as we do. And it is a commonplace thought that our moral responsiveness can be trained, improved, expanded through education, arts, travel, and so on. As we mature we learn the fine-grained distinctions between, say, guilt, shame, regret, and remorse. McDowell concludes that these everyday practices and commonplace beliefs commit us to the reality of values, not as first-natural primary qualities, but rather as "second nature," what Hegel called *Sittlichkeit*: cultural norms, values, justifying reasons and practices constituting an "objective ideal" world for its members.[22] And of course the second disanalogy to perception lies in the fact that moral responses exhibit motivational internalism in that they are at least dispositionally intrinsically motivating: to evaluate or "see" an action as cruel is to be moved to moral disapproval of the action and compassion with the person who was affected by it.[23]

3. Note that this conception of moral emotions as a unitary state of cognitive, conative, and affective dimensions and the related sensibility theory already fits two of the Tolstoyan conditions of adequacy we identified at the outset of chapter 6. In this view moral emotions ontologically have an intentional relation to the evaluative response-dependent properties they detect and hence they sustain a correctness or justification condition. And because sensibility theory conceives the awareness of the morally salient features of a situation on the analogy of perception, epistemologically this awareness is immediate and non-inferential, in that it provides immediate fallible knowledge without inferential justification. The virtuous person sees the other's behavior *as* rude, or *as* cruel; she does not draw an inference, but understands the morally salient features immediately.[24]

The epistemological analogy with perception includes a further respect beyond that of immediate, non-inferential knowledge: emotional sensibility, like perceptual acuity, can be improved as a *skill* through training and habituation. Many philosophers distinguish between propositional knowledge (or "knowing-that") and non-propositional knowledge manifested in skills and abilities (or "knowing-how"). For instance, a chess master can "see" the next move in a game, even if she cannot formulate that knowledge in terms of propositionally articulated beliefs or rules. Perceptual locutions express this know-how, skill, or ability: one comes to "see" what is to be done. Similarly, becoming habituated to a practice can be seen as acquiring a skill or ability, as McDowell notes: "if one cannot formulate what someone has come to know when he cottons on to a practice, say one of concept-application, it is natural to say that he has seen something."[25] The skills model suggests a similar line of reasoning regarding the perceptual analogy of moral emotions: the possession of a moral sensibility at once allows one to see what to do and motivates one to do it. The virtuous person is the person whose moral-emotional responses are appropriately attuned to the situation such that they act in the morally appropriate way. So a kind person sees what is required in a given concrete situation and is motivated to do it, without explicit reflection on codes, norms, or rules.

An integral aspect of this account of moral emotions is that one's responsiveness to ethical situations will not be a matter of universal, objective rules, but rather of one's moral upbringing as a process of habituation. As McDowell writes, "In moral upbringing what one learns is not to behave in conformity with rules of conduct, but to see situations in a special light, as constituting reasons for acting."[26] The special way of seeing characteristic of the virtuous person more closely resembles a skill than a set of beliefs. To have a skill—the sensibility that is characteristic of virtue—is at once to have the ability to see what to do and the motivation to do it.[27] Just as one can be trained up to be sensitive to the phonemes of one's native language, or to be sensitive to finely grained facial expressions conveying surprise, fear, or astonishment, so too the virtuous person is habituated to perceive evaluative properties of actions, persons, and situations. The more cognitively sharpened emotional responses are also rationally revisable. If emotional responses reveal evaluative features of the world as second nature, what about conflicting second natures? McDowell responds:

> Any second nature of the relevant kind, not just virtue, will seem to its possessor to open his eyes to reasons for acting. What is distinctive about virtue, in the Aristotelian view, is that the reasons a virtuous person takes himself to discern really are reasons; a virtuous person gets this kind of thing right.[28]

This may seem hopelessly epistemologically self-serving in the age of multiculturalism, but what McDowell is denying is the possibility of an external, non-subjective grounding for justifying when an emotional response discerns a genuine reason for acting: "the necessary scrutiny does not involve stepping outside the point of view constituted by an ethical sensibility"; instead, the genuineness of the reasons to act discerned by our sensibility is "vindicated from within the relevant way of thinking."[29] Given the skill aspect of moral responsiveness, one way such revision or improvement can occur is by means of an expert who can, through training and habituation, improve the moral-perceptual skill of the novice, who will help her "see by feeling" (that is, emotionally respond in an appropriate or fitting way) the right thing to do in a given situation. Artworks as extolled by Tolstoy can function as such experts, habituating people to ethical knowledge (in the sense of knowing what to do and being moved to do it) by describing persons, actions, and situations in an affect-laden language (verbal, visual, or musical) that both elicits emotional responses and calibrates those responses with fine-grained descriptions of the morally salient features of the person, action, or situation.

Thus the skills model makes plausible the sensibility theorist's claim that evaluative aspects in general, and moral aspects in particular, of the world can be seen by feeling, in the sense that they are rendered salient by the emotional response manifest in a particular sensibility. The upshot of this account is that moral emotions are sui generis, neither simply cognitive states (beliefs, judgments, construals, appraisals, etc.) nor simply conative states (desires), but irreducible unitary states including cognition, motivation (action readiness tendenies), and often phenomenology and distinctive physiological states, events and processes. And this correlates to what they respond to and track in the world, for values too are "primitive, *sui generis*, incurably anthropocentric, and as unmysterious as any properties will ever be to us."[30]

4. There remains one other ontological constraint on moral emotions from our discussion of Tolstoy in earlier chapters. Recall that Tolstoy advocates two types of art that are distinguished by the different types of feelings they convey or inculcate: "universal art" conveys "the simplest everyday feelings of life, such as are accessible to everyone in the world," and "religious art" conveys "feelings coming from a religious consciousness of man's position in the world with regard to God and his neighbor."[31] Universal feelings thus seem to be moral emotions common to human nature, while religious feelings are in some sense culturally specific moral emotions trained and habituated as second nature.[32] While our exposition of sensibility theory seems to explicate how religious feelings might work, since one can be trained and habituated in the skill of their responsive recognition, what about universal feelings? A recent variant of sensibility theory called *sentimentalism* ("neo-sentimentalism" would be more accurate) is promising in this context. Sentimentalist theories hold that the appraisal and appreciation of evaluative features depends not on moral responsiveness understood as an inculcated second nature, but rather, invoking David Hume, "depends on some internal sense or feeling, which nature has made universal in the species."[33] These universal feelings are in this view *sentiments* that are constituents of human nature, which nowadays are called basic or anthropologically universal emotions. It is an open question whether such emotions exist, how many exist, how they are individuated, whether non-human animals have them, and so on, but for our purposes we can state that there appears to be general consensus that such sentiments include at least the following: happiness, sadness, anger, fear, surprise, and disgust.[34] Like second-natural moral emotions, these sentiments are response-dependent on their corresponding evaluative features (e.g., fear is response-dependent on the dangerous, etc.)

but are not culturally constructed because anchored in anthropologically universal sensitivities.[35] Response-dependent evaluative properties provide a common subject matter that does not preclude normative disputes about the instantiation of those properties on specific occasions. That is, the common shared evaluative response of fear and its dependence relation with the dangerous (fear-eliciting evaluative property) provides the agreement in meaning required for genuine disagreement about whether one should feel fear at a particular situation, that is, whether the particular situation is a reason to feel fear, whether the common sentiment of fear is *fitting* or appropriate to the particular situation.[36] It is therefore plausible that Tolstoy's "universal feelings" can be interpreted as some subset of these sentiments.[37]

Moreover, it is also plausible that at least some moral emotions themselves are associated with, and possibly developed from, these basic emotions or sentiments. For instance, moral resentment as anger at another whom one believes has wronged one[38] might be a more cognitively developed, or reticulated form of the basic emotion of simple anger (elicited by the frustration of a desire); indignation might be yet another.[39] Thus as an infant matures, it is inculcated with propositionally articulated judgments and concepts like RESENTMENT and INDIGNATION and WRONG, which enrich the cognitive and conative dimensions of the basic emotion of anger. And concomitantly the child learns more reticulated patterns of response-eliciting features, and correspondingly reticulated patterns of emotional response. Unlike the simple eliciting factor for the basic emotion of sadness (elicited by the perceived loss of something or someone dear to one), these developed and subtle patterns in turn are enriched into further refinements of concept, response, and behavior, as for instance when one learns to differentiate REGRET and REMORSE from GUILT. John Deigh has suggested that one's sentimental education in part consists in these basic emotional responses being trained up to include a normative relation. The infant who is innately disposed to react with disgust to milk gone bad is habituated to extend that emotional response to, say, morally disgusting behavior, like perfidy.[40] One of the virtues of this developmental theory is that it can answer the chief objection to cognitivist theories of emotion (discussed in the previous chapter), for it grants that non-human animals and human infants possess emotions (namely, some or all of the "basic" ones) but also can account for the development among mature humans of more refined moral emotions. And this account dovetails nicely with Tolstoy's emphasis on general or universal emotions: pity, compassion, motherly succor all appear to be more closely related to universal "basic emotions" than do, say, more reticulated emotions such as righteous indignation, social status embarrassment, and so on. This general developmental view, that pan-cultural, physiological "basic" emotions or "affect program" emotions can form the basis for more acculturated specifically "moral" emotions, reaches back to Aristotle's virtue theory, as Myles Burnyeat suggests:

> Being a human being [the well-brought up young person] has the physiologically based appetites as well. The object of these is, of course, pleasure . . . , but they can be modified and trained to become desires for the proper enjoyment of bodily pleasures; this . . . is what is involved in acquiring the virtue of temperance. There are also instinctive reactions like fear to be trained into the virtue of courage. In a human being these feelings cannot be eliminated; therefore, they have to be trained.[41]

Jesse Prinz advocates a similar, albeit cultural-historical rather than individual-aretaic, account of the development of distinctly moral emotions from non-moral emotions, and offers one just-so genealogical account along those lines:

> Imagine that certain behaviors cause emotions that are not yet specific to the moral domain. An act of cruelty might cause anger on the part of the victim, and sympathy among others. The perpetrator may be ostracized, criticized, and punished. This may cause the perpetrator to feel sad. If these responses are stable, then cruelty is governed by a kind of rule. The rule consists in the fact that cruelty is discouraged as a result of these emotional responses. The emotions guarantee a predictable pattern of behavior. Cruelty is less likely to occur, and when it does, certain emotions and corresponding behaviors will follow. After this pattern is established, the emotions that once had no moral significance take on new meaning. Sadness is not just a generic loss-response, but a feeling associated with violating a rule. Anger is not a generic response to a threat, but a feeling directed at rule violators. Guilt and righteous anger are born. At the very moment these emotions are born, the rule takes on new meaning. It is now a rule enforced by moral emotions. It is a moral rule.[42]

Such an account might offer independent explanation for Tolstoy's bifurcation of moral emotions into universal feelings and religious feelings, for we can understand the two categories as occupying opposite ends of an ontogenetically developmental spectrum from non-moral universal basic emotions on one side to culturally, religiously specific emotions on the other. "Universal feelings" would be those emotions that are as it were minimally morally modulated forms of non-moral basic emotions: for example, happiness that has been minimally modulated with a sense of expectation (on the way to becoming full-blown moral obligation), as for instance Tolstoy's example of motherly succor developing into another of his examples, a stranger's distress eliciting aid. That after his crisis Tolstoy dedicated himself to writing children's tales and parables would be relevant here as well. At the other extreme would be feelings that are maximally modulated with institutionally or culturally specific moral cognitive and conative aspects, such as Christian selflessness, righteous indignation, guilt, and so on. These "thick concepts" include an evaluative attitude and specification in terms of moral conduct (transgressions or obligations), which in turn incorporate more elaborate narrative considerations in these concepts' application conditions. Righteous indignation at someone's reneging on a promise in turn requires understanding the practice of promising, and so on. Such "narrative density" in turn suggests that the inculcation and habituation of these "religious feelings" require more elaborate storytelling than does that of "universal feelings."

This ontological account of the nature of moral emotions along the spectrum from universal feelings to religious feelings, together with the epistemological account of moral responsiveness as a version of sensibility theory, provides the reconstruction required to understand the content of Tolstoy's claim regarding the kinds of emotions that an artwork communicates or with which it infects an audience. It is to that aesthetic claim of an artwork's capacity to express and elicit emotions that we now turn.

Chapter 8

Reconstructing Tolstoy III: Expression in Art

> Art is a kind of expression. Good art is complete expression.
>
> —Wittgenstein

> A theme, not less than a face, wears an expression.
>
> —Wittgenstein

Having outlined an understanding of emotions in general, and then of moral emotions in particular, that fulfills the ontological and epistemological constraints that arose in the earlier chapters of this study, I turn now to the topic of an artwork's expression or elicitation of such emotions and, perhaps surprisingly, find similar tensions between the causal and normative relations in the area of philosophical aesthetics often termed "aesthetic expressivism."[1]

As with the earlier discussion of emotions, caveats must be made here as well. First, some theorists rightly caution against overgeneralization and abstraction in the discussions of art, even *within* a single aesthetic medium or genre (such as instrumental music), and suggest that aesthetic experience will vary with artwork, audience, and occasion.[2] Such particularist cautionary reminders mean that any theoretical position is liable to empirical (dis)confirmation unless carefully qualified. Second, several theorists claim that the emotions expressed or elicited by artworks are in some sense not genuine or full-fledged emotions, because they lack the motivational states or "action readiness" tendencies on the one hand, or often lack intentional objects on the other, all of which constitute integral components of emotions.[3] These reductive accounts of emotion by philosophers of aesthetics parallel the "add-on" theories of emotion put forward by philosophers of emotion, and they can be answered in similar fashion. We shall see that the construal of emotion as merely causally elicited feelings parallels the "feeling" theories of emotion discussed in chapter 6 and underlying the "Nietzschean threat" Tolstoy found in Schopenhauer's philosophy of art. Regarding the lack of behavioral action in one's emotional response to art, recall that the motivational state accompanying a genuine emotion is conceived as an "action readiness" disposition. Just as a motivational state *qua* disposition can be suppressed, overridden, or silenced by another motivational or cognitive state (one might have the disposition to lash out when angered, but one usually does not), one's knowing that one is undergoing an aesthetic experience "contextually checks," as it were, the action readiness disposition's actualization. In what follows therefore, it is assumed that the emotions elicited or expressed by art are of the same type of emotion outlined and defended in the previous two chapters.

1. Clearly artistic works that *represent* moral emotions (e.g, by naming or describing the moral emotions felt by literary or dramatic characters), or represent morally salient characters or actions (e.g., by describing such characters and actions in evaluative language or suggesting moral salience in the use of evaluatively connotative imagery) can habituate and train the audience in the skillful perception of and emotional responsiveness to morally salient situations, and the broadly "Aristotelian" tradition in literary criticism elaborates and at times advocates how such morally affective reading can and should occur. For instance, in a programmatic article Martha Nussbaum writes:

> The Aristotelian conception [of virtue theory] contains a view of learning to support the claims of literature. For teaching and learning, here, do not simply involve the learning of rules and principles. A large part of learning takes place in the experience of the concrete. This experiential learning, in turn, requires the cultivation of perception and responsiveness: the ability to read a situation, singling out what is relevant for thought and action. This active task is not a technique; one learns it by guidance rather than by formula. [Henry] James plausibly suggests that novels exemplify and offer such learning: exemplify it in the efforts of the characters and the author, engender it in the reader by setting up a similarly complex activity.[4]

Much of Tolstoy's psychologically realist fiction, like this tradition's favorite modern example, the works of Henry James, would just as clearly illustrate the tenets of this way of reading: the audience reads, hears, and imagines literary characters and the moral situations, choices, and consequences they confront, and thereby is trained and habituated in skilled moral responsiveness along the lines outlined in the previous chapter. However, were this the whole story, Tolstoy's theory would be far less provocative, for he seems to be championing the inculcation, transmission, and elicitation of morally worthwhile emotions regardless of genre, indeed, regardless of whether the art forms in question are *representational* or not. Therefore, in this final chapter I turn to the "hard case" of the non-representational art form of instrumental music and argue that even here—in what Wittgenstein called "the most sophisticated art of all"[5]—Tolstoy's theory of moral-emotionally expressive art can be vindicated.

2. Modern philosophical work on the relation between art and emotion has focused on "pure" or "absolute" music, that is, instrumental music unaccompanied by text, title, or program, because this music offers the "hard case" of an art form that does not *represent* anything (as do pictorial and narrative art forms), including emotions, and yet can and regularly does *express* emotions: it seems undeniable that instrumental music manifests and engenders emotions in listeners. Understanding and explaining how pure music relates to emotions is presumably logically prior to understanding and explaining how "mixed" or "impure" art forms relate to emotion; so, philosophers of music reason, providing a philosophical account of the emotional expressiveness of pure music must precede more complicated accounts of mixed art forms.[6] The problem can be stated easily: we experience music as expressive of emotion, as when we say that a funeral march is sad; yet music is not sentient, and not the kind of thing that can experience an emotion to which it gives expression. So what is required is an account of music's emotional expressiveness.[7]

Theorists seem agreed that minimally what is at issue is a certain experience, that the claim that a piece or passage of music is sad in effect is the claim that the experience of hearing it has a certain affective (phenomenological, perhaps also physiological and behavioral) characteristic to which an emotion term like "sad" refers. As in our earlier discussion, here too emotion terms refer to response-dependent concepts or properties: to claim that the music is sad is minimally to claim that understanding listeners typically undergo the emotion of sadness when experiencing the music. And we must add a slight qualification: we can speak of emotional responses to art as empathetic responses, as when the audience feels sad because the music is sad, or as sympathetic responses, as when the audience feels pity for the sadness of a fictional character, or even as antipathetic responses, as when the audience is irritated by a surprising occurrence of aesthetic harmony, say; in the interests of clarity and simplicity I ignore these complications in my discussion of musical expressiveness and emotional response in this chapter.

3. In his overview of theories of emotional responses to pure music, Jerrold Levinson helpfully divides the field into two approaches, the general contours of which will be familiar to readers of chapter 6. Levinson suggests that there are two different sorts of mechanisms responsible for the elicitation of emotions in listeners. The first case, the "sensory, or cognitively unmediated route," refers to music's "power to induce sensations, feelings and even moods by virtue of its basic musical properties, virtually without any interpretation or construal on the listener's part. Particular timbres, rhythms, intervals, dynamics, and tempi exemplify this power most clearly. Such properties need only be registered to have their effect, at least for an auditor acclimatized to a given musical culture."[8]

The most common theory in the literature explicating this "cognitively unmediated route" is a causal-dispositional account, called the "arousal theory" of art. This theory accounts for the emotional response by citing its cause: to invoke the common toy example, sad music is music that causes the emotion of sadness in its listeners. The expressive property or properties of sad music consists of its dispositional properties to induce an experience of sadness in appropriate listeners.[9] For instance, in her recent and sophisticated version of arousal theory, Jenefer Robinson writes that "*expressive qualities* are *qualities that can be grasped through the emotions that they arouse*."[10] Thus the order of explanation proceeds from effect to cause: the emotions aroused in the listener are taken to be indications of the expressive qualities of the music, understood as dispositions to reliably cause just those emotions. Such emotions "alert listeners to what is *expressed* in the music"[11] because the aroused emotions are constitutive of the musical expressiveness. Thus the fundamental claim of the arousal theory is that music has certain properties that cause certain emotional responses, and the resulting experience (of the music and of the emotions) is constitutive of musical expression.

Readers of this study will recognize the arousal theory as a version of the causal-dispositional account of meaning discussed in chapter 1, but here transposed into philosophical aesthetics. It inherits the same problems.[12] If the expressive qualities of a passage of music are just whatever causally induces an emotional response, the theory must first accommodate "deviant causal chains." If an obviously joyful piece of music causes me to be sad because of idiosyncratic associations (say, because my dog died when I first heard that music), it would follow that the music is in fact sad. And statistical generalizations will not suffice: suppose the majority of the people have a similar association (say, because they learned of the 9/11 attacks while that music was playing on the radio); nonetheless we would think it normatively false that the music has sad expressive qualities. Relatedly, a mere causal conjunction does not suffice for the conclusion desired. If I stumble on a tree root, which arouses irritation in me, it does not follow that the tree root expresses irritation or has an expressive property of irritation.[13] The causal relation is not sufficient because it omits an *intentional* relation: if what is aroused is an emotion, rather than a mere sensation, it must be directed toward or about something, must have an intentional object or intentional property. And it is that intentional relation that provides the rationality and intelligibility of our emotional response. If our emotional response is merely causal, it is pointless to ask whether it makes sense for us to respond to the sounds in the way that we do, whether our emotional response is *right* or *appropriate* or *fits* the expressive character of the music, and we take the presence of the correct emotional response to be indicative of understanding the music.[14]

Robinson's sophisticated version of the arousal theory tries to accommodate the necessity of an intentional relation and correctness conditions through a temporalized and compartmentalized division of labor, as it were, in what she calls the "Jazzercise" effect of musical expression:

> How can happy music make people happy, and calm music calm people down? The answer in a nutshell is that music with a happy, sad, calm, or restless character causes *physiological changes, motor activity*, and *action tendencies*, that are experienced as happiness, sadness, serenity, or restlessness. These states are *emotional* rather than merely physiological states in that they bring in their wake not only characteristic subjective feelings but also characteristic cognitive activity: people have a tendency to view the world in characteristic ways. However, although the world gets "regestalted," so that we are more inclined to take a certain point of view on things or view the world in a certain way, there is no affective appraisal of some particular event or situation (and certainly no "cognitive object" of emotion) that sets off the emotion process. The points of view we take tend to be global [that is, moods]: we view ourselves and the world in general in a positive or negative, reassuring or uncertain way.[15]

This account strongly recalls the James-Lange "feeling" theory of emotions: music causes "affective" (physiological, phenomenological, behavioral-dispositional) changes in the listener which, however, conduce merely to a general point of view or mood, but not yet an emotion.[16] Subsequent "cognitive monitoring" includes one's labeling the affective state, in effect individuating it into one emotion rather than another (recall from our discussion in chapter 6 that "affective" changes are not sufficient to individuate emotions: excitement, rapture, and anger all share basic physiological traits): "In short, emotion begins in bodily changes which in turn induce a mood and make us readier to get into some emotional state. Which emotional state we get into is the result of interpreting our bodily state by reference to the context in which we find ourselves." She concludes her book with a generalization of this conclusion that invokes Tolstoy's famous metaphor: "The Jazzercise effect is a quite general capacity of music—whether Brahms, rock, or folk music—to 'infect' us with a mood by a kind of contagion or motor mimicry. Music evokes moods by means of effecting autonomic changes, motor activity, and action tendencies, so as to put listeners into a mood state, a state in which they more readily ascribe emotions to themselves. Different listeners label their states by reference to different contexts, and that is one big reason why different people say they feel somewhat different emotional states in response to the very same music."[17] That is, because the affective feeling caused by an expressive passage of music is underdetermined *qua* emotion, because it lacks the intentional relation inherent in the cognitive dimension of emotions, which emotion the mood state is resolved into by "cognitive monitoring" will essentially depend on contextual factors, including presumably the character of the listener.[18] She also accepts the unwelcome consequence of her theory, namely that since any cognition, intentional relation, or correctness condition comes far downstream in the experience, that it makes no sense to ascribe a specific emotion to the expressiveness of music.[19] Music is at most the causal trigger of a diffuse affective psychological state, the potential individuation of which into a specific emotion-type depends on the context of the listener, not on any properties of the music. Thus Robinson's theory restates and radicalizes the "Nietzschean threat" we identified in chapter 5.

4. In answer to these and other shortcomings of the various versions of non-cognitivist arousal theory, some philosophers opt for the second category of Levinson's twofold division, the "perceptual-imaginative, or cognitively mediated route." In addition to presenting sonic features, this group of theories holds that "music offers the appearance of human emotion, or of persons outwardly manifesting emotional states . . . , the degrees of resemblance between the shape of the music and the behaviors through which emotions are commonly expressed in life will have something . . . to do with our being disposed to hear music in such ways . . . It is the perceptual-imaginative aspect, manifested in our disposition to hear emotion or emotion expression in music, that is surely primarily responsible for the complex, more robustly emotional responses to music."[20] There are several major varieties of perceptual-imaginative, cognitivist theories of musical expression. Critically evaluating them will lead us to a position reminiscent of the argumentation in chapter 1.

One strand of cognitivist theories can be termed inferentialist, in that they hold that the expressiveness of a passage of music is arrived at through the listener's drawing an inference to the best explanation, where the inference results in the ascription of a psychological state to the imagined utterer of the passage, or to the imagined protagonist as determined by an overall interpretation of the work, or a best hypothesis by the listener regarding the state of mind the composer intended the listener to hear in the passage.[21] The common objection brought against these theories is that they falsify the epistemology of the listener's emotional response: she does not take the musical properties, or her experience of them, as *evidence* for inferring or judging that the music is emotional; rather, she *perceives* (*hears*) the emotion *in* the music or *hears* the music *as* expressive. The analogy with perceptual knowledge is perspicuous here: one does not infer from one's experience that an apple is red, say; rather, one sees the redness in it, or perceives it as red. The perceptual knowledge is immediate and non-inferential. The transition from a perception as of a sad passage of music or as of a red apple to the belief that the passage is sad or that the apple is red, is justified without the need of any inference. If asked why one has such a belief, the justification is something like "because I hear (or see) that it is" or "because I know what sadness sounds like (or what red looks like)."[22]

A second, and more promising, strand of cognitivist theories is the "resemblance theory," advanced and vigorously defended by Stephen Davies.[23] According to Davies, emotion predicates are used primarily to refer to felt emotional states, and are used secondarily, but literally, to describe appearances in persons ("she looks sad"), non-human animals ("the basset hound looks sad"), natural objects ("the willow looks sad"), and works of art ("that musical passage sounds sad"). In this secondary usage, emotion predicates describe "emotion characteristics in appearance," and these constitute musical expressiveness: "the expressiveness of music consists in its presenting emotion characteristics in its appearance . . . Emotion characteristics in appearance are attributed without regard to the feelings or thoughts of that to which they are predicated. These expressive appearances are not emotions that are felt, take objects, involve desires or beliefs—they are not occurrent emotions at all. They are emergent properties of the things to which they are attributed."[24] Thus conceived, this musical expressiveness "depends mainly on a resemblance we perceive between the dynamic character of music and human movement, gait, bearing, or carriage." The resemblance is thus cross-modal, for Davies believes that "the likeness between music and the voice is slight."[25] Thus the principal claim of the resemblance theory is that emotions "are heard in music as belonging to it, just as appearances of emotion are present in the bearing, gait, or deportment of our fellow humans and other creatures."[26] Whereas Davies holds that the chief respect in which properties of a passage of music can be said to cross-modally resemble properties of human expressiveness is movement (e.g., we experience the slowness of music as resembling the slowness of a person's gait), Paul Boghossian advocates a more inclusive form of the theory, which allows resemblance between sound and voice as well: "A passage P is expressive of E just in case P sounds the way a person would *sound* who was expressing E vocally, or sounds the way a person would *look* who was expressing E gesturally."[27] Boghossian's formulation is helpful also because it clearly is a metaphysical claim regarding the nature of musical expressiveness conceived as a kind of response-dependent property. Davies by contrast sometimes seems to be making this claim, but sometimes seems to slip into an epistemological claim, as when he writes that the listener has "an experience of resemblance between the music and the realm of human emotion."[28] If Davies is here claiming that the listener experiences and recognizes a resemblance, and *based on that* recognition, responds emotionally, then we have an inferentialist account once again, which is problematic, as we saw above. So it is better to understand Davies to be claiming that the emotional response is immediate and non-inferential, but that upon reflection the listener can adduce a resemblance relation as that which partially constitutes the content of her perception. The perceptual analogy would be something along the lines of a person responding to the question of why the apple is red by invoking its resemblance to a fire engine. Thus this explanation can provide the rationality and intelligibility for our emotional responses to music that we found goes unexplained in the causal-dispositional accounts, without having to incorporate inferential reasoning into our account.

Jerrold Levinson has raised the following metaphysical objection to Davies's resemblance theory:

> [The theory is] a matter, when a passage displays an emotion characteristic in its medium of sound sequences, of an appearance *similar* to that presented by a person in some state. But since everything is similar to everything else to some degree, the issue then becomes one of *how* similar such an appearance must be to one presented by human behavior in order to constitute an emotion-characteristic-in-sound of the emotion in question, or else, as Davies sometimes puts it, of how similar the *experience* of musical movement and of expressive behavior must be, in order for the appearance generated by such movement to constitute an emotion-characteristic-in-sound of the emotion in question.[29]

In effect, Levinson is raising the worry that a resemblance relation is always underdetermined, or that the rule for determining what constitutes the acceptable degree of resemblance between a musical passage and a type of human expressive behavior is in principle underdetermined. This is recognizably a version of the worry raised by Kripke in chapter 1 regarding the underdetermination of the rule of addition, and Levinson opts for a version of Kripke's "sceptical solution" (see chapter 1, section 11): what counts as the acceptable degree of resemblance just is whatever the community of appropriate listeners deem it to be by their responses. Boghossian provides a helpful gloss: "If you say that sad music is music that resembles sad sound, [Levinson] observes, you have to say to what degree, since everything resembles everything else to some degree. But the degree of resemblance required cannot be specified in terms of some fixable degree of resemblance between the two. It can only be specified as whatever resemblance is sufficient to induce appropriate listeners to hear the music as sad."[30] Levinson locates the normativity of the resemblance relation in the listener's causal-dispositional responses to passages of music. He writes:

> I think it is plain that there is no answer to this except by appeal to our disposition to *hear* that emotion—rather than another, or none at all—in the music, that is, by appeal to our disposition to aurally construe the music as an instance of personal expression, perceiving the human appearances in the musical ones. . . . Only if this occurs does the music have the expressiveness in question, regardless of the degree of similarity between the music's appearances and the human appearances in relation to which it ends up being expressive, or alternatively, the degree of similarity between the experiences of those appearances.[31]

Levinson's initial formulation of his dispositional theory is as follows:

> A passage of music P is expressive of an emotion or other psychic condition E if and only if P, in context, is readily and aptly heard by an appropriately backgrounded listener as the expression of E, in a sui generis, "musical," manner, by an indefinite agent, the music's persona.[32]

The music's "persona" is the imaginatively projected "expresser" of expressive music: "if expressive music is, as I maintain, music readily heard as, or as if, expression, and if, in addition, expression requires an expresser, then personae or agents, however minimal, just *are* presupposed in the standard experience of such music."[33] I will consider musical personae presently, but for the moment the key issue is the use of "aptly" in the above formulation, for with it we have yet another example of normativity being smuggled into a putatively causal-dispositional account, for "aptly" amounts to the qualification that the disposition of "hearability" is functioning *correctly*.[34] In response to this objection, Levinson reformulated his theory as "a passage of music P is expressive of an emotion E if and only if P, in context, is readily heard, by a listener experienced in the genre in question, as an expression of E."[35] Levinson thus now shifts the bearer of normativity from the disposition to the experienced listener or the community of "properly backgrounded listeners," by which he means "listeners demonstrably competent at understanding such music, such competence being manifested through various recognitional, continuational, and descriptive abilities, and whose other judgments of expressiveness are in line with established ones in uncontroversial cases." But this merely shifts the problem of smuggled normativity: it does not resolve it.

Why does Levinson unwittingly opt for a variant of Kripke's "sceptical solution," which, as we saw in chapter 1 serction 11, is no solution at all? Because Levinson sees himself confronted with a dilemma: a suspect metaphysical Platonism of fixed degrees of resemblance on the one hand, or a communal dispositionalism on the other:

> There's the rub, for as we all know, everything resembles everything else, yet the degree of resemblance to an emotion required to make a musical appearance a musical emotion characteristic in appearance of that emotion cannot be specified in terms of some fixable degree of resemblance between the two. It can only be specified, it seems, as whatever resemblance is sufficient to induce appropriately backgrounded listeners to *hear* the music as sad, or as expressing sadness.[36]

Levinson has, perhaps unwittingly, reproduced the dilemma between meaning Platonism and communal dispositionalism that we examined in the context of theories of meaning in chapter 1. As Wittgenstein argued, the dilemma is a false one, because it overlooks the picture of meaning—and here transposed into philosophical aesthetics, the picture of resemblance—as nothing more, but also nothing less, than an ongoing practice, composed of interests, human "natural history" *qua* second nature, and inculcated via training and guidance by which the relevant resemblances are perceived immediately, without explicit justification. In this way listeners directly perceive emotions in music that are grounded in resemblances between expressive characteristics of the music and expressive characteristics of human beings.

5. Why do all these theorists speak of the expressiveness or the expressive characteristics or qualities or properties of an artwork, rather than the artwork's expression; why the claim that an artwork is *expressive of* an emotion rather than that it *expresses* an emotion? This is, I believe, the final problem for a successful reconstruction of Tolstoy's theory, for Tolstoy (at least in certain passages) seems to hold that an artwork expresses its creator's emotions, rather than merely being expressive of an emotion, and that the audience responds (usually empathetically, or sympathetically) to that expressed emotion. In non-artistic cases of human expression, we take the person's expression to reveal her psychological state, and her psychological state to explain her expression. More strongly, there is a logical, that is, a non-contingent and *constitutive* relationship between many psychological states and their expressions: part of what it means to be sad is to have (at least the disposition to have) an expression of sadness. She *manifests* her sadness in her expression, and we *see* her sadness *in* her expression. In the case of an artwork, however, the tradition holds that there is no such relationship between expression and psychological state. Peter Kivy provides a quick *reductio* to support the denial of such a relationship in the context of musical expression:

> Many, and perhaps most, of our emotive descriptions of music are logically independent of the states of mind of the composers of that music, whereas whether my clenched fist is or is not an expression of anger is logically dependent upon whether or not I am angry. It is unthinkable that I should amend my characterization of the opening bars of Mozart's G-minor Symphony (K.550) as somber, brooding, and melancholy, if I were to discover evidence of Mozart's happiness . . . during its composition. But that is exactly what I would have to do, just as I must cease to characterize a clenched fist as an expression of anger if I discover that the fist clencher is not angry. This is a matter of logic.[37]

It is this argument from "logical independence" that motivates the distinction between something *expressing* an emotion and its being *expressive of* that emotion. The former exhibits the logically dependent or constitutive relation between expression and psychological state, whereas the latter does not. The illustrative example repeated in the literature is that of the St. Bernard or basset hound, whose face is expressive of sadness independently of whatever psychological state of mind the dog may be in. Artworks, the argument runs by analogy, can thus be expressive of emotions without being expressions of their creators' emotional states. If artworks are logically independent of their creators' emotional states, then Tolstoy's expressive theory of art would require a significant qualification: in the *weaker* version of the theory, one could speak of the artwork's expressiveness or suggestiveness of emotion, while the *stronger* version would hold that an artwork can transmit or convey an emotion to its audience by expressing that emotion.

Carefully and successfully evaluating this claim of "logical independence" requires identifying and setting aside three misleading lines of thought. The first misleading thought is that an expressive artwork has merely an *instrumental* relationship to the emotion it conveys or elicits. Here the logical independence is taken to be a contingent relationship between the expressive features of the artwork on the one hand and the transmission of emotion on the other. If the emotion is separable from the nature of the artwork, because the latter is a mere vehicle or means for the former, then the function of the artwork could be replaced by any other means—another artwork, or a drug, or hypnosis—that reliably produces the emotional response. Conceiving the emotional response of a specific artwork as somehow detachable in this way seems to falsify genuine aesthetic experience, as when Wittgenstein writes:

> It has sometimes been said that what music conveys to us are feelings of joyfulness, melancholy, triumph, etc., etc. and what repels us in this account is that it seems to say that music is an instrument for producing in us sequences of feelings. And from this one might gather that any other means of producing such feelings would do for us instead of music.—To such an account we are tempted to reply "Music conveys to us *itself!*"[38]

A second misleading thought is the line of reasoning that proceeds from the observation that people sometimes conceal or feign their emotional state to the conclusion that outer expressiveness and inner psychological state must therefore be non-constitutive, merely contingent. This is a misleading argument because feigning an emotional state rests parasitically on the genuine expression of emotion, which is logically prior: the concept of feigned emotion, like the concept of false promise, logically presupposes the concept of genuine emotional expression and sincere promises. Likewise, perhaps a happy Mozart composed a somber symphony analogously to a happy person feigning a somber mood: the very possibility, let alone success, of the feint depends on the logically prior relationship of an emotional state being constitutively manifested in the emotional expression.[39] A third misleading thought is the line of reasoning that proceeds from the observation that many human emotional expressions are natural, whereas the expressive capacities of artworks are artificial, in the sense that they often are thoroughly dependent on conventions. But this line of thinking rests on an equivocation in the word "artificial," a shift from the sense of being the opposite of "natural" to the sense of being the opposite of "genuine." But while some human expressions of emotion are natural (e.g., my face turning red with anger), many expressions of emotion are conventional, such as linguistic expressions ("How dare you!") or gestures (elevating a certain finger). And in ordinary, non-artistic contexts, we take these conventional expressions to be just as much genuine manifestations of emotional states as we do genuine natural expressions of the same states.[40]

While I have sought to undermine the motivations for the distinction between expression and expressiveness from the side of human expression, as it were, one can also do so from the side of aesthetic expression. Recall that Jerrold Levinson's "persona" theory, examined above as a putative correction to Davies's "resemblance theory," claims that in order to perceive emotions in musical passages, the listener must imagine an "indefinite agent" or persona, a subject to whom the emotional state can be attributed imaginatively, because "if expressive music is . . . music readily heard as, or as if, expression, and if, in addition, expression requires an expresser, then personae or agents, however minimal, just *are* presupposed in the standard experience of such music."[41] The imaginative projection of a persona is one remove from the perception of the creator's emotional state in her artistic work, and it reflects the continuing presence of the "logical independence" claim. But it is an unnecessary complication that arises only in certain situations. Consider the case where I receive a handwritten letter from a friend, and I discern that his handwriting looks "angry." On Levinson's account, I am entitled to imaginatively project a "persona" or "indefinite agent," distinct from the letter writer, to whom I imaginatively attribute (Levinson claims this usually happens unconsciously) the state of being angry. But these recommended or required philosophical somersaults are indicative that something has gone wrong, for in my ordinary life I immediately see that my friend is angry because his anger is manifested, apparent in his handwriting. It is only if other considerations come to my attention (that a recent hand injury has affected his writing ability, that he is feigning anger in order to manipulate my feelings, that he is starting a new game of "pretend handwriting," etc.) that I will retreat to the more circumspect and skeptical attitude of postulating an intermediary "persona" and then asking to what degree this persona might coincide with my friend. Recall that in chapter 3 we considered an observation by Wittgenstein of one's everyday understanding of a linguistic symbol:

> What happens is not that this symbol cannot be further interpreted, but: I do no interpreting [*Ich deute nicht*]. I do not interpret, because I

> feel at home [*heimisch*] in the present picture. When I interpret, I step from one level of thought to another.[42]

That is, I feel at home, as it were, seeing my friend's anger expressed in his handwriting, Such perception is immediate and non-inferential, and I am "exiled" from that familiarity only by the impingement of exceptional circumstances that incite my *will* to question and interpret. Wittgenstein seems to suggest similar thinking in the case of understanding a musical theme:

> Understanding a sentence is much more akin to understanding a theme in music than one may think. What I mean is that understanding a sentence lies nearer than one thinks to what is ordinarily called understanding a musical theme.[43]
>
> This musical phrase is a gesture for me. It creeps into my life. I make it my own.[44]

Here too, when one is at home with the music, one hears the emotion *in* the music, without the skeptical inclination to search for an explanation or justification: "When a theme, a phrase, suddenly says something to you, you don't have to be able to explain it to yourself. Suddenly *this* gesture too is accessible to you."[45]

6. What gives rise to the philosophical distinction between expressing an emotion and being expressive of an emotion or the surmise of the imaginative projection of a persona in the experience of emotionally expressive music? I submit that *au fond* it is yet another version of Cartesianism, the posited gulf between inner mental state and outer bodily or behavioral appearance, for that gulf entails that outer appearance is detachable from the emotion, the latter now relegated to an independent and merely introspectable inner realm rather than the human being in her entirety. The Wittgensteinian alternative to this Cartesianism is to embrace a holistic understanding of psychological concepts, including emotion concepts, as including mental representations, phenomenological and physiological qualities, and behavioral dispositions: "It comes to this: only of a living human being and what resembles (behaves like) a living human being can one say: it has sensations; it sees; is blind; hears; is deaf; is conscious or unconscious."[46]

One might object that in cases of pretense, physical failure (say, due to facial paralysis), and so on, it only *seems* as if a person's face is expressing an emotion (sadness, say): like the basset hound, the person's face is expressive of, or has the *appearance* of sadness, but does not *really* express sadness in such cases; one is tempted to say that the corresponding inner, mental state is not itself one of sadness. Therefore what is common to both false (insincere, etc.) and veridical expressions of emotion is merely the identical, independent *appearance*, and an observer has epistemic access only to the appearance, not the inner emotional state of the person. And one might go on to extrapolate this line of reasoning to the aesthetic experience of artworks, and likewise conclude that the audience has access only to the artwork's expressive qualities (the "emotion characteristics in appearance"), but that the artwork does not express emotion.

Note that an unwelcome consequence of the objector's line of reasoning is that one can never know the emotional state of another, because at best one can have a belief with some degree of confidence based on the appearance of the other. The appearance—false or veridical—will always be an independent epistemic intermediary between the observer and the inner state of the other, and thus always invite skepticism. The objector's error lies in his conception of the appearance (false or veridical) as being identical, rather than allowing of two different determinations of appearance: an appearance being either a case of the subject's manifesting her emotional state or of its merely seeming to the observer that she is. Adopting this alternative, disjunctive conception of emotional expression also shows how the objector's reasoning is fallacious. Because there can be cases of failure in the expression of emotion by a person, it does *not* follow that when there is no such failure (when the person is not feigning, when her facial muscles are not damaged, etc.) her appearance is not directly manifesting her emotional state and that another person does not immediately perceive the emotional state in her appearance. Mutatis mutandis a similar argument can be made regarding an artwork's expression of emotion and recognition of the emotion by the artwork's audience.[47] A musical theme, no less than a face, may wear an expression, as Wittgenstein claims, where this means not merely exhibiting emotional expressiveness, but rather expressing a determinate emotion.

I have therefore provided independent arguments to make plausible Tolstoy's claim that an artwork can express or communicate a distinctive emotion, even in the hard case of "pure" music. Moreover, my account of the nature of emotion, and the roles of moral emotions in virtue theory construed as sensibility theory and neo-sentimentalism, provide the theoretical framework sufficient to explain how an artwork can convey or elicit a moral emotion in its recipient. Thus my reconstruction over this and the previous two chapters also vindicates Wittgenstein's claim, quoted at the outset of this study, that "there is *much* to be learned from Tolstoy's false theorizing about how a work of art conveys 'a feeling.'"[48]

CONCLUSION

> "The aim of music: to communicate feelings."
>
> Connected with this: We may say correctly "his face has the same expression now as previously"–even though measurement yielded different results on the two occasions.
>
> How do we use the words "the same facial expression"?— How do we know that someone is using these words correctly? But do I know that *I* am using them correctly?
>
> —Wittgenstein

We can now return to Tolstoy and explicate his theory of aesthetic expression according to our reconstruction. His programmatic definition in *What Is Art?* reads:

> *To call up in oneself a feeling once experienced and, having called it up, to convey it by means of movements, lines, colors, sounds, images expressed in words, so that others experience the same feeling—in this consists the activity of art. Art is that human activity which consists in one man's consciously conveying to others, by certain external signs, the feelings he has experienced, and in others being infected by those feelings and also experiencing them.*[1]

The aesthetic means that Tolstoy lists and summarizes under the term "external signs" should be understood as the conventions of artistic media, forms, and genres that are artificial in the sense of "non-natural" but not in the sense of "not genuine" expressions of the artist's emotional state, which in the default cases is what is expressed by the artwork (or suitable part of the artwork), and only derivatively, contextually, to be attributed to the expressive properties or imagined "persona" of the artwork.[2] Wittgenstein says something similar regarding architecture as an art form: "Architecture is a *gesture*. Not every purposive movement of the human body is a gesture. Just as little as every functional building is architecture."[3] And regarding music he writes: "'I sing it [a musical passage] with a quite particular expression.' This expression is not something that can be separated from the passage. It is a different concept. (A different game.)"[4] And more strongly still: "A theme has a facial expression just as much as a face does."[5] Thus for Wittgenstein an artwork is (at least partly) constituted by its being an expressive gesture in analogy with human expressive gestures: aesthetic and human gestures are just as holistically conceived.[6] Since the expressiveness of the artwork consists in its emotional response-dependent properties, the audience will experience the emotion immediately, non-inferentially, and hence perceive the artist's[7] (or derivatively, a persona's) emotion *in* the artwork as his or her expression:

> Such words as "pompous" and "stately" could be expressed by faces. Doing this, our descriptions would be much more flexible and various than they are as expressed by adjectives. If I say of a piece of Schubert's that it is melancholy, that is like giving it a face . . . In fact, if we want to be exact, we do use a gesture or a facial expression.[8]

The theory of moral emotions developed in chapter 7 entails that artworks can "infect" their audiences with determinate moral emotions in two ways. Artworks for young children will express "basic," pan-cultural emotions (our reconstruction of Tolstoy's "universal feelings") which will be cultivated and reticulated as the child matures to include finer-grained cognitive aspects by which the emotions will be more finely individuated in explicitly moral terms. These finer-grained and cognitively reticulated emotions, which may include specifically local, cultural inflections, correspond in my reconstruction to Tolstoy's "religious feelings." Thus the basic emotion of anger would be developed, through aesthetic and non-aesthetic inculcation, into more morally reticulated emotions such as indignation, affront, moral resentment, and so on. My account of central emotions, especially moral emotions, as sui generis states integrally composed of cognitive, conative, behavioral-dispositional, physiological, and phenomenological dimensions, and their role in a sensibility theory of virtue, can accommodate this developmental account. In this way aesthetic expressivism, as the felt perception of moral emotions in aesthetic experience, would cultivate virtue and qualify as a case of "art as a moral institution," in Friedrich Schiller's famous phrase. Such cultivation would necessarily be a contingent process, dependent on the qualities of the specific artworks as much as the specific characters of their recipients, for the model here is the cultivation of a skill—practical, moral-emotional responsiveness—rather than the learning of principles, norms, or rules; and it is that essential contingency—the "Nietzschean threat" that he perceived in Schopenhauer's account of the decontextualized influence of musical emotions—that tempted Tolstoy to fall back into meaning Platonism. Instead, we should understand the skill being cultivated as the immediate, non-inferential emotional responsiveness to morally salient properties of a situation, person, or action.

The retreat to interpretation in the sense of providing an explicit justification for the moral-emotional response, typically the invocation of a relevant resemblance between aesthetic expression and human expression, will occur only if such immediate understanding has failed to occur or if its legitimacy is being questioned in a context that motivates adopting a skeptical attitude. That is, only very specific contexts will tempt or elicit the *will* to interpret, which in turn may prompt the potentially endless search for ultimate justification that is a consequence of Derridean meaning skepticism.

But if that occurs, we will no longer be thinking and feeling with Tolstoy and Wittgenstein, but rather without them.

NOTES

Introduction

The epigraphs for the introduction are from Ludwig Wittgenstein, *Culture and Value*, rev. ed., trans. Peter Winch (Oxford: Blackwell, 1998), 67 and 41, respectively.

1. On Dostoevsky in the context of existentialism, see Walter Kaufman, *Existentialism from Dostoevsky to Sartre* (New York: Meridian Books, 1956); and George Steiner, *Tolstoy or Dostoevsky: An Essay in the Old Criticism* (New York: Knopf, 1959). Philosophers in the Anglo-American tradition who have drawn on Tolstoy for psychological insights include Peter Goldie, *The Emotions: A Philosophical Exploration* (Oxford: Clarendon, 2000), and Graham Oddie, *Value, Reality, and Desire* (Oxford: Clarendon, 2005). The problem of the "paradox of fiction" (why we feel apparently genuine emotions regarding fictional characters whom we know do not exist) was famously motivated by consideration of *Anna Karenina* in Colin Radford and Michael Weston, "How Can We Be Moved by the Fate of Anna Karenina?" *Proceedings of the Aristotelian Society*, suppl. vol. 49 (1975): 67–93.

2. Jonathan Glover, "*Anna Karenina* and Moral Philosophy," in *Well-Being and Morality: Essays in Honour of James Griffin*, ed. Roger Crisp and Brad Hooker (New York: Oxford University Press, 2000), 159. Glover emphasizes Tolstoy's advocacy of the role of moral emotions together with moral beliefs in practical reasoning, and likens that role to a kind of perception.

3. In 1931 Wittgenstein compiled a list of influences on his thinking: "Boltzmann, Hertz, Schopenhauer, Frege, Russell, Kraus, Loos, Weininger, Spengler, Sraffa." Wittgenstein, *Culture and Value*, 16.

4. Ray Monk, *Ludwig Wittgenstein: The Duty of Genius* (New York: Penguin, 1990), 115–16. Other examples: "Tolstoy was as much in his thoughts as Frege" (Allan Janik and Stephen Toulmin, *Wittgenstein's Vienna* [New York: Simon and Schuster, 1973], 200); in a letter of 1912 to Russell: "I have just read 'Hadji Murat' by Tolstoy! Have you read it? If not, you ought to for it is *wonderful*" (Ludwig Wittgenstein, *Cambridge Letters: Correspondence with Russell, Keynes, Moore, Ramsey and Sraffa*, ed. Brian McGuinness and G. H. von Wright [Oxford: Blackwell, 1995], 20); "F. R. Leavis recalls that Wittgenstein knew *A Christmas Carol* practically by heart, and the book is, in fact, placed by Tolstoy in his treatise *What Is Art?* in the very highest category of art 'flowing from the love of God'" (Monk, *Ludwig Wittgenstein*, 569); "[Wittgenstein] went on to recommend Tolstoy, and encouraged me to read the *Twenty Three Tales*; and when I had bought a copy he marked those which he thought most important. These were *What Men Live By; The Two Old Men; The Three Hermits*, and *How Much Land Does A Man Need?*. 'There you have the essence of Christianity!' he

said" (Rush Rhees, ed., *Ludwig Wittgenstein: Personal Recollections* [Oxford: Blackwell, 1981], 87–88).

5. Paul Engelmann, *Letters from Ludwig Wittgenstein, with a Memoir* (Oxford: Oxford University Press, 1967), 91, does not tell us *which* of Tolstoy's conclusions Wittgenstein had in mind. For good summaries of the recorded evidence, see E. B. Greenwood, "Tolstoy, Wittgenstein, Schopenhauer: Some Connections," in *Tolstoi and Britain*, ed. W. Gareth Jones (Oxford: Berg, 1995), 239–49; and R. M. Davison, "Wittgenstein and Tolstoy," in *Wittgenstein and His Impact on Contemporary Thought*, ed. E. Leinfellner, W. Leinfellner, H. Berghel, and A. Hübner (Vienna: Hölder, Pichler, Tempsky, 1978), 50–53.

6. Davison, "Wittgenstein and Tolstoy," 51.

7. The publisher Ludwig von Ficker describes the impression he had on first meeting Wittgenstein as "a picture of poignant solitude at first glance (reminding one, say, of Alyosha [Karamazov] or Prince Myshkin)," in his "Rilke und der unbekannte Freund," *Der Brenner* 18 (1954): 236.

8. The concluding chapter of Gary Saul Morson's *"Anna Karenina" in Our Time: Seeing More Wisely* (New Haven, Conn.: Yale University Press, 2007) invokes Aristotelian *phronêsis* and several tantalizing quotations from both early and late Wittgenstein to support his characterization of the novel as "prosaic," where "all realist works, by definition, contain many particularities and ordinary events; prosaic novels regard such events as the locus of value. . . . Prosaic novels *redefine* heroism as the right kind of ordinary living and sainthood as small acts of thoughtfulness that are barely perceived" (28–29). Since Wittgenstein seeks to return metaphysical speculation to the everyday, and acknowledges the limitations of language, Morson concludes: "it is as if Wittgenstein had set himself the task of arriving at Tolstoy's conclusions by a different route. Each work can serve as a gloss on the other" (210). One of the goals of this study is to make precise, qualify, and partially vindicate this supposition through careful analysis, exposition, and argument.

9. Michael Fischer, *Stanley Cavell and Literary Skepticism* (Chicago: University of Chicago Press, 1989) draws on Cavell's Wittgenstein to respond to a deconstructive version of other-minds skepticism. John Gibson, *Fiction and the Weave of Life* (Oxford: Oxford University Press, 2007) draws on the later Wittgenstein's account of criteria and standards of representation (like the Paris meter stick) to argue that literature is neither mimetically referential nor linguistically self-referential (as some adherents of deconstruction suggest), but rather that it reveals and imaginatively considers those standards of representation. Students of Wittgenstein will note that while I mainly draw on the later Wittgenstein's thoughts on psychological concepts, expression, and meaning, I also deploy arguments and views that are continuous, or at least implicitly consistent, between the early and the later Wittgenstein, for example, skepticism as a distinct failure in ordinary understanding, anti-Cartesianism, values as conditions of a signifying practice, and so on. On the relation between Wittgenstein's early and later philosophy, see David Pears, *The False Prison: A Study of the Development of Wittgenstein's Philosophy*, 2 vols. (Oxford: Clarendon, 1987).

10. The expression "rational reconstruction" appeared in Jürgen Habermas, *Communication and the Evolution of Society*, trans. Thomas McCarthy (Boston: Beacon Books, 1979), to mean making explicit and theoretically systematizing the implicitly known presuppositions of communicative discourse. My aim is

somewhat similar but applied to the discourse (literary and essayistic) of late Tolstoy. The principle of charity, coined by Neil L. Wilson and adopted by W. V. O. Quine and Donald Davidson, "constrains the interpreter to maximize the truth or rationality in the subject's sayings." For an overview see Simon Blackburn, *The Oxford Dictionary of Philosophy* (Oxford: Oxford University Press, 1994), from which this quote, p. 62.

11. L. N. Tolstoi, *Polnoe sobranie sochinenii*, 90 vols. (Moscow: Gosudarstvennoe izdatel'stvo "Khudozhestvennaia literatura," 1928–58).

12. Arthur Schopenhauer, *Sämtliche Werke* (Frankfurt: Suhrkamp, 1986). Ludwig Wittgenstein, *Werkausgabe* (Frankfurt: Suhrkamp, 1984).

Chapter 1

The epigraph for chapter 1 is from Wittgenstein, *Remarks on the Foundations of Mathematics*, edited by G. H. von Wright, R. Rhees, and G. E. M. Anscombe (Cambridge, Mass.: MIT Press, 1983), VII-44; see also VII-48.

1. See Ludwig Wittgenstein, *Philosophical Investigations*, trans. G. E. M. Anscombe, 2nd ed. (Oxford: Blackwell, 1958), §§143, 186–90; and John McDowell, "Meaning and Intentionality in Wittgenstein's Later Philosophy," in his *Mind, Value and Reality* (Cambridge, Mass.: Harvard University Press, 1998), 263–78.

2. Wittgenstein, *Philosophical Investigations*, §193. On this point see also Saul Kripke, *Wittgenstein on Rules and Private Language* (Cambridge, Mass.: Harvard University Press, 1982), 33–39.

3. See Wittgenstein, *Philosophical Investigations*, §§193–95; and Kripke, *Wittgenstein on Rules and Private Language*, 22–38, for an extended critical discussion of dispositional accounts. For an attempt to offer a double-dispositional account in response, see Graeme Forbes, "Skepticism and Semantic Knowledge," in *Rule-Following and Meaning*, ed. A. Miller and C. Wright (Montreal: McGill-Queen's University Press, 2002), 16–27.

4. Wittgenstein, *Philosophical Investigations*, §218.

5. See Kripke, *Wittgenstein on Rules and Private Language*, 1–54.

6. For a very helpful comparison of Cartesian, Kantian, and Wittgensteinian varieties of skepticism, see James Conant, "Varieties of Scepticism," in *Wittgenstein and Scepticism*, ed. Denis McManus (New York: Routledge, 2004), 97–136.

7. John McDowell, "Wittgenstein on Following a Rule," in *Mind, Value and Reality* (Cambridge, Mass.: Harvard University Press, 1998), 226–27.

8. See Kripke, *Wittgenstein on Rules and Private Language*, 69–71: "it seems that no matter what is in my mind at a given time, I am free in the future to interpret it in different ways" (107).

9. Ludwig Wittgenstein, *The Blue and Brown Books* (New York: Harper, 1958), 34.

10. Wittgenstein, *Philosophical Investigations*, §218.

11. See, for example, Kripke, *Wittgenstein on Rules and Private Language*, 53–54.

12. David Pears, *The False Prison. A Study in the Development of Wittgenstein's Philosophy* (Oxford: Clarendon, 1987), 1: 10.

13. Wittgenstein, *Philosophical Investigations*, §195; see also §193.

14. Kripke, *Wittgenstein on Rules and Private Language*, 54.

15. Jacques Derrida, *Speech and Phenomena and Other Essays on Husserl's Theory of Signs*, trans. with intro. David B. Allison (Evanston, Ill.: Northwestern

University Press, 1973), 5, 9. Derrida uses the same locution—"metaphysical presupposition"—in *Of Grammatology*, trans. Gayatri Chakravorty Spivak (Baltimore: Johns Hopkins University Press, 1997), 28–29. In chapter 1 of part II of *Logical Investigations* Husserl defines the "expressive relation or function" as conveying an ideal sense or meaning which is the same in different acts of assertion or of understanding it. Such ideal "meaning entities" he also terms "meaning-intentions." See Edmund Husserl, *Logical Investigations*, trans. J. N. Findlay (London: Routledge and Kegan Paul, 1970), 1: 269–98.

16. Jacques Derrida, "Différance," in *Speech and Phenomena*, 147.

17. Jacques Derrida, *Limited, Inc.*, trans. Samuel Weber and Jeffrey Mehlman (Evanston, Ill.: Northwestern University Press, 1988), 15.

18. Derrida, *Of Grammatology*, 16; "It [the transcendental signified] is the unique experience of the signified producing itself spontaneously, from within the self, and nevertheless, as signified concept, in the element of ideality and universality" (20).

19. For an excellent introduction to the set of commitments identified in contemporary philosophy of mind as "Cartesianism," see Gilbert Ryle, *The Concept of Mind* (New York: Barnes and Noble, 1949), chap. 1.

20. Some scholars, such as Henry Staten, in his *Wittgenstein and Derrida* (Lincoln: University of Nebraska Press, 1986), claim that Derrida's deconstructive arguments are similar to Wittgenstein, but here a caveat is in order: they are similar to Kripke's Wittgenstein, but as I shall argue, Kripke misreads Wittgenstein.

21. Rodolphe Gasché, *The Tain of the Mirror* (Cambridge, Mass.: Harvard University Press, 1986), and his introduction in his *Inventions of Difference: On Jacques Derrida* (Cambridge, Mass.: Harvard University Press, 1994). In *Limited, Inc.*, Derrida writes: "Doubtless the concept of iterability is not a concept like the others (nor is *différance*, nor trace, nor supplement, nor parergon, etc.). That it might belong *without* belonging to the class of concepts of which it must render an accounting, to the theoretical space that it organizes in a (as I often say) 'quasi-'transcendental manner, is doubtless a proposition that can appear paradoxical, even contradictory in the eyes of common sense or of a rigid classical logic" (127; see also 152). However, it is clear that what Gasché calls "infrastructures" (to distinguish them from concepts classically understood) fulfill a transcendental function for Derrida, in that they are in part his answer to the inquiry into the conditions of possibility of meaning *überhaupt*.

22. Derrida, *Of Grammatology*, 45–46.

23. Depending on the specific context of his reading, Derrida has coined a variety of variations of the trace, including "supplement," "mark," "spacing," and of course, "*différance*."

24. Derrida, *Of Grammatology*, 7, 9.

25. Ibid., 23–24.

26. Ibid., 57.

27. Ibid., 62–63. A similar hypostatization occurs in Derrida's *Speech and Phenomena*: "The absence of intuition [that is, reference]—and therefore of the subject of that intuition—is not only *tolerated* by speech; it is *required* by the general subject of signification, when considered *in itself*. It is radically requisite: the total absence of subject and object of a statement—the death of the writer and/or the disappearance of the objects he was able to describe—does not

prevent a text from 'meaning' something. On the contrary, this possibility gives birth to meaning as such, gives it out to be heard and read." Derrida, *Speech and Phenomena*, 93.

28. Derrida, *Of Grammatology*, 50–51. See also: "The study of the functioning of language, its *play*, presupposes that the substance of *meaning* and, among other possible substances, that of *sound*, be bracketed. The unity of sound and of sense is indeed here, as I proposed above, the reassuring closing of play" (57, translation modified).

29. Derrida, "Différance," 142–43.

30. Ibid., 139–40. There are obvious affinities to Wittgenstein's arguments against a "private language" in the *Philosophical Investigations* that I cannot consider here.

31. Martin Stone, "Wittgenstein on Deconstruction," in *The New Wittgenstein*, ed. Alice Crary and Rupert Read (New York: Routledge, 2000), 83–117. Stone draws on McDowell's reading of Wittgenstein and extends it to Derrida, as do I. Stone and I differ, however, in our choice and interpretation of Derrida's texts.

32. Jacques Derrida, "The Supplement of Origin," in *Speech and Phenomena*, 103.

33. There is a similar argument in the offing for meaning holism understood along the lines of inferential relations among concepts; for instance, if one holds that to know the meaning of "red" is to know what conditions entitle one to claim "this is red" (for instance, seeing something red, under normal visual conditions, among English speakers, etc.) and what inferentially follows from claiming "this is red" (e.g., "this is colored," "this is not [completely] blue or yellow," etc.), then it can be argued that such conditions and such inferential relations are potentially innumerable.

34. Derrida draws this conclusion explicitly: "it is always possible that it [an expression] has no decidable meaning." Jacques Derrida, *Spurs: Nietzsche's Styles* (Chicago: University of Chicago Press, 1981), 133.

35. Wittgenstein, *Philosophical Investigations*, §217.

36. Wittgenstein, *Remarks on the Foundations of Mathematics*, VI-28.

37. Derrida, *Limited, Inc.*, 62.

38. Ibid., 15. Compare also "rigorous purity" (20), "a stability that is absolute, eternal, intangible, natural, etc." (146).

39. Ibid., 119.

40. This line of argument is also found in Derrida, "The Force of Law: The 'Mystical Foundation of Authority,'" in *Deconstruction and the Possibility of Justice*, ed. Drucilla Cornell et al. (New York: Routledge, 1992), 3–67.

41. Derrida, *Limited, Inc.*, 126.

42. Ibid., 20. See also "but this condition of possibility turns into a condition of impossibility" (Derrida, *Of Grammatology*, 74).

43. In *Limited, Inc.*, Derrida explains this possibility of misapplication or radical reinterpretability of an expression explicitly in terms of his earlier work on quasi-transcendental infrastructures, identifying the ground for an expression's alterability in "the nonpresent remainder of a differential mark cut off from its putative 'production' or origin" (10); Compare ". . . the possibility of disengagement and citational graft which belongs to the structure of every mark, spoken or written, and which constitutes every mark in writing before and outside of every

horizon of semio-linguistic communication; in writing, which is to say, in the possibility of its functioning [that is, being interpretable] being cut off, at a certain point, from its 'original' desire-to-say-what-one-means [*vouloir-dire*] and from its participation in a saturable [i.e., determinate] and constraining context" (12).

44. " . . a possibility—a possible risk—is *always* possible, and is in some sense a necessary possibility" (Derrida, *Limited, Inc.*, 15); Derrida's rhetorical question: "is this risk rather [language's] internal and positive condition of possibility?" (17). Compare: "the essential and irreducible *possibility* of *mis*understanding, or of '*in*felicity' must be taken into account in the description of those values said to be positive" (147). Hence "the condition of possibility of those effects [of signature, i.e., of responsibility for the meaning of one's utterance] is simultaneously, once again, the conditions of their impossibility, of the impossibility of their rigorous [i.e., determinate] purity" (20).

45. "Above all, this essential absence of intending the actuality of utterance, this structural unconsciousness, if you like, prohibits any saturation of the context. In order for a context to be exhaustively determinable . . . conscious intention would at the very least have to be totally present and immediately transparent to itself and to others, since it is the determining center of context. The concept of—or the search for—the context thus seems to suffer at this point from the same theoretical and 'interested' uncertainty as the concept of the 'ordinary,' from the same metaphysical origins: the ethical and teleological discourse of consciousness" (Derrida, *Limited, Inc.*, 18). Compare: "This essential drift [*dérive*] bearing on writing as an iterative structure, cut off from all absolute responsibility, from *consciousness* as the ultimate authority . . ." (8).

46. There can be no "absolutely meaningful speech" (Derrida, *Limited, Inc.*, 15); see also: "determinate content, identifiable meaning, describable value," "ideal content" (6).

47. Derrida, *Limited, Inc.*, 15.

48. Ibid., 151.

49. Ibid., 133. Compare: "the essential and irreducible *possibility* of *mis*understanding or of '*in*felicity' must be taken into account in the description of those values said to be positive" (147).

50. Ibid., 157, n. 9.

51. John McDowell offers this interpretation of Kripke in "Wittgenstein on Following a Rule." For helpful discussion see also David H. Finkelstein, *Expression and the Inner* (Cambridge, Mass.: Harvard University Press, 2003), chap. 4.

52. Kripke, *Wittgenstein on Rules and Private Language*, 66.

53. Ibid., 68–69, 70–71, and 77.

54. Ibid., 91–92.

55. Wittgenstein, *Philosophical Investigations*, §85. See also §28: "That is to say: an ostensive definition can be variously interpreted in *every* case." See also Wittgenstein, *Blue and Brown Books*, 33.

56. An example of the hypostatizing move in Derrida: "The absence of intuition—and therefore of the subject of that intuition—is not only *tolerated* by speech; it is *required* by the general subject of signification, **when considered *in itself*"** (Derrida, "The Supplement of Origin," in *Speech and Phenomena*, 93 [bold emphasis mine]).

57. Wittgenstein, *Philosophical Investigations*, §198; see also §87.

58. Ibid., §199.

59. Compare these types of account with a dispositional account, namely, "That's how I (or: we) react to sign-posts," where such a response is susceptible to Kripke's objections discussed earlier.

60. Wittgenstein, *Philosophical Investigations*, §201.

61. "As part of the system of language, one may say, the sentence has life. But one is tempted to imagine that which gives the sentence life as something in an occult sphere, accompanying the sentence. But whatever accompanied it would for us just be another sign." Wittgenstein, *Blue and Brown Books*, 5. See also Wittgenstein, *Philosophical Investigations*: §194; Ludwig Wittgenstein, *Zettel*, ed. G. E. M. Anscombe et al., trans. G. E. M. Anscombe (Berkeley: University of California Press, 1967), §290, §139.

62. For recent defenses of the claim that an experiential state may serve as warrant for a judgment known immediately or non-inferentially, see James Pryor, "There is Immediate Justification," in *Contemporary Debates in Epistemology*, ed. M. Steup and E. Sosa (Oxford: Blackwell, 2005), 181–201. Compare McDowell's similar definition of the epistemological distinction between inferential and non-inferential knowledge; "knowledge is inferential if the only way to vindicate its status as knowledge is to invoke the goodness of an inference to what is known from something independently within the knower's epistemic reach . . . Contrast . . . someone who knows that something is green by seeing that it is. That she sees that the thing is green entails that the thing is green." McDowell, "Brandom on Observation," in *Reading Brandom*, ed. B. Weiss and J. Wanderer (London: Routledge, 2010), 141.

Chapter 2

The epigraph for chapter 2 is from Wittgenstein, *Philosophical Investigations*, part II, section v.

1. See Boris Eikhenbaum, "Tolstoi i Shopengauer: K voprosu o sozdanii 'Anny Kareninoi,'" *Literaturnyi Sovremennik* 11 (1935): 134–49; Eikkhenbaum, *Tolstoi in the Seventies*, trans. Alber Kaspin (Ann Arbor, Mich.: Ardis, 1982), 137–47; and Donna Tussing Orwin, *Tolstoy's Art and Thought, 1847–1880* (Princeton, N.J.: Princeton University Press, 1993), 143–70.

2. The older scholarship maintains the division between the pre- and post-conversion Tolstoy, although Richard Gustafson, in *Leo Tolstoy: Resident and Stranger* (Princeton, N.J.: Princeton University Press, 1986) has challenged the view, arguing for the continuity of Tolstoy's religious beliefs and their narrative embodiment throughout his life.

3. For a helpful overview of readers' reactions, see A. V. Knowles, "Russian Views of *Anna Karenina*, 1875–1878," *Slavic and East European Journal* 22 (1978): 301–12.

4. Tolstoy, *Polnoe sobranie sochinenii*, 62: 268–69. Vladimir Alexandrov, in *Limits to Interpretation: The Meanings of "Anna Karenina"* (Madison: University of Wisconsin Press, 2004), esp. 104–6, but passim, expands upon Tolstoy's suggestion of linkages between "images, actions, situations" by theorizing the linkages in terms of metonymic and metaphoric relations (as in classical structuralism), to show how such relations "function as generators of meaning that is polyvalent within relatively circumscribed borders, or that is both plural and limited" (99).

5. See Elisabeth Stenbock-Fermor, *The Architecture of "Anna Karenina"* (Lisse: Peter de Ridder, 1975); Sydney Schultze, *The Structure of "Anna Karenina"* (Ann Arbor, Mich.: Ardis, 1982); and William M. Todd III, "The Responsibilities of (Co-)Authorship: Notes on Revising the Serialized Version of *Anna Karenina*," in *Freedom and Responsibility in Russian Literature*, ed. E. C. Allen and G. S. Morson (Evanston, Ill.: Northwestern University Press, 1995), 159–69.

6. This is Tussing Orwin's conjecture, in her *Tolstoy's Art and Thought*, 154.

7. Leo Tolstoy, *Anna Karenina*, trans. Richard Pevear and Larissa Volokhonsky (New York: Penguin: 2000), 227. The semiotician Iurii Lotman describes very similar inversions in native-foreign binary possibilities of behavior in his "Poetics of Everyday Behavior in Eighteenth-Century Russian Culture," in *The Semiotics of Russian Cultural History*, ed. A. D. Nakhimovsky and A.S. Nakhimovsky (Ithaca, N.Y.: Cornell University Press, 1985), 30–66.

8. Tolstoy, *Anna Karenina*, 7 (translation modified).

9. Ibid., 61. Lydia Ginzburg offers illuminating commentary along these lines regarding Vronsky's happiness in having "a code of rules which unquestionably defined everything that ought and ought not to be done" (Tolstoy, *Anna Karenina*, 304), in Ginzburg, *On Psychological Prose*, trans. Judson Rosengrant (Princeton, N.J.: Princeton University Press, 1991), 348.

10. Tolstoy, *Anna Karenina*, 128–29.

11. Ibid., 174 (translation modified).

12. For example, Vronsky refers to his "regimental connections," and his mother refers to an extramarital affair as "*sviaz'*" in part 2, chap. 18 (173–74).

13. Tolstoy, *Anna Karenina*, 211, 213. See also also part 4, chapter 1: "The Karenins, husband and wife, went on living in the same house, met every day, but were completely estranged from each other. Alexei Alexandrovich made it a rule [*za pravilo postavil*] to see his wife every day, so as to give the servants no grounds for conjecture . . ." (353).

14. Tolstoy, *Anna Karenina*, 415 (translation modified). Russian "*koleia*" can mean "rut" or "railway track" (my thanks to William Mills Todd III for this observation).

15. Ibid., 433.

16. See *Russkaia povest' XIX veka: Istoriia i problematika zhanra*, ed. B. C. Meilakh (Leningrad: Nauka, 1973), 169–99.

17. Tolstoy, *Anna Karenina*, 483–84.

18. On the new railroads in Russia as both "spiritual destruction and material progress" see James Billington, *The Ikon and the Axe: An Interpretive History of Russian Culture* (New York: Vintage, 1970), 382–83. For an enumeration of the more than thirty occurrences of the theme of "railway" in the novel and an attempt to interpret them as emotionally charged narrative "linkages," see Schultze, *The Structure of "Anna Karenina,"* 117–22.

19. Gary Jahn, "The Image of the Railroad in *Anna Karenina*," *Slavic and East European Journal* 25 (1981): 6.

20. *Oxford English Dictionary*, s.v. "rail." Compare the related German words *Riegel* ("bar") and *Regel* ("rule"). The explicitly aesthetic term "role," however, derives from the rolled-up parchments upon which plays were recorded.

21. Tolstoy, *Anna Karenina*, 173.

22. Leo Tolstoy, "The Memoirs of a Madman," trans. Louise and Aylmer Maude, in *Tolstoy's Short Fiction*, ed. Michael Katz (New York: Norton, 1991), 295–304.

23. This is at least in part the influence of the "insidious poison" of Schopenhauer's philosophy, according to Tussing Orwin, *Tolstoy's Art and Thought*, 154–55. See also Sigrid McLaughlin, "Some Aspects of Tolstoy's Intellectual Development: Tolstoy and Schopenhauer," *California Slavic Studies* 5 (1970): 187–245.

24. Tolstoy, "The Memoirs of a Madman," 304.

25. There may also be a reference here to the cultural-religious figure of the "holy fool" (*iurodivyi*) who imitates Christ's virtues to the point of being considered a fool or madman by bourgeois society.

26. Tolstoy, "The Memoirs of a Madman," 300 (translation modified).

27. Ibid., 300 (translation modified).

28. Ibid., 295.

29. Tolstoy, *Anna Karenina*, 2–3. The translators note that the passage likely alludes to *Reflexes of the Brain* by I. M. Sechenov, published in 1863.

30. Oblonsky in particular, as a comic figure, seems to possess mental states that are mere effects of physical causes. Another example: "Having finished the newspaper, a second cup of coffee, and a kalatch with butter, he got up, brushed the crumbs from his waistcoat and, expanding his broad chest, smiled joyfully, not because there was anything especially pleasant in his soul—the smile was evoked by good digestion" (Tolstoy, *Anna Karenina*, 8, translation modified). There is a parallel, a linkage here, between the secondary characters of Oblonsky and Karenin. Oblonsky's mental life and behavior are all too often determined by physical causes; Karenin's are all too often determined by codes and habits of conduct, first of polite society and officialdom, later of the church. For example, we are told why he proposed to Anna, that he was "honor-bound and had to propose," and that "his relations with these people were confined to one sphere, firmly defined by custom and habit, from which it was impossible to depart" (507).

31. Tolstoy, *Anna Karenina*, 24.

32. Varenka's "excitement" (*volnenie*) at the expected proposal causes physiological effects as well: "she felt herself blush, then turn pale, then blush again" (Tolstoy, *Anna Karenina*, 565).

33. Tolstoy, *Anna Karenina*, 564–65.

34. Of course, according to Schopenhauer's metaphysics, their actions are the expression of a deeper, unconscious, and unfathomable will.

35. Scholars diverge strikingly in their interpretations of this scene. Justin Weir sees the initial unity of the lovers broken by their digression into convention: "The failure of the proposal is not a failure of communication but an instance of the misery of convention, which now has its way with the unlucky couple. . . . They betray their love because they think it will develop on its own" when in fact it requires "skill and work." Weir, *Leo Tolstoy and the Alibi of Narrative* (New Haven, Conn.: Yale University Press, 2011), 134. By contrast, Amy Mandelker reads the scene as an unqualified pastoral critique in which "Tolstoy counters Victorian victimizing conventions, both literary and social, with a native Russian version of the courtship plot, an 'anti-proposal' scene." Mandelker, *Framing "Anna Karenina": Tolstoy, the Woman Questions, and the Victorian Novel* (Columbus: Ohio State University Press, 1993), 169.

36. Tolstoy, *Anna Karenina*, 61 (my emphasis).

37. Ibid., 81, 82–83 (my emphasis).
38. Ibid., 105.
39. Ibid., 149.
40. Ibid., 150.
41. Ibid., 188.
42. Ibid., 314.
43. Ibid., 182. Echoed six pages later when Vronsky sees Anna: "Besides that, her [Anna's] excitement [*volnenie*] communicated itself physically to him" (188).
44. Ibid., 314.
45. Ibid., 668.
46. The reasons why skeptical doubt creeps into Anna's and Vronsky's relationship are many, and their explication would take us too far afield, into the area of self-deception (e.g., Anna's "deliberate refusal to understand her position," and Vronsky's fancying himself a painter). One reason, however, certainly has to do with the *will*, in the form of countervailing *desires*. Vronsky's commitment to Anna causes him to lose the regimental and social connections, rules and codes within which he understands himself and feels at home. Once those have been lost, his desire moves from object to object, and he begins to lose interest in Anna.

> Vronsky . . . was content, but not for long. He soon felt arise in his soul a desire for desires, an anguish. Independently of his will [*Nezavisimo ot svoei voli*], he began to grasp at every fleeting caprice, taking it for a desire and a goal. . . . outside the sphere of conventional social life that had occupied their time in Petersburg. . . . And as a hungry animal seizes upon every object it comes across, hoping to find food in it, so Vronsky quite unconsciously seized now upon politics, now upon new books, now upon painting. (Tolstoy, *Anna Karenina*, 465)

Ultimately Vronsky finds that he cannot express his innermost attitudes to Anna (627), and they come to misunderstand each other's looks (641). Such a breakdown ushers in precisely the Cartesian divide: "[Vronsky] did not reproach her [Anna] in words, but in his soul he did reproach her" (549).
47. Tolstoy, *Anna Karenina*, 396. Immediately thereafter they play the parlor game whereby each divines words and sentences from initial letters given by the other. Later they finish each other's sentences in speech (559).
48. Ibid., 444.
49. Ibid., 446.
50. Ibid., 457–58.
51. Ibid., 297–98. Full disclosure: the difference in usage is not observed without exception by Tolstoy. At one point in the novel we read: "and Varenka—something Kitty had not seen before—melted into weak but infectious laughter [*raskisala ot slabogo, no soobshchaiushchegosia smekha*], provoked in her by the prince's witticisms" (233), but the verb is "to communicate itself," *not* "to infect." After all, Tolstoy wrote and serialized the novel over several years, and ultimately is not a philosopher honor-bound to keep his terminology in line.
52. Tolstoy, *Anna Karenina*, 401.
53. Ibid., 579.
54. Ibid., 586.
55. Ibid., 591.

56. As quoted of Amfiteatrov in Eikhenbaum, *Tolstoi in the Sixties*, trans. Duffield White (Ann Arbor, Mich.: Ardis, 1982), 120.
57. Tolstoy, *Anna Karenina*, 440.
58. Ibid., 587.
59. Ibid., 170.
60. Compare Levin's reaction to Western treatises on political economy and agriculture: "he found laws deduced from the situation of European farming; but he simply could not see why those laws, not applicable in Russia, should be universal. He saw the same in the socialist books: these were either beautiful but inapplicable fantasies, such as he had been enthusiastic about while still a student, or corrections, mendings of the state of affairs in which Europe stood and with which Russian agriculture had nothing in common" (Tolstoy, *Anna Karenina*, 341–42).
61. Tolstoy, *Anna Karenina*, 238.
62. Ibid., 396.
63. Ibid., 678 (translation modified).
64. Ibid., 786. Note that the secondary character emblematically called Sviyazhsky (suggesting "*sviaz'*," "connection," "liaison")—whose thoughts and actions are completely divorced from each other—serves as a contrast to Levin's introspections: "Sviyazhsky was one of those people, always astonishing to Levin, whose reasoning, very consistent though never independent, goes by itself, and whose life, extremely well defined and firm in its orientation, goes by itself, quite independent of and almost always contrary to their reasoning" (326; see also 337). Also, this "linkage" has another set of nodes revolving around the use of "pretend" and "pretense" in the novel, which I will not follow here, except to note that Dolly's children feel no shyness towards Levin, as they do toward other adults, because Levin does not "pretend" (267).
65. Ludwig Wittgenstein, *Tractatus Logico-Philosophicus*, trans. D. F. Pears and B. F. McGuinness (London: Routledge, 1961).
66. Ludwig Wittgenstein, *On Certainty* (New York: Harper, 1969), 5.
67. Robert Fogelin, *Wittgenstein*, 2nd ed. (London: Routledge, 1987), 232–33.
68. Lydia Ginzburg, *On Psychological Prose*, trans. J. Rosengrant (Princeton, N.J.: Princeton University Press, 1991); and relatedly, Aleksandr Skaftymov, "Idei i formy v tvorchestve L. Tolstogo," in *Nravstvennye iskaniia russkikh pisatelei* (Moscow: Khudozhestvennaia literatura, 1972), 144–45; and the diary entry (March 21, 1898) by Tolstoy: "How good it would be to write a work of art in which one could clearly express the fluidity [*tekuchest'*] of a person; the fact that one and the same man is now a villain, now an angel, now a wise man, now an idiot, now a strong man, now the most important creature of all." Leo Tolstoy, *Tolstoy's Diaries*, ed. and trans. R. F. Christian (New York: Charles Scribner's Sons, 1985), 2: 457 (translation modified); Tolstoi, *Polnoe sobranie sochinenii*, 53: 187.
69. Tolstoy, *Anna Karenina*, 797 (original emphasis).
70. This is John McDowell's felicitous expression.
71. Wittgenstein, *On Certainty*, 44 (no. 341). Some examples Wittgenstein provides: describing something, naming something, measuring something, following a road sign, issuing or obeying a command, understanding a human face.
72. See Wittgenstein, *Philosophical Investigations*, §§85, 454.

73. I take this view to be one of the lessons of McDowell, "Wittgenstein on Following a Rule."

74. Tolstoy, *Anna Karenina*, 251, 252. Compare: "Having lived the major part of his life in the country and in close relations with the peasantry, Levin always felt during the work period that this general peasant excitement *communicated itself* [*soobshchaetsia*] to him as well" (792).

75. Tolstoy, *Anna Karenina*, 791. Note that "*doroga*" ("road") alone may also be translated as "railway."

76. Leo Tolstoy, *A Confession and Other Religious Writings*, trans. Jane Kentish (New York: Penguin, 1987), 20–21 (translation modified). Schopenhauer's pessimism, as above, is at work here: "Can it be that only Schopenhauer and I have been intelligent enough to understand the meaninglessness and evil of life?" (47).

77. Tolstoy, *A Confession*, 58 (translation modified).

78. In the interests of fairness it must be noted that it seems Tolstoy does *not* make the difference between *unsinnig* and *sinnlos* that Wittgenstein will in the *Tractatus*. Thus Tolstoy finds that he cannot think of infinite matters (matters beyond space and time, such as goodness or value) from within the spatio-temporal context of finite, scientific thinking (which is based on causality). He concludes:

> It is somewhat similar to what happens in mathematics when, trying to resolve an equation, we get an identity. The method of deduction is correct, but the only answer obtained is that a equals a, and x equals x, or 0 equals 0. Precisely the same thing was happening with my reasoning concerning the meaning of life. The only answers the sciences give to this question are identities. (Tolstoy, *A Confession*, 52)

Such passages would, in Tractarian terms, be *sinnlos*, as are logical tautologies: vacuously true but contentless (see *Tractatus* 4.4611). On this point see Caleb Thompson, "Wittgenstein, Tolstoy and the Meaning of Life," *Philosophical Investigations* 20 (1997): 112–13; and James Conant, "Must We Show What We Cannot Say?" in *The Senses of Stanley Cavell*, ed. R. Fleming and M. Payne (Lewisburg, Pa.: Bucknell University Press, 1989), 242–83.

79. Tolstoy, *A Confession*, 69.

80. Ibid., 78.

Chapter 3

The epigraphs for chapter 3 are from J. W. Goethe, *Maximen und Reflexionen* (Frankfurt: Insel, 2000), no. 1115; and Arthur Schopenhauer, *The World as Will and Representation*, trans. E. F. Payne (New York: Dover), 1: 271.

1. See Tolstoi, *Polnoe sobranie sochinenii*, 60: 288, where he calls *War and Peace* a "beautiful lie."

2. Leo Tolstoy, *Walk in the Light and Twenty-Three Tales*, trans. Louise und Aylmer Maude (Farmington, Penn.: The Plough Publishing House, 1998), 44 (translation modified); Tolstoi, *Polnoe sobranie sochinenii*, 26: 282.

3. Classic touchstones of this story are M. H. Abrams, *The Mirror and the Lamp: Romantic Theory and the Critical Tradition* (New York: Oxford University Press, 1971); and Charles Taylor, *Hegel* (Cambridge: Cambridge University Press,

1977), chap. 1. For a general introduction to the concept of aesthetic expression, see Dabney Townsend, *An Introduction to Aesthetics* (Oxford: Blackwell, 1997), 79–91; Noël Carroll, *Philosophy of Art: A Contemporary Introduction* (London: Routledge, 1999), 58–106; Aaron Ridley, "Expression in Art," in *The Oxford Handbook of Aesthetics*, ed. Jerrold Levinson (Oxford: Oxford University Press, 2003), 211–27; and Gordon Graham, *Philosophy of the Arts: An Introduction to Aesthetics*, 3rd ed. (London: Routledge, 2005), 31–51.

4. It is important here to note briefly that my characterization of expressivism differs from Krystyna Pomorska's semiotic explication of the meaning of "natural" for Tolstoy: "It is the non-mediated, intuitive cognition and behavior, the capacity that every person—unspoiled by rule and learning—is endowed with from birth. Or . . . it is a special way of learning comparable to learning one's native language: a process based not on rules, but on memory, in which one remembers a number of 'texts' in their numerous usages" (Pomorska, "Tolstoy—Contra Semiosis," *International Journal of Slavic Linguistics* 25–26 [1982]: 383). While expressivism does entail immediate (non-inferential) understanding, that understanding need not be instinctual or intuitive, as opposed to learned or trained. As shall be argued in chapter 8, both "natural" and "conventional" signs can express genuine emotions; if not, then most artworks, by virtue of their conventions, could not express emotions. Tolstoy does at times seem to affirm this view in *What Is Art?*, incorrectly, I believe. Furthermore, Pomorska (385) associates natural communication (as not based on learned knowledge) with iconic rather than indexical signification (according to Peirce's semiotic taxonomy), but iconic signification, based on similarity, differs from expressivism as the direct manifestation of meaning content.

5. Gary Saul Morson, *Hidden in Plain View: Narrative and Creative Potentials in "War and Peace"* (Stanford, Calif.: Stanford University Press, 1987), 37. Rimvydas Silbajoris, in the conclusion to his book-length study of Tolstoy's aesthetics, goes even further, claiming that *What Is Art?* should be read as "withdrawal from all conventional standards and concepts of art carried onwards through history by the rising tide of civilization" and "the entire enormous structure of aesthetics that was built through long centuries" (Silbajoris, *Tolstoy's Aesthetics and His Art* [Columbus, Oh.: Slavica, 1990]: 263).

6. Gustafson (*Leo Tolstoy: Resident and Stranger*) in his exposition of Tolstoy's understanding of genuine aesthetic experience as "ecstatic" from the vantage point of Orthodox theology perhaps unwittingly draws on Longinus, who at the outset of "On the Sublime" cautions that "the effect of elevated language upon an audience is not persuasion but transport" (1.4, ll. 3–4), the latter of which is "*ekstasis*" in the original. Gustafson lauds Tolstoy for his use of hyperbaton in indirect discourse as a successful way to involve the reader in the character's thoughts and perceptions, precisely in the way Longinus praises the use of hyperbaton as "an imitation that approaches nature" my mimicking unpremeditated speech and thought (22.3). On the other hand, Amy Mandelker (*Framing "Anna Karenina,"* 46–80) tries to read *What Is Art?* as a version of the *Kantian* sublime, but I think this is less than illuminating; although concepts of power, intensity, and effect/affect—all central to Longinus and the naturalized sublime of Burke—are in play, for Kant the experience of the sublime reflexively reveals cognitive aspects of subjectivity and the subject's relationship to normativity (the

supersensible), whereas for Longinus, and for Tolstoy, the effect of the sublime is primarily one of passion and communication.

7. Dionysius Longinus, *Libellus de Sublimate*, ed. D. A. Russell (Oxford: Oxford University Press, 1968), 3.1 (ll. 22–3); see also 11.2 (ll. 7–9).

8. See, for example, Jürgen Habermas, *The Philosophical Discourse of Modernity*, trans. Frederick Lawrence (Cambridge, Mass.: MIT Press, 1987), 83–106.

9. Jean-François Lyotard, *Des dispositifs pulsionnels* (Paris: Union générale d'éditions, 1973), 266; see also Lyotard, "The Sublime and the Avant-Garde," in *The Lyotard Reader*, ed. A. Benjamin (Oxford: Blackwell, 1989), 196–211; and Susan Sontag, "Against Interpretation," in *A Susan Sontag Reader* (New York: Vintage, 1983), 104.

10. Leo Tolstoy, *What Is Art?* trans. Richard Pevear and Larissa Volokhonsky (New York: Penguin, 1995). Art as "spiritual nourishment" (138) recurs throughout the treatise; see also 35, 88, 114.

11. Ibid., 131–32.

12. The early chapters of the treatise are devoted to rejecting previous aesthetic theories based on the concept of beauty or aesthetic pleasure, and need not concern us directly here.

13. Tolstoy, *What Is Art?* 37.

14. Ibid., 39–40 (original emphasis).

15. Tolstoy's younger brother Dmitry Nikolaevich Tolstoy died of consumption on January 21, 1856; the experience formed the basis for Levin visiting his dying brother in *Anna Karenina*. Tolstoy's eldest brother Nikolai Nikolaevich Tolstoy died of consumption on September 20, 1860, at Hyères in the south of France. See A. N. Wilson, *Tolstoy* (New York: W.W. Norton, 1988), 132–35 and 156–57.

16. Wilson, *Tolstoy*, 44.

17. See for example, Richard Shusterman, *Pragmatist Aesthetics. Living Beauty, Rethinking Art*, 2nd ed. (Lanham, Md.: Rowman and Littlefield, 2000).

18. Tolstoy, *What Is Art?* 41. See also 135 (where he includes "porcelain dolls") and 155: ". . . the whole enormous realm of popular children's art—jokes, proverbs, riddles, songs, dances, children's games, mimicry . . ."

19. Tolstoy, *What Is Art?* 88.

20. Ibid., chap. 15. Caryl Emerson notes that "sincerity" (*iskrennost'*) "is built off *iskra*, a 'spark': that which flashes momentarily and either catches fire or dies. The artistic effect either takes, or fails to take." Emerson, "Tolstoy's Aesthetics," in *The Cambridge Companion to Tolstoy*, ed. Donna Tussing Orwin (Cambridge: Cambridge University Press, 2002), 244. And Tolstoy likens the effect of genuine art to that of a spark: "It sometimes happens that people, while together, are, if not hostile, at least alien to each other in their moods and feelings, and suddenly a story, a performance, a painting, even a building or, most frequently, music, will unite them all with an electric spark [*kak elektricheskoi iskroi*], and instead of their former separateness, often even hostility, they all feel unity and mutual love." Tolstoy, *What Is Art?* 130–31.

21. Tolstoy, *What Is Art?* 81. See also 38.

22. Ibid., 81; my emphasis.

23. This scene echoes a related scene early in *Anna Karenina* in which the spiritually stricken Levin is not infected by singing peasant women: "Levin was

envious of this healthy merriment; he would have liked to take part in expressing this joy of life. But he could do nothing and had to lie there and look and listen. When the peasants and their song had vanished from his sight and hearing, a heavy feeling of anguish at his loneliness, his bodily idleness, his hostility to the world, came over him" (Tolstoy, *Anna Karenina*, 275).

24. Tolstoy, *What Is Art?* 118–19. On a first approximation, these examples illustrate or elicit the following emotions: (1) joy, gaiety; (2) motherly succor; (3) pity or compassion; (4) a child's love for its mother, and subsequently, sadness.

25. For example: "Once the spectators or listeners are infected by the same feeling the author has experienced, this is art" (Tolstoy, *What Is Art?* 39)

26. This "persona" theory of expression has been advocated by philosophers of aesthetics including Bruce Vermazen, Jerrold Levinson, and Jenefer Robinson, and is discussed in chapter 8.

27. Tolstoy, *What Is Art?* 139.

28. Ibid., 150.

29. Ibid., 39.

30. Ibid., 121 (emphasis in original). Caryl Emerson ("Tolstoy's Aesthetics," 244–45) resists the claim that Tolstoy seems to be making: that a particular emotion is transmitted from artist to audience. She cites the following passage from *What Is Art?* (122): "And since each man is unlike all others, this feeling will be particular for all other men, and will be the more particular the more deeply the artist penetrates, the more heartfelt and sincere he is," to support her claim that "art destroys separation—but emphasizes individuality" and "the primary value that is 'caught' by the receiver is sincerity." But this is misleading. Sincerity is a disposition or trait possessed by a person, and is arguably a relation (person P is sincere regarding the expression E of something F.), while an emotion does not have this logical structure. I read the passage cited above to be about the *individuation* of the feeling: Tolstoy is conceding that the feeling conveyed may be individuated more finely or coarsely for each person. For instance, one person may differentiate between regret and remorse, while another may not: for the first person the feeling conveyed would be more particular than for the second, but from this it does not follow that what is conveyed is mere "sincerity."

31. Tolstoy, *What Is Art?* 122. Compare: "Thus art is distinguished from non-art, and the worth of art as art is determined, regardless of its content, that is, independently of whether it conveys good or bad feelings" (123).

32. It should be noted that in his own presentation in *What Is Art?* Tolstoy does not observe the strict division between the criterion of genuine art (infectiousness of feeling) and the criterion of good art (content of conveyed feeling): see chapter 6, where he introduces thoughts he will develop in chapter 16.

33. Tolstoy, *Anna Karenina*, 787.

34. "In the cathedral Levin, lifting his hand and repeating the words of the archpriest along with the others, swore with the most terrible oaths to fulfill all the governor's hopes. Church services had always had an effect on him, and when he uttered the words, 'I kiss the cross,' and turned to look at the crowd of young and old people repeating the same thing, he felt himself moved" (Tolstoy, *Anna Karenina*, 647).

35. Tolstoy recounts a similar process in *A Confession* and "The Memoirs of a Madman," as we saw in chapter 2. In this sense Levin contrasts most starkly

with Karenin, who wholly subjects himself first to bureaucratic officialdom and subsequently "was now guided by the Scriptures in all things," but remains coldly detached from whatever codes and rules he is observing, because his fundamental attitude towards rules as such has *not* changed: "As for me, I am fulfilling my duty" (Tolstoy, *Anna Karenina*, 516–18).

36. Recall Wittgenstein in the *Tractatus* (6.51): "Skepticism is *not* irrefutable, but obviously nonsensical, when it raises doubts where no question can be asked. For a doubt can exist only where a question exists, a question only where an answer exists, and an answer only where something *can be said*." To ask for the meaning, the value, of life, is to ask for a necessary, absolute thing or statement which names or describes a contingent, accidental state of affairs. If it's absolute, then it cannot truthfully describe a contingent state of affairs; if it can describe it, then it's not absolute.

37. Tolstoy, *Anna Karenina*, 817 (translation modified).

38. Fogelin, *Wittgenstein*, 97. And he notes that these views "clearly derive from Kant and Schopenhauer" (ibid.). Compare Wittgenstein in the notebooks written during his work on the *Tractatus*: "Ethics does not treat of the world. Ethics is a condition of the world, like logic." Ludwig Wittgenstein, *Notebooks 1914–1916*, ed. G. E. M. Anscombe and G. H. von Wright, trans. G. E. M. Anscombe (Oxford: Basil Blackwell, 1961), 77 (July 24, 1916). On this general topic, see Martin Stokhof, *World and Life as One: Ethics and Ontology in Wittgenstein's Early Thought* (Stanford, Calif.: Stanford University Press, 2002).

39. Tolstoy, *What Is Art?* 42.

40. ". . . more or less needed for people's good" (Tolstoy, *What Is Art?* 124). More generally, see Thomas Barran, "Rousseau's Political Vision and Tolstoy's *What Is Art?*," *Tolstoy Studies Journal* 5 (1992): 1–12.

41. Tolstoy, *What Is Art?* 42.

42. *Poniatie* can also mean "concept," but that would flatly contradict Tolstoy's claim that it is undefinable by reason.

43. Tolstoy, *What Is Art?* 52.

44. Ibid., 43, 53. Thus *What Is Art?* is also the theoretical vindication of the artist Mikhailov's rejection of mere mechanical "technique" (Vronsky's talent), and the compliment he pays the artist: "He knew that it implied a mechanical ability to paint and draw, completely independent of content. He had often noticed, as in this present praise, that technique was opposed to inner virtue, as if it were possible to make a good painting out of something bad" (Tolstoy, *Anna Karenina*, 474). For further interpretation along these lines, see Alexandrov, *Limits of Interpretation*, 83–88.

45. Tolstoy, *What Is Art?* 129. And here we recall the devotion with which Wittgenstein read Tolstoy's exegesis of the Gospels.

46. Tolstoy, *What Is Art?* 131–32.

47. Ibid., 156.

48. See, for example, Wittgenstein, *Notebooks* entry for 9.11.14; *Tractatus*, 5.5423; *Blue and Brown Books*, 162–79; and *Philosophical Investigations*, part II, 193–229.

49. This construal of the distinction shifts Wittgenstein's diagnosis into the proximity of Sellars's "Myth of the Given" in Wilfrid Sellars, *Empiricism and the Philosophy of Mind* (Cambridge, Mass.: Harvard University Press, 1997).

50. Wittgenstein, *Zettel*, §225; see also §§490, 503–14. Compare *Blue and Brown Books*, 162ff., and *Philosophical Investigations*, §§536ff., also part II, section vi.ff.

51. Wittgenstein, *Blue and Brown Books*, 168–79.

52. Wittgenstein, *Philosophical Investigations*, part II, section iv.

53. Wittgenstein, *Culture and Value*, 26.

54. Alan Tormey, *The Concept of Expression: A Study in Philosophical Psychology* (Princeton, N.J.: Princeton University Press, 1971), 32.

55. J. L. Austin, "Other Minds," in *Philosophical Papers*, ed. J. O. Urmson and G. J. Warnock (Oxford: Oxford University Press, 1979), 108–9.

56. Wittgenstein, *Zettel*, §234.

57. In later writings Wittgenstein will speak of "methods of projection."

58. Denis McManus, *The Enchantment of Words: Wittgenstein's "Tractatus Logico-Philosophicus"* (Oxford: Clarendon, 2006), 39–40. See also Eli Friedlander, *Signs of Sense: Reading Wittgenstein's "Tractatus"* (Cambridge, Mass.: Harvard University Press, 2001), chap. 6.

59. Wittgenstein, *Culture and Value*, 25 and 67. See also Ludwig Wittgenstein, *The Big Typescript: TS 213*, ed. and trans. C. Grant Luckhardt and Maximilian A. E. Aue (Oxford: Blackwell, 2005), sec. 86.

60. Tolstoy, *What Is Art?* 94–95.

61. For an excellent and accessible introduction to the problematic of causal vs. normative relations in the theory of mind, a version of which recurs in the present study, see Tim Crane, *The Mechanical Mind: A Philosophical Introduction to Minds, Machines and Mental Representation*, 2nd ed. (London: Routledge, 2003), chap. 5.

62. One might speculate that Tolstoy avoided the use of the verb "to communicate itself" (*soobshchat'sia*) perhaps to avoid any suggestion of normative intentionality *necessarily* being attributed to the work of art and thereby to avoid some of the problems that arise in aesthetic expressivism, as for instance the contingent relationship between what an author might be feeling when composing a work and what the work itself expresses: a work might convey or elicit sadness, although its author was not sad when composing it. My thanks to Barry Scherr for raising this question, which I attempt to address in chapter 8.

63. *Obshchenie* is the nominalized derivative of the verb *obshchat'*; Dal' defines the latter as "to unite, share, consider together" and sets the former equivalent to *soobshchenie* (the nominalized derivative of the verb *soobshchat'*, "to communicate") and defines it as "communication, connection, mutual relation with someone." Vladimir I. Dal', *Tolkovyi slovar' zhivogo velikorusskogo iazyka* (Moscow: "Russkii Iazyk," 1981), 2: 634.

64. Tolstoy, *What Is Art?* 38.

65. Lexically, Tolstoy seems to prefer to use "feeling" (*chuvstvo*) to cover the spectrum, rather than "sensation" (*oshchushenie*) or the foreign calque term "emotion" (*emotsiia*).

66. Richard Wollheim, *On the Emotions* (New Haven, Conn.: Yale University Press, 1999). makes a compelling and psychologically rich case for emotions being mental dispositions, or "attitudes towards the world." On this understanding, distinctively moral emotions would seem to be similar if not equivalent to what Wittgenstein calls a good or evil will. Likewise Allan Gibbard writes: "An

emotion, we can say, involves a special way of experiencing one's world, a way that will be difficult to express and perhaps can only be whistled" (*Wise Choices, Apt Feelings: A Theory of Normative Judgment* [Cambridge, Mass.: Harvard University Press, 1990], 131), echoing Frank Ramsey's riposte to Wittgenstein regarding the latter's claim that the very propositions of the *Tractatus*, including ethical propositions, cannot be said.

67. Anthony Kenny, *Action, Emotion and Will* (London: Routledge and Kegan Paul, 1963), 60ff. See also Tormey, *The Concept of Expression*, 10–17 on prepositional objects of intentional states in contrast to sensations.

68. The modern resurrection of intentionality and intentional objects in the European philosophical tradition dates to Franz Brentano's *Psychologie vom empirischen Standpunkt* (1874), English translation Brentano, *Psychology from an Empirical Standpoint*, trans. Rancurello, Terrell and McAlister (London: Routledge and Kegan Paul, 1973); and Edmund Husserl's *Logische Untersuchungen* of 1900–1901.

69. Kenny, *Action, Emotion and Will*, 189.

70. Thus Heidegger distinguishes between fear (*Furcht*) and anxiety (*Angst*) precisely according to this criterion in *Sein und Zeit* (Tübingen: Niemeyer, 1986), §30. By contrast, Tormey (*The Concept of Expression*, 33–35) argues that moods, as emotions, have vague or diffused objects, and marshals Freud's analysis of anxiety (*Angst*) to support his claim.

71. How exactly the cognitive dimension of emotions should be understood receives various answers from philosophers of emotion. Some identify an emotion with a form of judgment or belief (e.g., Martha Nussbaum, *Upheavals of Thought: The Intelligence of Emotions* [Cambridge: Cambridge University Press, 2001]; Robert Solomon, "Emotions and Choice," in *Explaining Emotions*, ed. A. O. Rorty [Berkeley: University of California Press, 1980]), or evaluation (e.g., William Lyons, *Emotion* [Cambridge: Cambridge University Press, 1980]), or sets of beliefs and desires (Joel Marks, "A Theory of Emotion," *Philosophical Studies* 42 [1982]: 227–42).

72. Thus Amélie Rorty, "Explaining Emotions," in *Explaining Emotions*, holds that some emotions (e.g., unconscious resentment) do not involve propositional content. Michael Stocker's ("Psychic Feelings: Their Importance and Irreducibility," *Australian Journal of Philosophy* 61 [1983]: 5–26) famous "fear of flying" example (I know that it is irrational to fear flying, but my fear persists) and Patricia Greenspan's (*Emotions and Reasons: An Inquiry into Emotional Justification* [New York: Routledge, 1988]) examples of conflicting emotions (I'm happy my colleague won a fellowship, but also jealous that she did) suggest that emotions are more like desires than beliefs.

73. William James, "What Is an Emotion?" *Mind* 9 (1884): 190.

74. Wollheim, *On the Emotions*, 123.

75. Gary Jahn, "The Aesthetic Theory of Leo Tolstoy's *What Is Art?*," *Journal of Aesthetics and Art Criticism* 34 (1975): 62. See also Magdalene Zurek, *Tolstojs Philosophie der Kunst* (Heidelberg: C. Winter, 1996), 279–81.

76. Douglas Robinson, *Estrangement and the Somatics of Literature: Tolstoy, Shklovsky, Brecht* (Baltimore: Johns Hopkins University Press, 2008) interprets Tolstoyan "infection" as "somatic mimeticism," defined by two criteria: "somatic transfer" ("a somatic orientation in one body is transferred to another body")

and "somatic guidance" (the orientation should guide "thought and behavior"). He then connects them by drawing on a neurological theory of causal associationism (the "somatic marker" theory: a certain somatic orientation will trigger past memories, whose accompanying sensations of pleasure or pain will subconsciously affect the person's will and resulting behavior). Robinson thus collapses the distinction between *causal* somatic transfer and *normative* guidance into a causal-dispositional theory of decision and behavior, which effectively denies the normative dimension of meaning. See Kripke, *Wittgenstein on Rules and Private Language*, 22–38 for criticisms of the causal-dispositional view. I pursue this line of criticism in greater depth in chapter 6.

Chapter 4

The epigraphs from chapter 4 are from Plato, *Republic*, book III, 401d.; G. W. F. Hegel, *Aesthetics: Lectures on Fine Art*, trans. T. M. Knox (Oxford: Oxford University Press, 1975), 2: 903.; and Friedrich Nietzsche, *Jenseits von Gut und Böse*, "Sprüche und Zwischenspiele," §106.

1. Harry Walsh, "The Place of Schopenhauer in the Philosophical Education of Leo Tolstoi," in *Schopenhauer*, ed. E. von der Luft (Lewiston, N.Y.: Mellen, 1988), convincingly argues that Tolstoy's "philosophical fragments" (*filosofskie nabroski*), probably dating from the 1840s, reveal the influence of the subjective idealism of Fichte and early Schelling.

2. Tolstoi, *Polnoe sobranie sochinenii*, 61: 219; quoted by Sigrid McLaughlin, "Some Aspects of Tolstoy's Intellectual Development: Tolstoy and Schopenhauer," *California Slavic Studies* 5 (1970): 188.

3. Tolstoi, *Polnoe sobranie sochinenii*, 61: 219.

4. Tolstoi, *Polnoe sobranie sochinenii*, 50: 123. But then again on October 23, 1909, he describes Schopenhauer as one of the "greatest thinkers" (ibid., vol. 57: 158).

5. Studies of Schopenhauer's influence on Tolstoy include Eikhenbaum, *Tolstoi in the Seventies*, 144–47; Tussing Orwin, *Tolstoy's Art and Thought*, 143–70; Inessa Medzhibovskaya, *Tolstoy and the Religious Culture of His Time: A Biography of a Long Conversion, 1845–1887* (Lanham, Md.: Lexington Books, 2008), 121–84; McLaughlin, "Some Aspects of Tolstoy's Intellectual Development"; and Walsh, "The Place of Schopenhauer in the Philosophical Education of Leo Tolstoi." See here especially Walsh, "Schopenhauer's *On the Freedom of the Will* and the Epilogue to *War and Peace*," *Slavonic and East European Review* 57 (1979): 572–75.

6. Schopenhauer, *The World as Will and Representation*, 2: 195.

7. In fact, following Kant, Schopenhauer claims that self-consciousness, as "inner sense," is subject only to the transcendental form of intuition of *time*, but not space or causality, and so concludes that the agent is aware of temporal manifestations of our noumenal being rather than having an awareness of our noumenal being in itself. Schopenhauer, *The World as Will and Representation*, 2: 318.

8. Compare, for instance, the will as a "blindly urging force" and "endless striving" (Schopenhauer, *The World as Will and Representation*, 1: 117, 164).

9. Schopenhauer, *The World as Will and Representation*, 1: 178–79.

10. "But now, what kind of knowledge is it that considers what continues to exist outside and independently of all relations, but which alone is really essential

to the world, the true content of its phenomena, that which is subject to no change, and is therefore known with equal truth for all time, in a word, the *Ideas* that are the immediate and adequate objectivity of the thing-in-itself, of the will? It is *art*, the work of genius. It repeats the eternal Ideas apprehended through pure contemplation, the essential and abiding element in all the phenomena of the world." Schopenhauer, *The World as Will and Representation*, 1: 184.

11. Arthur Schopenhauer, *On the Basis of Morality*, trans. E. F. J. Payne (Providence, R.I.: Berghahn Books, 1995), 143–44 (translation modified). This general approach to ethics—sentimentalism—finds an early voice in Adam Smith (*The Theory of Moral Sentiments* [Oxford: Clarendon, 1976 (1759)], 10):

> When we see a stroke aimed, and just ready to fall upon the leg or arm of another person, we naturally shrink and draw back our own leg or our own arm; and when it does fall, we feel it in some measure, and are hurt by it as well as the sufferer. The mob, when they are gazing at a dancer on the slack rope, naturally writhe and twist and balance their own bodies as they see him do, and as they feel that they themselves must do if in his situation. Persons of delicate fibres and a weak constitution of body complain, that in looking on the sores and ulcers which are exposed by beggars in the streets, they are apt to feel an itching or uneasy situation in the correspondent part of their own bodies. The horror which they conceive at the misery of those wretches affects that particular part in themselves more than any other, because that horror arises from conceiving what they themselves would suffer, if they really were the wretches whom they are looking upon, and if that particular part in themselves was actually affected in the same miserable manner. The very force of this conception is sufficient, in their feeble frames, to produce that itching or uneasy sensation complained of.

12. Lauren Wispé, "History of the Concept of Empathy," in *Empathy and Its Development*, ed. H. Eisenberg and J. Strayder (Cambridge: Cambridge University Press, 1987), 17–37.

13. "Consideration of what it feels like to have sympathetic feelings towards another's physical pain, say on slamming his fingers in a car door, is sufficient to show this: the feelings you have are feelings of sympathy, not feelings of pain as of slamming your fingers in a car door," Goldie, *The Emotions: A Philosophical Exploration*, 214, used to substantiate his claim that "it is entirely mistaken to assume that in addition to this recognition of, feeling towards, and response to another's difficulties, sympathy also involves undergoing difficulties and having feelings *of the same sort* as the other person's." Michael Slote argues similarly that empathy is a "matter of feeling, for example, someone else's pain, whereas sympathy involves feeling *for* the pain of another. Clearly, too, I can feel for someone else's embarrassment, feeling sympathy for it, without feeling anything like embarrassment myself, so the concepts [of empathy and sympathy] are definitely different," in his "Moral Sentimentalism and Moral Psychology," in *Oxford Handbook of Ethical Theory* (Oxford: Oxford University Press, 2006), 227. This line of reasoning goes back to Max Scheler, *The Nature of Sympathy*, trans. Peter Heath (London: Routledge and Kegan Paul, 1954). See Stephen Darwall, "Empathy, Sympathy, Care," *Philosophical Studies* 89 (1998): 261–82. Empirical

research using neuro-imaging suggests that an observer of another's distress feels similar distress without imagining the sensation that causes the distress. See T. Singer, B. Seymour, J. O'Doherty, H. Kaube, R. J. Dolan, and C. D. Firth, "Empathy for Pain Involves the Affective but Not Sensory Components of Pain," *Science* 303 (2004): 1157–62; and general discussion in Jesse Prinz, *The Emotional Construction of Morals* (Oxford: Oxford University Press, 2007), 82–84.

14. Schopenhauer, *On the Basis of Morality*, 147. Schopenhauer's view thus is to be distinguished from Adam Smith, who holds: "By the imagination we place ourselves in his situation, we conceive ourselves enduring all the same torments, we enter as it were into his body, and become in some measure the same person with him, and thence form some idea of his sensations." Smith, *The Theory of Moral Sentiments*, 9. See also Goldie, *The Emotions: A Philosophical Exploration*, 218.

15. Schopenhauer, *On the Basis of Morality*, 203.

16. Ibid., 209–10.

17. Ibid., 211.

18. Tolstoy, *What Is Art?* 52.

19. Ibid., 81.

20. Ibid., 94.

21. Friedrich Nietzsche, *The Birth of Tragedy*, ed. R Geuss and R. Speirs, trans. R. Speirs (Cambridge: Cambridge University Press, 1999), 30. Compare Schopenhauer: "music differs from all the other arts by the fact that it is not a copy of the phenomenon, or more exactly, of the will's adequate objectivity, but is directly a copy of the will itself, and therefore expresses the metaphysical to everything physical in the world, the thing-in-itself to every phenomenon." Schopenhauer, *The World as Will and Representation*, 1: 262.

22. Nietzsche, *The Birth of Tragedy*, 33.

23. Ibid., 79–80.

24. Schopenhauer, *The World as Will and Representation*, 1: 257.

25. Ibid., 1: 262–63.

26. Ibid., 1: 256. Schopenhauer has a normative understanding of music, which by definition rules out programmatic music because it imitates nature, that is, is an artistic representation of a natural representation of the will.

27. Ibid., 1: 261–62 and 264.

28. For reflections on non-observational "practical knowledge" see G. E. M. Anscombe, *Intention* (Cambridge, Mass.: Harvard University Press, 2000).

29. For arguments for a dual-aspect theory, see Brian O'Shaughnessy, *The Will: A Dual Aspect Theory* (Cambridge: Cambridge University Press, 1980), especially vol. 2. Christopher Janaway in his *Self and World in Schopenhauer's Philosophy* (Oxford: Clarendon, 1989), 221–29 argues for the similarity of their views.

30. Arthur Schopenhauer, *Prize Essay on the Freedom of the Will*, trans. E. F. J. Payne (Cambridge: Cambridge University Press, 1999), 10. This expansion of the scope of the concept "will," beyond acts of the will, allows Schopenhauer's theory to address a prime objection to dual-aspect theories: that it cannot adequately explain *tryings*, that is, willed actions that do not occur. See Janaway, *Self and World in Schopenhauer's Philosophy*, chap. 8.

31. Schopenhauer, *Prize Essay on the Freedom of the Will*, 12. See also Schopenhauer, *On the Fourfold Root of the Principle of Sufficient Reason*, trans.

E. F. J. Payne (La Salle, Ill.: Open Court, 1974), 70–74; Schopenhauer, *The World as Will and Representation*, 1: 368.

32. Schopenhauer, *On the Fourfold Root*, 41–42.

33. Ibid., 72.

34. Ibid., 214 (original emphasis).

35. A caveat. We are dealing here with the human will and human acts of the will. In Schopenhauer's grander metaphysics, all events, including non-human, natural events, are "objectifications of the will," where the will here is the Kantian thing-in-itself, beyond space, time, and causality. Acts of the will are a species of this genus, distinguished by their mode of immediate awareness to the subject and their being caused by motives.

36. Schopenhauer, *The World as Will and Representation*, 1: 138–39.

37. Schopenhauer, *Prize Essay on Freedom of the Will*, 41–42.

38. Schopenhauer's and Nietzsche's analyses of the affective influence of music themselves develop a philosophical tradition that reaches back to Socrates's trope of "magnetic rings" of enthusiasm in *Ion*, the surrender of rational self-control and judgment in the rhapsode's audience in book 10 of the *Republic*, and the notion of catharsis in Aristotle's *Poetics*. For instance, in *Compendium Musicae*, Descartes argues that music can affect the listener's emotions through tone and rhythm. And Hume explicitly likens a person's emotions ("passions") to music: "Now if we consider the human mind, we shall find that with regard to the passions, tis not of the nature of a wind instrument of music, which in running over all the notes immediately loses the sound after the breath ceases; but rather resembles a string instrument, where after each stroke the vibrations still retain some sound, which gradually and insensibly decays. The imagination is extremely quick and agile, but the passions are slow and restive . . . though the fancy may change its views with great celerity; each stroke will not produce a clear and distinct note of passion, but the one passion will always be mixt and confounded with the other." Hume, *A Treatise of Human Nature*, ed. L. A. Selby-Bigge and P. H. Nidditch (Oxford: Clarendon, 1975), 440–41. Jean-Jacques Rousseau's thoughts on music's ability to convey emotion (e.g., in his *Essai sur l'origine des langues* [1764] and *Dictionnaire de musique* [1768]) were likely known to Schopenhauer and Tolstoy. See Ruth Rischin, "Allegro Tumultuoissimamente: Beethoven in Tolstoy's Fiction," in *In the Shade of the Giant: Essays on Tolstoy*, ed. Hugh McLean (Berkeley: University of California Press, 1989), 15–18.

39. Malcolm Budd puts this point well in the chapter on Schopenhauer in his *Music and the Emotions* (London: Routledge and Kegan Paul, 1985): "music cannot represent the thought a certain kind of emotion may involve but only that aspect of the emotion which is not representation but is a function of the will: pleasure and pain, desire and satisfaction. . . . Schopenhauer defines an emotion as 'a stirring of the will' by a motive, and he regards something as affecting the will only if it is felt pleasantly or painfully. But a motive just is a representation: it is either a sensuous representation of one of the senses, as is always so in the case of non-human animals, or an abstract representation, a concept, as is nearly always so in the case of human beings. Hence, Schopenhauer's claim that music expresses only the essential nature of an emotion, not its motive, implies that music can express only the element of pleasure or pain an emotion contains, and

not any perception or concept sometimes, usually or necessarily involved in the experience of the emotion" (91–92).

40. Arthur Schopenhauer, *Parerga and Paralipomena*, trans. E. F. J. Payne (Oxford: Clarendon, 1974), 2: 430 (§218). For extended discussion of this point in the context of "faculty psychology," see Robert Hall, "Schopenhauer: Music and the Emotions," *Schopenhauer-Jahrbuch* 83 (2002): 151–61.

41. Schopenhauer, *Prize Essay on Freedom of the Will*, 44.

42. Schopenhauer, *The World as Will and Representation*, 2: 448–49.

43. Ibid., 2: 448. Note that there is some ambiguity or uncertainty in Schopenhauer's account regarding the relationship between music and the expression or elicitation of feeling as an "affect of the will." Schopenhauer sometimes appears to hold that consonance and dissonance of tones constitute analogues respectively of pleasure/satisfaction and pain/dissatisfaction, and thereby provide a picture or image (*Bild*) of the will's manifestations rather than the manifestations—the feelings—themselves. Thus according to Schopenhauer music does not elicit emotions themselves but rather the listener's cognitive recognition of them: "Only in this way does music never cause us actual suffering, but still remains pleasant even in its most painful chords; and we like to hear in its language the secret history of our will and of all its stirrings and strivings with their many different delays, postponements, hindrances, and afflictions, even in the most sorrowful melodies. On the other hand, where in real life and its terrors our *will itself* is that which is roused and tormented, we are then not concerned with tones and their numerical relations; on the contrary, we ourselves are now the vibrating string that is stretched and plucked." Schopenhauer, *The World as Will and Representation*, 2: 451. See also Malcolm Budd's commentary: "The sense in which music is a representation of the will is that the most important elements of musical structure are close counterparts of the essential features and forms of the will as it manifests itself in time and, consequently, the experience we have in listening to music is formally analogous to the will's nature. Hence, our experience of music more closely relates us to the will than does any perceptual representation of something whose being-in-itself is the will" (*Music and the Emotions*, 93–96, here 94–95). But in his criticism Budd acknowledges that "Schopenhauer himself falls into difficulties when he tries to give an accurate description of the experience of music which at the same time conforms to his requirement that the will should not be excited in aesthetic experience. . . . If [Schopenhauer's] apparent references to the effects of music were intended to be understood strictly, the experience of music would not merely be an analogue of the will's activity—it would essentially involve it: if a dissonant chord arouses a desire for a further chord, when we listen to music our will is *not* at rest. This uncertainty in Schopenhauer's account is mirrored by the uncertainty we sometimes experience in reading musical theorists as to whether they are describing in figurative terms features we hear in music or, instead, are describing literally our responses to what we hear" (97–98, my emphasis). For a helpful discussion of Schopenhauer's reliance on the Pythagorean acoustical theory of Rameau to underwrite his claims that due to "numerical relations" of harmony and disharmony in music "all movements of the human heart, i.e., of the will . . . can be faithfully portrayed and reproduced in all their finest shades and modifications . . . by means of the invention of the melody" (Schopenhauer, *The World as Will and Representation*,

2: 451), see Lawrence Ferrara, "Schopenhauer on Music as the Embodiment of Will," in *Schopenhauer, Philosophy, and the Arts*, ed. Dale Jacquette (Cambridge: Cambridge University Press, 1996), 183–99.

Schopenhauer's view of music and the emotions is echoed in Eduard Hanslick's influential *On the Musically Beautiful* (trans. G. Payzant [Indianapolis, Ind.: Hackett, 1986]) of 1854, in which he argues that music cannot express or represent "definite feelings" because it cannot represent the "specific representations or concepts" that determine particular emotions. More recently, Annette Baier ("What Emotions Are About," *Philosophical Perspectives* 4 [1990]: 1–29) has argued independently along similar lines, by suggesting that certain emotions like love have, in addition to a formal object (the lovable, which is a thin property), deep objects ("the ghosts of all the other objects which that specific sort of emotion has had in this person's history, and maybe also the shadows of those that it will have," 4) that at least partly constitute a particular person's specific emotional responsiveness, an "intentional depth" that can be triggered by music: "What music may do is arouse the 'precipitate of a reminiscence' by a shortcut—not via a current object, but by a more direct revival of the memory of past loved ones or lost ones, or of the *general* common features or such ones (the formal object), without needing to or providing us with any current focus for that emotion" (12).

44. Tolstoy, *Anna Karenina*, 685. On the other hand, at times Tolstoy valorizes the emotional effect of pure music, as in this diary entry from January 20, 1905:

> Music is the stenography of feelings [*chustv*]. What I mean is: the quick or slow succession of sounds, their pitch, their volume [*sila ikh*]—all this, in speech, embellishes words and their meaning, indicating those shades of feelings which are associated with our parts of speech. Music without speech takes these expressions of feelings and shades of feelings [*vyrazheniia chustv i ottenkov ikh*] and combines [*soediniaet*] them, and we get a play of feelings without the things that gave rise to them. For this reason music has such a particularly strong effect, and for this reason the combination of music with words is a weakening [*oslablenie*] of the music, a retrogression, a writing out in letters of stenographic signs. (Tolstoi, *Polnoe sobranie sochinenii*, 55: 116–17)

45. Wittgenstein makes an analogous observation regarding the underdetermination of intentional contexts of a smiling face in *Philosophical Investigations*, §539.

46. Tolstoy, *What Is Art?* 97.

47. Ibid., 14 (translation modified).

48. The locus classicus for this thought is Wittgenstein: "Let us not forget this: when 'I raise my arm,' my arm goes up. And the problem arises: what is left over if I subtract the fact that my arm goes up from the fact that I raise my arm?" *Philosophical Investigations*, §621.

Chapter 5

The epigraph for chapter 5 is from Theodor W. Adorno, *Aesthetic Theory*, trans. Robert Hullot-Kentor (Minneapolis: University of Minnesota Press, 1996), 198.

1. For detailed presentation of the drafts of the novella, see N. K. Gudzii, "Kreitserova sonata," in Tolstoi, *Polnoe sobranie sochinenii*, 27: 561–624; and

V. A. Zhdanov, *Ot "Anny Kareninoi" k "Voskreseniiu"* (Moscow: Kniga, 1967), 155–84.

2. See, for instance, L. D. Opul'skaya, *Lev Nikolaevich Tolstoi: Materialy k biografii c 1886 po 1892 god* (Moscow: Nauka, 1979), chaps. 3 and 4.

3. See, for instance, Tolstoy's diary entries for May 15, 16, and 17, 1889.

4. "O tom, chto nazyvaetsia iskusstvom," *Literaturnoe nasledstvo* 37–38 (Moscow: Akademii Nauk SSSR, 1939): 62–63. Tolstoy's belief that music conveys emotion goes back to the early fragment "A Definition of Music" (June 17, 1850), in which he writes: "There is a fourth meaning of music—a poetic meaning. Music in this sense is the means to arouse certain feelings, or to transmit them, through sounds." Tolstoi, *Polnoe sobranie sochinenii*, 1: 245. Quoted in Rischin, "*Allegro Tumultuosissimamente*," 15.

5. Tolstoi, "O tom, chto nazyvaetsia iskusstvom," 67.

6. A. B. Gol'denveizer, "Tolstoi i muzyka," *Literaturnoe nasledstvo* 37–38 (Moscow: Akademia Nauk SSSR, 1939): 591 (original emphasis underlined).

7. Ibid., 592.

8. Schopenhauer, *The World as Will and Representation*, 1: 261 (final emphasis only mine).

9. Leo Tolstoy, *The Kreutzer Sonata and Other Stories*, trans. David McDuff (New York: Penguin Books, 1985), 96–97.

10. Ibid., 96. Compare *What Is Art?* chap. 5.

11. Tolstoy, *Kreutzer Sonata*, 96.

12. Tolstoy, *What Is Art?* 121.

13. Ibid., 132.

14. Ibid., 134.

15. Ibid., 135.

16. Tolstoy, *Kreutzer Sonata*, 97.

17. Ibid., 34.

18. Ibid., 37.

19. Ibid., 45.

20. Ibid., 43.

21. Ibid., 44. I pause at this description somewhat, because I think a case can be made that Pozdnyshev's desires may be more expansive. Such evidence includes his obsession with Trukhachevsky (even when he is headed back to confront his wife, Pozdnyshev recounts that rather "all my thoughts led back to him" (104), his descriptions of his beauty ("moist eyes, like almonds, smiling red lips . . . his face was handsome in a vulgar sort of way . . . he had a particularly well-developed posterior, as women have, or as Hottentots are said to have," 80) and his fawning upon him ("Some peculiar, fatal energy led me not to repulse him, get rid of him, but, on the contrary, to bring him closer," 85), and his quite bizarre description of his honeymoon ("It's something similar to what I experienced when I was learning how to smoke. I felt like vomiting, my saliva flowed, but I swallowed it and pretended I was enjoying myself," 52–53) that would seem to belie his asseverations of being a Don Juan. I think scholars have not explored Pozdnyshev as an *unreliable narrator* with anything approaching the necessary attentiveness. However, see David Herman, "Stricken by Infection: Art and Adultery in *Anna Karenina* and *Kreutzer Sonata*," *Slavic Review* 56 (1997): 15–36; and Stephen Baehr, "Art and *The Kreutzer Sonata*: A Tolstoian

Approach," *Canadian-American Slavic Studies* 10 (1976): 39–46 (reprinted in *Tolstoy's Short Fiction*, ed. M. Katz [New York: Norton, 1991], 448–56) for very perceptive remarks in this direction.

22. Tolstoy, *Kreutzer Sonata*, 51.

23. In this regard *The Kreutzer Sonata* rivals the confessional intricacies of Dostoevsky's narrator in *Notes from the Underground*. See J. M. Coetzee, "Confession and Double Thoughts: Tolstoy, Rousseau, Dostoevsky," *Comparative Literature* 37 (1985): 193–232.

24. Tolstoy, *Kreutzer Sonata*, 100.

25. Ibid., 46.

26. Ibid., 54. At this juncture Pozdnyshev also explicitly links his strategy of naturalizing ideals and sentiments to his understanding of Schopenhauer: "But why should we live? If life has no purpose, if it's been given us for its own sake, we have no reason for living. If that really is the case, then the Schopenhauers and the Hartmanns, as well as all the Buddhists, are perfectly right" (ibid.). So here too Tolstoy is artistically reworking his own spiritual crisis, as he had in *Anna Karenina*, "The Memoirs of a Madman," and *A Confession*.

27. Ibid., 91. Once again this is complicated by Pozdnyshev's vituperations *against* the "moral rot of materialism" and the elimination of moral guidance in chapter 15: "If you're living badly, it's because your nerves aren't functioning properly, or something of that sort." Is this a moment of lucidity that undermines his continual causal etiologies of his and society's behavior, or the converse? In the same chapter he says, "I'm supposed to be a kind of madman, you know. . . . I'm a wreck, a cripple. I've only got one thing. It's what I know. Yes, I know something it'll take other people quite a while to find out about." This Gordian knot of reliability can be loosened only so far, I believe.

28. Tolstoy, *What Is Art?* 32–33, 37.

29. Ibid., 89–90. Tolstoy's footnote in the passage describes a mechanical measuring device that records differences in muscle tension of the arm.

30. Ibid., 111.

31. Ibid., 116.

32. Tolstoy, *Kreutzer Sonata*, 34.

33. Ibid., 36: "The tea was really like beer, but I downed a glass" (translation corrected).

34. Pozdnyshev's wife made several suicide attempts, at least once with opium. One might wonder how she got hold of it.

35. Tolstoy, *Kreutzer Sonata*, 41. He also seemingly admits to being a frequent masturbator: of his youth he reports that "the hours I spent alone were not pure ones" (39), and shortly thereafter confides that "I became involved in all kinds of moral deviations" (41).

36. Ibid., 62.

37. Gustafson, *Leo Tolstoy: Resident and Stranger*, 352–55.

38. In her richly suggestive article, "Forms of Judicial Blindness, or the Evidence of What Cannot Be Seen: Traumatic Narratives and Legal Repetitions in the O. J. Simpson Case and in Tolstoy's *The Kreutzer Sonata*" (*Critical Inquiry* 23 [1997]: 738–88), Shoshana Felman is one of the few readers to point to Pozdnyshev's jealousy and sexual ambivalence towards Trukhachevsky. She interprets his self-confessed "swinishness" (*svinstvo*; Tolstoy, *Kreutzer Sonata*: 81, translation

modified) and self-confessed "real debauchery"—"genuine debauchery consists in liberating yourself from moral relations with the woman with whom you enter into physical relations [*obshchenie*]" (*Kreutzer Sonata*, 37, translation modified)—as an instantiation of the universal *différance* of human sexuality, "an inner schism or chasm not just *between the narrator and his wife* but *within the narrator's own sexual desire*; there is an abyss, precisely, that inhabits human sexuality, like an internal hollowness at the bottom of a whirling chaos of attractions and repulsions, of rivalries and of conflicting, secret sexual ambiguities. This abyss of difference (internal and external) cannot but become an abyss of conflict . . . an abyss that fatally and radically divides sexuality from itself, makes it different from itself" (Felman, "Forms of Judicial Blindness," 771–72). In providing a generalized explanation, however, Felman removes from consideration the aspects—causal vs. normative, a Wittgensteinian notion of "evil"—which, I believe, go towards explaining the *specificity* of Pozdnyshev's character.

39. Tolstoy, *Kreutzer Sonata*, 66 (my emphasis). See also: "If jealousy hadn't been the pretext, some other one would have been found. I insist on the fact that all husbands who live as I lived must either live in debauchery, get divorced, or kill themselves or their wives, as I did" (81); Pozdnyshev's narrative links "the wild beast of jealousy" (109) with extended images of animality (sensuousness, debauchery) in the novella.

40. Ibid., 105 (see 103–4 as well). I therefore must disagree with John Kopper's analysis that "by marrying, [Pozdnyshev] has located himself within a certain code of behavior that permits what he only later will conclude to be impermissible: jealousy, sex, and deceit" (Kopper, "Tolstoy and the Narrative of Sex: A Reading of 'Father Sergius,' 'The Devil,' and 'The Kreutzer Sonata'," in *In the Shade of the Giant: Essays on Tolstoy*, ed. H. McLean [Berkeley: University of California Press, 1989], 168). On my reading we are to consider the ethical character of Pozdnyshev himself, and not necessarily that of marriage (which, he says, exists for those who see it as a sacrament, but not for debauchers, chapter 2).

41. Tolstoy, *Kreutzer Sonata*, 109.

42. Ibid., 99.

43. Ibid., 104.

44. Ibid., 108.

45. Ibid., 109.

46. Ibid., 110. Notice the surprising similarity of descriptions between Pozdnyshev on the threshold of murder and Kitty attending to Levin's dying brother: "She had in her that excitement and quickness of judgment that appear in men before battle, a struggle, in dangerous and decisive moments of life, those moments when once and for all a man shows his worth and that his whole past has not been in vain but has been a preparation for those moments" (Tolstoy, *Anna Karenina*, 497). Both cases are paradigmatic instances of acts of will, actions that issue directly without a conflict of motives, perhaps with an allusion to the Aristotelian virtue of courage.

47. Tolstoy, *Kreutzer Sonata*, 111–12.

48. Ibid., 112 (translation modified, my emphasis).

49. Ibid., 104.

50. Justin Weir likewise suggests that Pozdnyshev may simply be creating rather than recounting his story, exercising his willed dependency on an addressee by

means of confabulation: "But the best way to account for the difference between *fabula* and *siuzhet* is to stop assuming there is a difference. Pozdnyshev's story is the creation of his telling it; that is why the plot and narrative accord so well with the violent staccato of the train, which is, of course, the perfect setting for a story of sex and murder if ever there was one . . . [The narrator] is seduced by Pozdnyshev's enthusiasm and strong tea and is soon quietly listening with understanding and sympathy." Weir, *Leo Tolstoy and the Alibi of Narrative* (New Haven, Conn.: Yale University Press, 2011), 164–65.

51. Cora Diamond, "Ethics, Imagination and the Method of Wittgenstein's *Tractatus*," in *The New Wittgenstein*, ed. Alice Crary and Rupert Read (London: Routledge, 2000), 153–54. See also J. C. Edwards, *Ethics without Philosophy: Wittgenstein and the Moral Life* (Tampa: University of South Florida Press, 1982). Christopher Janaway demonstrates Wittgenstein's reliance on his reading of Schopenhauer in this regard, in *Self and World in Schopenhauer's Philosophy* (Oxford: Clarendon, 1989), 336–42. Janaway also shows how Wittgenstein engaged with Schopenhauer's views on willing and acting in his notebooks but excluded such thoughts from the *Tractatus*.

52. Diamond illustrates this aspect of Wittgenstein with readings of Hawthorne's "The Birthmark" and the Grimm tale "The Fisherman and His Wife." In both stories the protagonists manifest ethical evil by issuing conditions to the world and, when those conditions are frustrated, in their unhappiness and *resentment at the world*.

53. Tolstoy, *Kreutzer Sonata*, 100.

54. Ibid., 105–6.

55. Compare Wittgenstein in his preliminary notes while working on the *Tractatus*: "I will call 'will' ["*Willen*"] first and foremost the bearer of good and evil" such that so long as even a paralyzed man is able to "think and *want* [wünschen] and communicate his thoughts" he is still "*in the ethical sense* . . . the bearer of a will [*Willens*]." Wittgenstein, *Notebooks*, 76–77 (July 21, 1916); thus "Good and evil only enter through the *subject*" (79, August 2, 1916).

56. Tolstoy, *What Is Art?* 52.

57. Ibid., 41.

58. Ibid., 42.

59. Tolstoy, *Kreutzer Sonata*, 96 (my emphasis).

60. Wittgenstein, letter to Ludwig von Ficker, in *Wittgenstein: Sources and Perspectives*, ed. C. Grant Luckhardt (Ithaca, N.Y.: Cornell University Press, 1979), 34–35.

61. Ludwig Wittgenstein, "A Lecture on Ethics," in Wittgenstein, *Philosophical Occasions 1912–1951*, ed. J. Klagge and A. Nordmann (Indianapolis, Ind.: Hackett, 1993), 44.

62. Leo Tolstoy, *The Gospel in Brief*, ed. F. A. Flowers III, trans. I. Hapgood (Lincoln: University of Nebraska Press, 1997), 127–43.

63. Gary Saul Morson, "The Reader as Voyeur: Tolstoy and the Poetics of Didactic Fiction," in *Leo Tolstoy: Modern Critical Views*, ed. H. Bloom (New York: Chelsea House, 1986), 189, quoted in David Herman, "Stricken by Infection: Art and Adultery in *Anna Karenina* and *Kreutzer Sonata*," *Slavic Review* 56 (1997): 32fn. Herman is the only critic of whom I am aware who has noticed the epigraph and its significance: "Here a portion of the audience is excluded from

the communal undertaking at the very outset. The epigraph suggests that only certain readers will really understand, namely those who can draw on their own experience to furnish an insight and a conviction that the text will not provide" (34). I am ignoring the infamous "Afterword" to *The Kreutzer Sonata*, which deserves extended treatment beyond this chapter. While it would seem to pose problems for my reading, since in it Tolstoy repeats, apparently *in propria persona* and apparently with approbation, Pozdnyshev's views on marriage and sex, one would need to consider the occasion of the "Afterword" (popular alarm, on my reading due to a profoundly disappointing *misreading* of *Kreutzer Sonata*'s poetics of address) as well as the question of intended addressee.

64. Tolstoy, *What Is Art?* 32.

65. "Just as people who think that the aim and purpose of food is pleasure cannot perceive the true meaning of eating, so people who think that the aim of art is pleasure cannot know its meaning and purpose, because they ascribe to an activity which has meaning in connection with other phenomena of life the false and exclusive aim of pleasure. People understand that the meaning of eating is the nourishment of the body only when they cease to consider pleasure the aim of this activity. So it is with art. People will understand the meaning of art only when they cease to regard beauty—that is, pleasure—as the aim of this activity" (Tolstoy, *What Is Art?* 35).

66. Stephen Baehr, "Art and *The Kreutzer Sonata*: A Tolstoian Approach," traces out some of the parallels, albeit under the motto "life is art."

67. Tolstoy, *Kreutzer Sonata*, 39.

68. Ibid., 67. Were Pozdnyshev syphilitic, that fact would be yet another respect in which Trukhachevsky would be a rival and double: "Once, when I'd asked Trukhachevsky's brother if he ever went to brothels, he'd replied that a respectable man wouldn't go to some dirty, loathsome place where he might run the risk of catching an infection, when it was always possible to find a respectable woman. And now his brother had found my wife" (103).

69. Tolstoy, *What Is Art?* 157.

70. Ibid., 157, 158.

71. Tolstoy acknowledges science as "another human spiritual activity" (Tolstoy, *What Is Art?* 157).

72. Ibid., 159.

73. Ibid., 165.

74. Ibid., 164.

75. Ibid., 123.

76. "So he lived, not knowing and not seeing any possibility of knowing what he was and why he was living in the world, tormented by this ignorance to such a degree that he feared suicide, and at the same time firmly laying his own particular definite path [*svoiu osobennuiu, opredelenuiu dorogu*] in life" (Tolstoy, *Anna Karenina*, 791).

77. Tolstoy, *What Is Art?* 166.

78. Ibid., 166–67 (my emphasis).

79. Unfortunately, book-length studies that consider the relationship between art and science in Tolstoy's treatise overlook this astounding passage: for instance, Rimvydas Silbajoris, *Tolstoy's Aesthetics and His Art*, 126–33; Magdalene Zurek, *Tolstojs Philosophie der Kunst* (Heidelberg: C. Winter, 1996), 322–23;

Konstantin Lomunov, *Estetika L'va Tolstogo* (Moscow: "Sovremennik," 1972), 14–65; and T.J. Diffey, *Tolstoy's "What Is Art?"* (London: Croom, 1985).

80. Wittgenstein, *Philosophical Investigations*, §218.

81. Liza Knapp, "Musical Mimesis: Platonic Aesthetics and Erotics in 'The Kreutzer Sonata,'" *Tolstoy Studies* 3 (1991): 25–42, aligns Tolstoy with Plato (of *The Republic)* against Schopenhauer and Nietzsche in a somewhat different relation: "In 'The Kreutzer Sonata,' Tolstoy responds indirectly to the musical theory dominant in his time, a musical theory in which the music of Beethoven played a pivotal role. Beethoven's music served as the model for the Schopenhaurian notion that music is a force that defies reason, that it is the language of feeling and passion, that it represents the will directly, without recourse to ideas or language, that it acts directly on the emotions . . . Whatever criticism of Beethoven's music is leveled in 'The Kreutzer Sonata' thus becomes a rebuttal of Schopenhauer's musical theory and a plea for music to remain unemancipated" from language (37).

Chapter 6

The epigraph for chapter 6 is from Wittgenstein, *Philosophical Investigations*, part II, section iv.

1. Wittgenstein, *Philosophical Investigations*, §§65–67 (here §66).

2. Jenefer Robinson ("Startle," *Journal of Philosophy* 92 [1995]: 53–74) argues for its being an emotion, while Richard Lazarus ("Thoughts on the Relations between Emotion and Cognition," *American Psychologist* 37 [1982]: 1019–24) asserts that "I do not consider startle an emotion. Emotion results from an evaluative perception . . . Startle is best regarded as a primitive neural reflex process" (1023).

3. For an extended analysis of jealousy, see Goldie, *The Emotions: A Philosophical Exploration*, chap. 8. For an analysis of grief, see Peter Goldie, "Grief: A Narrative Account," *Ratio* 24 (2011): 119–37. See also Gabriele Taylor, *Pride, Shame, and Guilt: Emotions of Self-Assessment* (Oxford: Clarendon, 1985). For an account of emotions as dispositional traits, see Richard Wollheim, *On the Emotions* (New Haven, Conn.: Yale University Press, 1999).

4. Thomas Dixon in *From Passions to Emotions: The Creation of a Secular Psychological Category* (Cambridge: Cambridge University Press, 2003) provides a rich history of definitions and theories of emotion and suggests that earlier delineations between passions, affections, appetites, and sentiments are more promising for research and theory than a single concept of emotion.

5. "Central" here does not mean essential, but rather indicates the relative density of resemblances, in keeping with the notion of family resemblance: "the strength of the thread does not reside in the fact that some one fibre runs through its whole length, but in the overlapping of many fibres." Wittgenstein, *Philosophical Investigations*, §67.

6. Aristotle, *De Anima* 403a29.

7. The notion of intentionality is due to Franz Brentano, *Psychology from an Empirical Standpoint* (London: Routledge and Kegan Paul, 1973; originally published 1874). For helpful discussion see Tim Crane, "Intentionality as the Mark of the Mental," in *Current Issues in Philosophy of Mind*, ed. Anthony O'Hear (Cambridge: Cambridge University Press, 1998), 229–51.

8. This aspect of emotion is explored extensively in Nico Frijda, *The Emotions* (Cambridge: Cambridge University Press, 1986).

9. Julien Deonna and Fabrice Teroni, *The Emotions: A Philosophical Introduction* (London: Routledge, 2012), lucidly discusses these various dimensions. Ronald de Sousa (*Rationality of Emotion*, 126, 181–84) formalizes the logical form of emotion as a seven-place relation R(Stfacmp), "where R stands for an emotion type, S for the subject, t the target, f the focal property, a the motivating aspect, c the cause, m the aim, p the proposition specifying the ground."

10. See E. Hatfield, J. T. Caicoppo, and R. L. Rapson, *Emotional Contagion* (New York: Cambridge University Press, 1994). For a survey of some empirical studies of emotional contagion, see D. McIntosh, D. Druckman, and R. B. Zajonc, "Socially Induced Affect," in *Learning, Remembering, Believing: Enhancing Human Performance*, ed. D. Druckman and R. A. Bjork (Washington, D.C.: National Academy Press, 1994), 251–76.

11. The "James-Lange" theory of the emotions refers in addition to William James to the Dutch physician who put forward a theory essentially similar to that of James. See C. G. Lange, *The Emotions*, trans. I. A. Haupt (Baltimore: William and Wilkins, 1922; original 1885).

12. James, "What Is an Emotion?" 189–90.

13. Ibid., 189, 194.

14. Ibid., 201–2. That is, the perception of some "exciting fact" causes some behavior, and feeling the bodily changes constituent of the behavior just is the emotion, which is as it were epiphenomenal, a product of the bodily changes. In his later formulation: "My theory . . . is that *the bodily changes follow directly the perception of the exciting fact, and that our feeling of the same changes as they occur is the emotion*" (William James, *The Principles of Psychology* [New York: Dover, 1950], 2: 449).

15. While Tolstoy appears to have shown little interest in James, the novelist was one of the latter's favorite authors after reading *War and Peace* and *Anna Karenina* in 1896, and James notoriously devoted part of a chapter of his *The Varieties of Religious Experience* to Tolstoy as an example of a "sick soul." While textual evidence is lacking, it is tantalizing to wonder whether James did not read *Anna Karenina* earlier, and find inspiration for his physiological theory of the emotions in the "infectiousness" of laughter there. On James and Tolstoy, see Donna Tussing Orwin, "What Men Live By: Belief and the Individual in Leo Tolstoy and William James," in *William James in Russian Culture*, ed. J. D. Grossman and R. Rischin (Lanham, Md.: Lexington Books, 2003), 59–80.

16. Wittgenstein, *Philosophical Investigations*, §476; see also Kenny, *Action, Emotion and Will*, 72. For a rejoinder, see Robert M. Gordon, *The Structure of Emotions: Investigations in Cognitive Philosophy* (Cambridge: Cambridge University Press, 1987), chap. 4, in which he argues that it is the cognitive state of non-deliberative uncertainty that is the cause of what he terms "epistemic emotions," including fear and other "forward-looking emotions."

17. Kenny, *Action, Emotion and Will*, 75.

18. On formal and apparent objects, see Kenny, *Action, Emotion and Will*. On paradigm scenarios, see De Sousa, *The Rationality of Emotions*, further developed by Annette Baier, "What Emotions Are About": "An adequate account of the intentionality of an emotion such as love or revulsion must then make room

not just for a deep as well as a formal and an apparent object, but should preferably be able to indicate whether or not the deep object is the same as the earliest apparent object. We need not only paradigm scenarios, that set the state for subsequent enactments of a given type of emotion, but also ultimate scenarios where that type of emotion really comes into its own, where it as it were finds its fulfillment" (14–15).

19. John Deigh, *Emotions, Values, and the Law* (Oxford: Oxford University Press, 2008), 34–35, has argued that the physiological states of ecstasy and anger are indistinguishable, so that their respective intentional objects must be invoked to differentiate the emotions. He refers to a famous experiment conducted by S. Schachter and J. Singer ("Cognition, Social, and Physiological Determinants of Emotional State," *Psychological Review* 69 [1962]: 379–99) that provided empirical evidence for a similar claim: that the bodily processes undergone by a person feeling some emotion themselves are insufficient to determine the type of emotion the person is feeling.

20. Baier, "What Emotions Are About," 11, 12–13. Baier concludes that the intentional objects of musically aroused emotions are "infantile so deep objects," that is, such emotions are directed at the originating paradigm scenarios of their first emergence for the subject, expressed in Freudian or possibly inherited species-memory.

21. Antonio Damasio, *Looking for Spinoza: Joy, Sorrow, and the Feeling Brain* (New York: Harcourt, 2003), 57, 88; Damasio, "William James and the Modern Neurobiology of Emotion," in *Emotion, Evolution and Rationality*, ed. D. Evans and P. Cruse (Oxford: Oxford University Press, 2004), 3–14; and Brian Massumi, "Fear [The Spectrum Said]," *Positions* 13 (2005): 36–37, all present their theories as endorsements and enhancements of James's theory of emotions.

22. Representative left-affect theorists include Brian Massumi, *Parables for the Virtual: Movement, Affect, Sensation* (Durham, N.C.: Duke University Press, 2002); William E. Connolly, *Neuropolitics: Thinking, Culture, Speed* (Minneapolis: University of Minnesota Press, 2002); *The Affective Turn: Theorizing the Social*, ed. Patricia Ticineto Clough and Jean Halley (Durham, N.C.: Duke University Press, 2007); Teresa Brennan, *The Transmission of Affect* (Ithaca, N.Y.: Cornell University Press, 2004); and Eve Kosofsky Sedgwick, *Touching Feeling: Affect, Pedagogy, Performativity* (Durham, N.C.: Duke University Press, 2003), all of whom draw inspiration from the work of Gilles Deleuze. See Ruth Leys, "The Turn to Affect: A Critique," *Critical Inquiry* 37 (2011): 434–72 for further bibliography of the turn to affect, especially its left-wing variety.

23. For this kind of view, see John Tooby and Leda Cosmides, "The Evolutionary Psychology of the Emotions and Their Relationship to Internal Regulatory Variables," in *Handbook of Emotions*, ed. M. Lewis, J. Haviland-Jones, and L. Feldman Barrett (New York: Guildford, 2008), 114–37.

24. See, for example, Paul Ekman, "Biological and Cultural Contributions to Body and Facial Movement in the Expression of Emotions," in *Explaining Emotions*, ed. A. O Rorty (Berkeley: University of California Press, 1980), 73–102; and Ekman, "Expression and the Nature of Emotion," in *Approaches to Emotion*, ed. K. Scherer and P. Ekman (Hillsdale, N.J.: Lawrence Erlbaum,1984), 319–43. This approach dates back to Darwin's classic study, *The Expression of the Emotions in Man and Animals* (1872). It is controversial how many, and which, emotions

are basic. Most scientists agree on the following: anger, fear, happiness, sadness, and surprise (disgust is sometimes contested). Sentimentalist theory (explained later) provisionally expands the list to include certain emotions often taken to be in some sense "moral": "amusement, anger, contempt, disgust, embarrassment, envy, fear, guilt, jealousy, joy, pity, pride, shame, and sorrow" (Justin D'Arms and Daniel Jacobson, "The Significance of Recalcitrant Emotion," in *Philosophy and the Emotions*, ed. A. Hatzimoysis [Cambridge: Cambridge University Press: 2003], 138), while acknowledging that ultimately such basic or natural emotions will be discovered by empirical science.

25. Paul Griffiths, *What Emotions Really Are: From Evolution to Social Construction* (Chicago: University of Chicago Press, 1997), 243. Griffiths holds that these basic emotions are evolutionarily selected natural kinds by virtue of the individuating character of their physiological markers (facial expression, neurophysiological mechanisms, etc.).

26. See the work by Joseph LeDoux (*The Emotional Brain: The Mysterious Underpinnings of Emotional Life* [New York: Simon and Schuster, 1996]) and Damasio (*Looking for Spinoza*) who coined the use of "substrate" in this context. In contrast to emotion as bearing an intentional relation or meaning, Brian Massumi (*Parables for the Virtual*, 27) defines affect as non-signifying, unconscious "intensity" or "energy."

27. Leys, "The Turn to Affect," 443. "Affect is the name for what eludes form, cognition, and meaning" (450). "The whole point of the turn to affect by Massumi and like-minded cultural critics is thus to shift attention away from considerations of meaning or 'ideology' or indeed representation to the subject's subpersonal material-affective responses, where it is claimed, political and other influences do their real work. The disconnect between 'ideology' and affect produces as one of its consequences a relative indifference to the role of ideas and beliefs in political, culture, and art in favor of an 'ontological' concern with different people's corporeal-affective reactions" (450–51). "In short, according to such theorists affect has the potential to transform individuals for good or ill without regard to the content of argument or debate" (451). Compare the definition provided on the first page of the editors' introduction to a popular collection of essays on affect theory: "Affect, at its most anthropomorphic, is the name we give to those forces—visceral forces beneath, alongside, or generally *other than* conscious knowing, vital forces insisting beyond emotion—that can serve to drive us toward movement, toward thought and extension, that can likewise suspend us (as if in neutral) across a barely registering accretion of force-relations, or that can even leave us overwhelmed by the world's apparent intractability." *The Affect Theory Reader*, ed. Melissa Gregg and Gregory J. Seigworth (Durham, N.C.: Duke University Press, 2010), 1. Recent literary criticism has embraced affect theory, as for example Hans Ulricht Gumbrecht, *Atmosphere, Mood, Stimmung: On a Hidden Potential of Literature* (Stanford, Calif.: Stanford University Press, 2012), who takes the expansive semantic field of German "*Stimmung*" (mood, atmosphere, climate) to license inferences from the affective tone of a literary work to conclusions regarding the author's biography (individual, subjective mood) as well as regarding the prevailing affective *Zeitgeist* (objective, collective climate).

28. Those commentators include Douglas Robinson (*Estrangement and the Somatics of Literature*), who offers a more extensive and explicit interpretation

via Damasio's "somatic marker hypothesis," and Michael Denner's elliptical appeal to neuroscience: "We are to understand that art accomplishes an almost physiological change in the mind [*sic*] of the perceiver. Were he writing today, Tolstoy would no doubt replace his train metaphor [in his claim that art will "train men to experience those same feelings under similar circumstances in actual life"] with something like 'art rewires the neural circuits.' It would be hard to imagine a more explicit rendering of Stalin's slogan about the artist being the 'engineer of the human soul.'" (Denner, "Accidental Art: Tolstoy's Poetics of Unintentionality," *Philosophy and Literature* 27 [2003]: 285–86). Caryl Emerson's metaphors point in a similar physiological direction when she writes that "in Tolstoy's view, every important truth had to prove itself on the individual body" and that the infectiousness of art "is almost involuntary, like radiation" (Emerson, "Tolstoy's Aesthetics," in *Cambridge Companion to Tolstoy*, ed. Donna Tussing Orwin [Cambridge: Cambridge University Press, 2002], 238–39).

29. Antonio Damasio, *Descartes' Error: Emotion, Reason, and the Human Brain* (New York: Putnam, 1994), 174; quoted in Robinson, *Estrangement and the Somatics of Literature*, 29.

30. Robinson, *Estrangement and the Somatics of Literature*, xiii–xiv. Damasio himself ascribes to the somatic marker the autonomic function of narrowing one's possible actions: "[The somatic marker] forces attention on the negative outcome to which a given action may lead, and functions as an automated alarm signal which says: Beware of danger ahead if you choose the option which leads to this outcome. The signal may lead you to reject, *immediately*, the negative course of action and thus make you choose among other alternatives. The automated signal protects you against future losses, without further ado, and then allows you *to choose from among fewer alternatives*. There is still room for using a cost/benefit analysis and proper deductive competence, but only *after* the automated step drastically reduces the number of options. Somatic markers may not be sufficient for normal human decision-making since a subsequent process of reasoning and final selection will take place in many though not all instances. Somatic markers probably increase the accuracy and efficiency of the decision process" (*Descartes' Error*, 173). This passage already intimates some of the problems to come: if the somatic marker constitutes a favorable or unfavorable appraisal of the likely future outcome of a possible action, then it does bear an intentional relation (it is *about* that likely outcome), and is not a purely causal relation. If it is a purely causal relation—say my immediately withdrawing my hand from a hot stove—then it would seem to be a fallacy to impute a *decision* or *choice* having been taken in that case, and indeed to view the movment as being *about* something (the outcome, say) rather than *caused by* something (the somatic marker as trigger).

31. Damasio, *Looking for Spinoza*, 75; see also 69–70 for a related experiment with crying and subsequent feelings of sadness. For related work see J. E. LeDoux, *The Emotional Brain* (New York: Simon and Schuster, 1996).

32. Damasio, *Looking for Spinoza*, 69. He recounts similar experiments by Paul Ekman whereby subjects were instructed to move certain facial muscles such that, unbeknownst to them, they formed a facial expression characteristic of a specific basic emotion; the subject subsequently came to feel the specific emotion associated with the specific facial expression.

33. Damasio, *Looking for Spinoza*, 115. See also G. Rizolatti and L. Craighero, "The Mirror-Neuron System," *Annual Review of Neuroscience* 27 (2004): 169–92.

34. Robinson, *Estrangement and the Somatics of Literature*, 26. Keith Oatley (*The Passionate Muse: Exploring Emotion in Stories* [New York: Oxford University Press, 2012]) has developed the theory that "mirror neurons" are activated by an action and by the perception of the same action-type in another into a general approach to literary understanding.

35. Wittgenstein, *Philosophical Investigations*, §192.

36. See also Peter Hacker's similar comments in M. Bennett, D. Dennett, P. Hacker, J. Searle, and D. Robinson, *Neuroscience and Philosophy: Brain, Mind, and Language* (New York: Columbia University Press, 2007), 151.

37. Jesse Prinz, *Gut Reactions: A Perceptual Theory of Emotion* (Oxford: Oxford University Press, 2004), which he subsequently developed into a theory of moral sentiments in his *The Emotional Construction of Morals.*

38. This is the "disjunctive problem": Jerry Fodor, *A Theory of Content and Other Essays* (Cambridge, Mass.: MIT Press, 1990), chap. 3.

39. This is the "semantic promiscuity problem": see, for instance, F. Adams and K. Aizawa, "'X' means X: Semantics Fodor-Style," *Minds and Machines* 2 (1992): 175–83.

40. See Tim Crane, *The Mechanical Mind: A Philosophical Introduction to Minds, Machines and Mental Representation*, 2nd ed. (London: Routledge, 2003), chap. 5 for an accessible account of the problematic. For more detailed accounts, see Fred Dretske, *Explaining Behavior: Reasons in a World of Causes* (Cambridge, Mass.: MIT Press, 1988); and Brian Loewer, "From Information to Intentionality," *Synthese* 70 (1987), 287–317, on error in informational semantics. For an overview of these criticisms, see Fred Adams and Ken Aizawa, "Causal Theories of Mental Content," *Stanford Encyclopedia of Philosophy*, http://plato.stanford.edu/entries/content-causal/. After canvassing criticisms of various causal theories for implicitly relying on semantic notions, the authors hold out Rob Rupert's "best test theory" for meanings of natural kind terms, whereby a certain natural kind expression "K" means a certain natural kind K if and only if members of K are statistically more efficient in causing tokenings of "K" in a thinker. If we assume with thinkers like Griffiths and Prinz that emotions are natural kinds, this might be a promising theory to explicate how emotions can be about their causal elicitors. But note that the best test theory can be taken to individuate causal tokenings according to an individual speaker or community, and in either case the meaning of a natural kind term could vary according to the environmental triggers, in which case the meaning of a natural kind term will be implicitly linked to the reference class we take to describe the environment's possible triggers. But defining a reference class amounts to inserting an intentional notion into an otherwise naturalistic theory, as Robert Brandom notes: "Relative to a choice of reference class, we can make sense of the idea of objective probabilities, and so of objective facts about the reliability of various cognitive mechanisms or processes—facts specifiable in a naturalistic vocabulary. But the proper choice of reference class is not itself objectively determined by facts specifiable in a naturalistic vocabulary. So there is something left over" (Brandom, "Insights and

Blindspots of Reliabilism," in his *Articulating Reasons: An Introduction to Inferentialism* [Cambridge, Mass.: Harvard University Press, 2000], 113).

41. John Deigh, "Concepts of Emotions," in *The Oxford Handbook of Philosophy of Emotion*, ed. Peter Goldie (Oxford: Oxford University Press, 2012), 36–37.

42. Prinz, *The Emotional Construction of Morals*, 64.

43. On the distinction between original and derived intentionality, see John Haugeland, "The Intentionality All-Stars," in his *Having Thought: Essays in the Metaphysics of Mind* (Cambridge, Mass.: Harvard University Press, 1998).

44. Barnaby D. Dunn, Tim Dalgleish, and Andrew D. Lawrence ("The Somatic Marker Hypothesis: A Critical Evaluation," *Neuroscience and Biobehavioral Reviews* 30 [2006]: 239–71) canvas the literature and raise significant doubts regarding the chief experiment in favor of the somatic marker hypothesis (SMH), including (1) the setup allows for more conscious awareness and explicit reasoning by the subjects, such that "the somatic marker signal could be interpreted as a consequence of the explicit knowledge rather than being of causal importance in the decision-making chain, making the SMH indistinguishable from other accounts of task performance" (249); (2) psychophysiological indications of somatic marker signals (e.g., skin conductance rates) could be interpreted as anticipatory expectations of reward or punishment *following* independent decision-making rather than inducing those decisions, so that "these signals may not play a causal role in shaping decision-making behavior" (250). For other doubts raised regarding experiments and conclusions drawn therefrom by other neuroscientists along similar lines, see Susan Pockett, William P. Banks, and Shaun Gallagher, *Does Consciousness Cause Behavior?* (Cambridge, Mass.: MIT Press, 2006), and Leys, "The Turn to Affect."

45. Leys, "The Turn to Affect," 455, 456–57; and M. R. Bennett and P. M. S. Hacker, *Philosophical Foundations of Neuroscience* (Oxford: Blackwell, 2003), 85–88, 111–14, 233–35.

46. Damasio, *Descartes' Error*, 173.

47. Examples of "pure" cognitivist theories, which equate emotions with judgments, include Robert Solomon, *The Passions*, 2nd ed. (Indianapolis, Ind.: Hackett, 1993); Martha Nussbaum, *Upheavals of Thought: The Intelligence of Emotions* (Cambridge: Cambridge University Press, 2001); and Robert Roberts, *Emotion* (Cambridge: Cambridge University Press, 2003), chap. 3.

48. Other definitions and descriptions include shame (1383b12–14), pity (1385b13–16), emulation (1388a32–5), etc. See Aristotle, *Rhetoric*, trans. W. Rhys Roberts, in *The Complete Works of Aristotle*, ed. Jonathan Barnes (Princeton, N.J.: Princeton University Press, 1984), volume 2.

49. For a helpful taxonomy of various types of cognitivist theories, see Robert Solomon, "Emotions, Thoughts and Feelings: What Is a 'Cognitive Theory' of the Emotions and Does It Neglect Affectivity?" in *Philosophy and the Emotions*, ed. Anthony Hatzimoysis (Cambridge: Cambridge University Press, 2003), 1–18.

50. That is, the correctness condition implies reference to rational norms that can provide warrant or justification for the emotional state. Some (e.g., Ruth Millikan, *Language, Thought, and Other Biological Categories: New Foundations for Realism* [Cambridge, Mass.: MIT Press, 1984] and subsequent work) have proposed instead teleological norms, that is, for our purposes, an emotion would

be appropriate if it promotes the biological fitness of its subject, social group, and so on. There are at least two problems with this account, however: first, it too amounts to a (in this case, inherited or selected-for) causal-dispositional account of intentionality, which is liable to the objections previously discussed; second, teleological norms can be irrational or immoral norms (e.g., fear of those who look different than one's group might have been selected for, but amounts to immoral prejudice, etc.).

51. "We can, however, consider an object *fearful* without being afraid *of* it, namely, if we judge it in such a way that we merely *think* of the case where we might possibly want to put up resistance against it, and that any resistance would in that case be utterly futile" (§28, 260). Kant, *Critique of Judgment*, trans. W. Pluhar (Indianapolis, Ind.: Hackett, 1987), 119–20. See also John Morreall, "Fear without Belief," *Journal of Philosophy* 90 (1993): 359–66.

52. Michael Stocker and Elizabeth Hegeman, *Valuing Emotions* (Cambridge: Cambridge University Press). See also Justin D'Arms and Daniel Jacobson, "The Significance of Recalcitrant Emotion (or, Anti-Quasijudgmentalism)," in *Philosophy and the Emotions*, ed. Anthony Hatzimoysis (Cambridge: Cambridge University Press, 2003), 127–36.

53. For a helpful discussion of this general objection, which she calls the "problem of mixed emotions," see Patricia Greenspan, *Emotions and Reasons* (New York: Routledge, 1988).

54. This objection has been made by John Deigh, *Emotions, Values, and the Law*, 17–38. It generalizes into an objection against intellectualist conceptions of experience, that is, theories claiming that experience requires concept possession. For helpful discussion, see Robert W. Lurz, ed., *The Philosophy of Animal Minds* (Cambridge: Cambridge University Press, 2009), especially the contributions by Eric Saidel and Robert Roberts.

55. Wittgenstein, *Philosophical Investigations*, §281. Hacker (in *Neuroscience and Philosophy*) explicitly likens this picture to that of Aristotle, for example, "It is mistaken to suppose that human beings are 'embodied' at all—that conception belongs to the Platonic, Augustinian, and Cartesian tradition that should be repudiated. It would be far better to say, with Aristotle, that human beings are *ensouled* creatures (*empsuchos*)—animals endowed with such capacities that confer upon them, in the form of life that is natural to them, the status of persons" (160; see also 131–32).

56. Bennett and Hacker, *Philosophical Foundations of Neuroscience*, 72. Compare their reformulation: "The third generation [of neuroscientists] retained the basic Cartesian structure by transforming it into brain-body dualism: substance-dualism was abandoned, structural dualism retained. For neuroscientists now ascribe much the same array of mental predicates to the brain as Descartes ascribed to the mind and conceive of the relationship between thought and action, and experience and its objects, in much the same way as Descartes—essentially merely replacing the mind by the brain." M. R. Bennett and P. M. S. Hacker, "The Conceptual Presuppositions of Cognitive Neuroscience," in *Neuroscience and Philosophy*, 131.

57. Behavior specifically, and physical processes in general are logical criteria for the application of these predicates. Because of the criterial connection between mental states and behavior, one should not make the separation between

mental phenomena and their external manifestation unless under special circumstances (e.g., phantom limb pain, hallucinations, etc.). But note Searle's objection to this use of Wittgenstein by Hacker: "Just as the old-time behaviorists confused the behavioral evidence for mental states with the existence of the mental states themselves, so the Wittgensteinians make a more subtle, but still fundamentally similar, mistake when they confuse the criterial basis for the application of the mental concepts with the mental states themselves. That is, they confuse the behavioral criteria for the *ascription* of psychological predicates with the *facts ascribed by these* psychological predicates, and that is a very deep mistake." (Searle, "Putting Consciousness Back in the Brain," in *Neuroscience and Philosophy*, 103). That is, folk psychology may be one thing, but the naturalistic description of human psychology another. In my view this distinction restates the normative vs. causal divide under discussion.

58. See Goldie, *The Emotions: A Philosophical Exploration*, 40–41.

Chapter 7

The epigraph for chapter 7 is from Wittgenstein, *Philosophical Investigations*, §287.

1. See Carla Bagnoli, "Introduction" in Bagnoli, ed., *Morality and the Emotions* (Oxford: Oxford University Press, 2011), 1–36; and Jesse Prinz, *The Emotional Construction of Morals* (Oxford: Oxford University Press, 2007): "moral emotions promote or detect conduct that violates or conforms to a moral rule" (68), whereas I would expand the *definiens* to include the promotion or detection of moral character as well as action. Aristotle makes the connection between emotion and virtue explicit when he writes that virtue requires not only acting well but also having the right emotions to the right degree and in the right way towards the appropriate objects. Aristotle, *Nicomachean Ethics* II.6, 1106b15–29. See L. A. Kosman, "Being Properly Affected: Virtues and Feelings in Aristotle's Ethics," in *Essays on Aristotle's Ethics*, ed. A. O. Rorty (Berkeley: University of California Press, 1980), 103–16. The understanding of the nature and ethical significance of emotions will depend on the specific account of morality in view; utilitarianism or Kantianism will therefore have different accounts of moral emotions. On this point see Justin Oakley, *Morality and the Emotions* (London: Routledge, 1992), 70–121.

2. Michael Smith, *The Moral Problem* (Oxford: Blackwell, 1994), 7. It should be noted that the "Humean picture" is a simplification of Hume's own more intricate views (e.g., his acknowledgment of "calm passions"). For a similar exposition of the dilemma, see Michael Stocker, "The Schizophrenia of Modern Ethical Theories," *Journal of Philosophy* 73 (1976): 453–66.

3. On the notion of motivational internalism (sometimes called "judgment internalism"), see David Brink, *Moral Realism and the Foundations of Ethics* (Cambridge: Cambridge University Press, 1989).

4. Smith, *The Moral Problem*, 11.

5. Smith's dilemma can be considered a version of J. L. Mackie's influential "argument from queerness," which reasons that, if values were part of "the fabric of the world" then "they would be entities or qualities or relations of a very strange sort, utterly different from anything else in the universe," because they would, simply by virtue of being known, impel the knower to act in certain ways,

thus bridging the gap between cognitive evaluation and desiderative motivation. Mackie, *Ethics: Inventing Right and Wrong* (Harmondsworth, Eng.: Penguin, 1977), 38. Subsequent philosophers have made sophisticated attempts to bridge the gap between cognition and motivation. On the one hand, Smith (*The Moral Problem*, 177–80) proposes that to have a normative reason means that, were we fully rational, we would desire to act on that reason, and we are rational just to the extent that we have the desires corresponding to what moral normativity rationally requires. He tries to bridge the divide by claiming that (full) rationality entails one's having the motivating desires that correspond to correct moral cognition. On the other hand, David Velleman (*Practical Reflection* [Princeton, N.J.: Princeton University Press, 1989], chap. 7) stipulates that a constitutive element of human agency just is having a motive to comply with the evaluations reason provides; he tries to bridge the divide by stipulating that human agency entails desires' complying with cognition. For a useful discussion of the issue, see Bennett Helm, "Emotions and Practical Reason: Rethinking Evaluation and Motivation," *Noûs* 35 (2001): 190–213.

6. Linda Zagzebski, "Emotion and Moral Judgment," *Philosophy and Phenomenological Research* 66 (2003): 107.

7. Of course, a motivational state does not necessarily issue in the corresponding action: it may be suppressed by other motivating states, conditions of *akrasia* ("weakness of the will"), and so on.

8. Zagzebski, "Emotion and Moral Judgment," 109, 113.

9. On "thick concepts" see Bernard Williams, *Ethics and the Limits of Philosophy* (Cambridge, Mass.: Harvard University Press, 1985).

10. Zagzebski, "Emotion and Moral Judgment," 115, 116–17. For related accounts of emotion as inseparable amalgams of cognitive, conative, and affective dimensions, see Goldie, *The Emotions*; Peter Goldie, "Emotion, Reason, and Virtue," in *Emotion, Evolution, and Rationality*, ed. D. Evans and P. Cruse (Oxford: Oxford University Press, 2004), 249–67; and Robert Hanna and Michelle Maiese, *Embodied Mind in Action* (Oxford: Oxford University Press, 2009), chap. 5.

11. Aristotle, *Nicomachean Ethics* 1144a30–1144b1.

12. The term "sensibility theory" was coined by Darwall, Gibbard, and Railton in their "Toward Fin de Siècle Ethics: Some Trends," *Philosophical Review* 101 (1992): 152–65, to describe theories put forward by John McDowell ("Values and Secondary Qualities," in his *Mind, Value and Reality* [Cambridge, Mass.: Harvard University Press, 1998], 131–50); David Wiggins ("A Sensible Subjectivism?" in his *Needs, Values, Truth*, 3rd ed. [Oxford: Clarendon, 1998], 185–214); and David McNaughton, *Moral Vision: An Introduction to Ethics* (Oxford: Blackwell, 1988), who argues that "a way of seeing a situation may itself be a way of caring or feeling" (113).

13. McDowell, "Values and Secondary Qualities," 132. Versions of ethical intuitionism have been attributed to G. E. Moore and H. A. Prichard. Moore claimed that values are metaphysically independent but intrinsically motivating "nonnatural properties," while Prichard claimed that to apprehend one's duty is at once to recognize an absolute moral truth and to be moved to act by it. Thus intuitionism makes two dubious stipulative claims: that there are non-natural properties directly accessible to one's "moral sense," and that these properties are intrinsically motivating (motivational internalism).

14. This account covers both an error theory of value (J. L. Mackie) and non-cognitivist/expressivist theories of value (Allan Gibbard's norm expressivism, Simon Blackburn's quasi-realism). The former holds that all judgments of value are false, because they correspond to no factual state of affairs. The latter interprets value judgments as prescriptive or expressive rather than assertoric, hence they are not truth-apt; rather, value judgments are more like commands or exhortations than statements of fact. For helpful discussion see Justin D'Arms and Daniel Jacobson, "Sensibility Theory and Projectivism," in *The Oxford Handbook of Ethical Theory*, ed. David Copp (Oxford: Oxford University Press, 2006), 186–218.

15. On internal realism see Hilary Putnam, *Reason, Truth and History* (Cambridge, Mass.: Harvard University Press, 1980): that the book is green or that her action was cruel is a fact, but that fact depends on our regarding the book as green or her action as cruel. Internal realism is mind-dependent factualism.

16. For helpful discussion on the controversies surrounding response-dependent concepts and properties, see R. Casati and C. Tappolet, eds., *Response-Dependence* (Stanford, Calif.: CSLI Publications, 1998).

17. So color definitions are as follows: "X is green if and only if X is such as to look green to normal human observers under standard conditions." The definition is circular (it uses "green" on both sides of the biconditional) but not viciously so, as it gives a substantive (non-tautological) account of greenness, in that it specifies the extension of the property GREEN by appealing to a particular sort of qualitative state (that of seeing green). On this account perceptual judgments are like ordinary predications: to judge something green is simply to ascribe the property of greenness to it.

18. David Wiggins, "Moral Cognitivism, Moral Relativism and Motivating Moral Beliefs," *Proceedings of the Aristotelian Society* 91 (1990): 74. There is a subtle but important point here. One might want to claim that value or evaluative properties like "funny" or "cruel" supervene on non-evaluative, or natural/physical properties, and thereby push the sensibility theorist to a primary-quality model of moral responsiveness. Thus one might claim that "funny" supervenes on "incongruity" or "unexpected juxtaposition," and that "cruel" supervenes on "gratuitously harmful." But our patterns of response are too variegated to permit reduction to a supervenience relation as proposed. Either the non-evaluative properties are too diverse to permit any kind of categorizing (e.g., a dog's teeth and an IRS audit are both "dangerous") or the categorizing smuggles in human responsiveness and so is viciously circular. Thus it seems that response and property are correlative concepts, reciprocally dependent for their definitions. Compare Wiggins: "there will often be no saying exactly what reaction a thing with the associated property will provoke without direct or indirect allusion to the property itself. Amusement for instance is a reaction we have to characterize by reference to its proper object, via something perceived as funny (or incongruous or comical or whatever). There is no object-independent and property-independent, 'purely phenomenological' or 'purely introspective' account of amusement" (Wiggins, "A Sensible Subjectivism," 195). That is, there is no priority between emotional responses (such as amusement, shame, and moral indignation) and their associated properties/concepts (FUNNY, SHAMEFUL and MORALLY WRONG); rather, these evaluative properties/concepts and responses arise together, in pairs, through a

co-evolution in which the character of the response and the extension of the predicate influence one another. Hence, no non-circular account of either concept or response is possible, because each depends essentially upon the other. For similar thoughts see McDowell, "Projection and Truth in Ethics," in his *Mind, Value and Reality*, 158. For a criticism of such circularity see Allan Gibbard, *Wise Choices, Apt Feelings: A Theory of Normative Judgment* (Cambridge, Mass.: Harvard University Press: 1990), 148.

19. That is, like perception, moral response in its cognitive dimension (as judgment, appraisal, construal, etc.) has a mind-to-world direction of fit; but in its conative/affective dimension (e.g., as action readiness tendency) it has a world-to-mind direction of it. It should also be noted that with respect to correctness conditions the analogy between moral perception and color perception is strained, because it is not clear that similar standard conditions and normal humans can be so readily specified. The appeal to an *ideal*, as for instance in Adam Smith (*The Theory of Moral Sentiments*), trivializes the problem because ideal is then defined to be whatever produces correct moral-emotional responses. The problem is specifying the subjective and objective conditions underlying that ideal responsiveness, and that is very much non-trivial. Hence theorists like Wiggins and McDowell acknowledge an irreducible non-vicious circularity between moral predicate and moral property.

20. McDowell, "Values and Secondary Qualities," 143.

21. Jesse Prinz (*The Emotional Construction of Morals*, 111–15) criticizes the "merit schema" of Wiggins and McDowell here for "shifting away from a merely causal model of the relationship between moral properties and moral sentiments" that underwrites his embodied appraisal view. Besides introducing an intentional and normative relation to sensibility theory, Wiggins's and McDowell's "metacognitive" view (Prinz's term) holds that "a moral judgment on this view is not itself an emotional response, but is rather a judgment to the effect that an emotional response would be appropriate. In other words, tokens of moral concepts *mention* emotions rather than *use* them" (112). But the sensibility theory under attack can answer this charge in two ways: first, on this view emotions are sui generis amalgams of cognitive, conative, and affective states, and therefore include a first-order cognitive component (appraisal, thought, representation, etc.); second, the judgment that an emotional response is fitting or appropriate is made not in lieu of the specific emotional response but rather *upon reflection*, so such judgment is at most entailed by the normative correctness of a specific emotional response.

22. McDowell, "Two Sorts of Naturalism," in his *Mind, Value and Reality*, 196–97. D'Arms and Jacobson ("Sensibility Theory and Projectivism," 203–4) object that the merit schema must provide a non-trivial, non-circular account of the correctness conditions in order to differentiate a merited response of shame, say, from an unmerited response of shame: that is, an account that says more than "the response of shame is merited when the eliciting action, person, situation is really shameful." A McDowellian response refuses to countenance the position of a "sideways on" observer of a *sittliche Welt*: the question and answer of evaluative properties has purchase only on a member of the practice. Although we must scrutinize our ethical responses, "the necessary scrutiny does not involve stepping outside the point of view constituted by an ethical sensibility"; rather, the reasons

to act revealed by our ethical sensibility are "vindicated from within the relevant way of thinking" (McDowell, "Projection and Truth in Ethics," 162–63). For McDowell, the position of an external observer is an illusion, that of a person who on the one hand possesses the evaluative concepts and emotional responses (and thus is within second nature) and on the other can stand outside of second nature and evaluate the practice. It is a mythic position to answer a temptation he locates in modernity: "what has happened to modernity is rather that it has fallen into a temptation, which we can escape, to wish for a foundation for ethics of a sort that it never occurred to Aristotle to supply it with" (McDowell, "Two Sorts of Naturalism," 195).

23. Simon Blackburn, "Errors and the Phenomenology of Value," in *Essays in Quasi-Realism* (New York: Oxford University Press, 1993), 149–65, outlines six disanalogies between moral properties and color properties in his criticism of Wiggins and McDowell.

24. Compare David Hume: "We do not infer a character to be virtuous because it pleases: But in feeling that it pleases after such a particular manner, we in effect feel that it is virtuous." Hume, *A Treatise of Human Nature*, ed. L. A. Selby-Bigge and P. H. Nidditch (Oxford: Clarendon, 1978), 471.

25. John McDowell, "Virtue and Reason," in his *Mind, Value and Reality*, 72–73.

26. John McDowell, "Are Moral Requirements Hypothetical Imperatives?" in his *Mind, Value and Reality*, 85.

27. On moral perception as a kind of skill, see Daniel Jacobson, "Seeing by Feeling: Virtues, Skills, and Moral Perception," *Ethical Theory and Moral Practice* 8 (2005): 387–409; Peter Goldie, "Seeing What Is the Kind Thing to Do: Perception and Emotion in Morality," *Dialectica* 61 (2007): 347–61; Sabine Döring, "Seeing What to Do: Affective Perception and Rational Motivation," *Dialectica* 61 (2007): 363–94.

28. McDowell, "Two Sorts of Naturalism," 189.

29. McDowell, "Projection and Truth in Ethics," 162–63.

30. Wiggins, "A Sensible Subjectivism?" 197. This conception of moral emotions might be deployed in support of Stanley Cavell's reframing the skeptical problem of other minds in terms not of knowledge but of "acknowledging" the other (say, his being in pain) as recognizing his demand for my recognition, my responsiveness. Cavell apparently grounds such responsiveness in a perceived kinship between oneself and a creature like oneself, with whom one identifies, via what he calls "empathetic projection," which at least suggests a more individualistic attitude then that associated with "second nature" in Wiggins and McDowell, as when Cavell writes: "I must settle upon the validity of my projection from within my present condition, from within, so to speak, my confinement from you. For there would be no way for me to step outside my projections." Stanley Cavell, "Knowing and Acknowledging," in *Must We Mean What We Say?* (Cambridge: Cambridge University Press, 1976), 238–66; Stanley Cavell, *The Claim of Reason: Wittgenstein, Skepticism, Morality, and Tragedy* (Oxford: Oxford University Press, 1979), quote p. 423. For helpful discussions of Cavell's thinking, see Stephen Mulhall, *Stanley Cavell: Philosophy's Recounting of the Ordinary* (Oxford: Clarendon, 1994); Espen Hammer, *Stanley Cavell: Skepticism, Subjectivity, and the Ordinary* (Cambridge, Eng.: Polity, 2002); and Charles

Altieri, "Cavell and Wittgenstein on Morality: The Limits of Acknowledgment," in *Stanley Cavell and Literary Studies: Consequences of Skepticism*, ed. Richard Eldridge and Bernard Rhie (London: Continuum, 2011), 62–77.

31. Tolstoy, *What Is Art?* 131–32.

32. This understanding of religious emotions contrasts with a common view, according to which religious feelings would include emotions such as divine reverence or awe (German *Ehrfurcht*), spiritual desolation, divine adoration, and so on. Certainly Tolstoy writes of such emotions, in *A Confession* and regarding Levin in *Anna Karenina*. Consideration of these emotions, perhaps in conjunction with specific tenets of various faiths, is beyond the scope of our study. On such emotions see Peter Goldie, "Intellectual and Religious Emotions," *Faith and Philosophy: Journal of the Society of Christian Philosophers* 28 (2011): 93–101.

33. David Hume, *Enquiries Concerning Human Understanding and Concerning the Principles of Morals*, ed. L. A. Selby-Bigge and P. H. Nidditch, 3rd ed. (Oxford: Clarendon, 1975), 173. For a clear account of neo-sentimentalism, see Justin D'Arms and Daniel Jacobson, "Sentiment and Value," *Ethics* 110 (2000): 722–48.

34. This is the list from Paul Ekman's seminal paper, "Universals and Cultural Differences in Facial Expressions of Emotion," in *Nebraska Symposium on Motivation 1971*, ed. J. Cole (Lincoln: University of Nebraska Press, 1972), 207–83. The individuation and enumeration of basic emotions has been controversial ever since. For a reassessment, see Paul Ekman, "All Emotions Are Basic," and Richard Lazarus, "Appraisal: The Long and Short of It," both in *The Nature of Emotion: Fundamental Questions*, ed. Paul Ekman and Richard Davidson (New York: Oxford University Press, 1994).

35. Thus while sensibility theorists like McDowell and Wiggins hold that any account of responsiveness and evaluative feature must be non-viciously circular, sentimentalism theorists claim priority for the sentiments. This anthropological universality between subject matter and sentiment does not entail univocity among people, however, for a variety of reasons, some of which are helpfully discussed in Justin D'Arms and Daniel Jacobson, "Sentimental Values and the Instability of Affect," in *The Oxford Handbook of Philosophy of Emotion*, ed. Peter Goldie (Oxford: Oxford University Press, 2010), 585–613. Note that D'Arms and Jacobson define sentiments similarly to how Zagzebski defines moral emotions, as sui generis states inseparably composed of cognitive, conative, and affective aspects: "The sentiments are syndromes of thought, feeling, and motivation, which constitute a core subset of the broad and diverse group of states that commonly get called emotions." D'Arms and Jacobson, "Anthropocentric Constraints on Human Value," *Oxford Studies in Metaethics* 1 (2006): 101. "[Basic emotions like amusement, disgust, and fear] are syndromes of cognitive, affective, motivational, and behavioral changes, which arise in patterns displaying some degree of consistency across times and cultures—perhaps because of our shared evolutionary history. Such natural emotions are amenable to study as distinctive psychological syndromes." D'Arms and Jacobson, "Sensibility Theory and Projectivism," 206.

36. "We can fix on a response . . . and then argue about what marks are of the property that the response is itself made for. And without serious detriment to the univocity of the predicate, it can now become essentially contestable what a thing

has to be like for there to be any reason to accord that particular appellation to it, and correspondingly contestable what the extension is of the predicate." Wiggins, "A Sensible Subjectivism?" 198. See Justin D'Arms ("Two Arguments for Sentimentalism," *Philosophical Issues* 15 [2005]: 13): "a shared response, or sentiment, somehow moors us in a common subject matter, making it possible for us to disagree substantively about what a thing has to be like in order to be such that we should feel *this* sentiment toward it. . . . It is because our evaluative concepts have a special tie to shared human sentiments that we are able to engage meaningfully in debates about their application. . . . A shared sentiment supplies a shared element in the intensions of our evaluative thoughts."

37. There is a controversy here that needs to be acknowledged, though it cannot be adequately discussed in the present context. Sensibility theorists hold that emotional response and eliciting evaluative property are correlative concepts, while sentimentalism theorists hold that basic emotional responses are logically and ontologically prior to their eliciting properties. Some sensibility theorists, for instance McDowell, seem to claim that disgustingness, the property that elicits the basic emotion disgust, is *not* an evaluative property at all, but rather merely a dispositional property: the disgusting is whatever reliably causes disgust, rather than what merits or deserves disgust ("Projection and Truth in Ethics," 157). This view would be in keeping with our earlier criticism of Right Affectivism, namely, that such basic emotions lack an intentional relation and intentional (formal) object, and hence a correctness condition: the disgusting is just whatever reliably causes the basic response of disgust. On the other hand, D'Arms and Jacobson claim that even disgust bears a normative relation, because a gap can arise between sentiment (emotional response) and value (the normative property associated with the response): "Not everything that nauseates, even regularly, is judged disgusting. Ever since an ugly food poisoning incident years ago, I cannot eat whitefish salad; but though it reliably disgusts me, I still consider it a delicacy—albeit one I can no longer enjoy. More generally, people often dispute such judgments . . . It thus seems that with disgust . . . sensibility theory must be prepared to concede the priority of emotional response to evaluative property" (D'Arms and Jacobson, "Sensibility Theory and Projectivism," 206). I think the objection can be answered in the following way: the author has first described a dispositional property (the disgusting as that which reliably causes the response of disgust) and then an evaluative property (being a delicacy), and it is only to the latter that a normative relation (merit, desert, justification) attaches. Or: the author has equivocated between a descriptive understanding of the concept disgusting (= reliably causing disgust) and a normative understanding of the concept disgusting (= worthy of, meriting disgust). Or, to anticipate the developmental story I will tell, the normative relation is a later, conceptual reticulation to the basic emotion of disgust, so that the causal response of disgust can in fact come apart from the judgment of "this is [not] disgusting."

38. Moral resentment of course must be distinguished from envious resentment and Nietzschean *ressentiment* (spiteful malice out of impotence). The idea that moral emotions derive from more basic emotions can be traced back to Adam Smith (*The Theory of Moral Sentiments*, 7.III.iii), and has received a contemporary inflection in Jesse Prinz, *The Emotional Construction of Morals*: "Indignation is not a basic emotion: it derives from anger. Indignation is anger

calibrated to [that is, associated with through learning] injustice" (69); "I think guilt is an extension of [the basic emotion of] sadness" (77); "Sympathy can be defined as a negative emotional response to the suffering of others. A sympathetic person feels bad that you feel bad. It's not clear empirically whether sympathy always refers to the same underlying emotion. If so, it's probably a species of sadness" (82).

39. John Rawls helpfully elucidates the distinction between emotion and moral emotion: "A person without a sense of justice may be enraged at someone who fails to act fairly. But anger and annoyance are distinct from indignation and resentment; they are not, as the latter are, moral emotions." John Rawls, *A Theory of Justice* (Cambridge, Mass.: Harvard University Press, 1971), 488. "In general, it is a necessary feature of moral feelings, and part of what distinguishes them from the natural attitudes, that the person's explanation of his experience invokes a moral concept and its associated principles. His account of his feeling makes reference to an acknowledged right or wrong" (Rawls, *A Theory of Justice*, 481).

40. Deigh, *Emotions, Values, and the Law*, 62–69.

41. M. F. Burnyeat, "Aristotle on Learning to Be Good," in *Essays on Aristotle's Ethics*, ed. A. O. Rorty (Berkeley: University of California Press, 1980), 82. See also Sabina Lovibond, *Ethical Formation* (Cambridge, Mass.: Harvard University Press, 2002).

42. Prinz, *The Emotional Construction of Morals*, 118–19. Using the example of "cruelty," arguably already a moral concept, might leave Prinz open to the charge of circularity; replacing it with "violence" would avert the issue.

Chapter 8

The epigraphs for chapter 8 are from Wittgenstein, *Notebooks* (September 19, 1916) and Wittgenstein, *Culture and Value*, page 59.

1. For a helpful introduction and overview of recent work, see *The Routledge Companion to Philosophy and Music*, ed. T. Gracyk and A. Kania (New York: Routledge, 2011); Aaron Ridley, *The Philosophy of Music: Theme and Variations* (Edinburgh: Edinburgh University Press, 2004); and Andrew Kania, "The Philosophy of Music," *Stanford Encyclopedia of Philosophy* (online).

2. Aaron Ridley cautions against overgeneralization and abstraction, and advocates a judiciously pragmatic approach to theorizing about specific artworks in *Music, Value and the Passions* (Ithaca, N.Y.: Cornell University Press, 1995) and "*Persona* Sometimes *Grata*: On the Appreciation of Expressive Music," in *Philosophers on Music: Experience, Meaning, Work*, ed. Karen Stock (Oxford: Oxford University Press, 2007), 130–46.

3. See Stephen Davies, *Musical Meaning and Expression* (Ithaca, N.Y.: Cornell University Press, 1994), 299–307; Jerrold Levinson, *Music, Art, and Metaphysics* (Ithaca, N.Y.: Cornell University Press, 1990), 319–22; and Colin Radford, "Emotions and Music: A Reply to the Cognitivists," *Journal of Aesthetics and Art Criticism* 47 (1989): 69–76. Peter Kivy, *Sound Sentiment: An Essay on the Musical Emotions* (Philadelphia: Temple University Press, 1989), chap. 12, claims that music elicits a sui generis "musical" emotion. Kendall Walton (*Mimesis as Make-Believe: On the Foundations of the Representational Arts* [Cambridge, Mass.: Harvard University Press, 1990], 240–55) describes our emotional responses to

expressive music as "quasi-emotions": causally elicited affective elements of emotion that we *imagine* to be genuine emotions.

4. Martha Nussbaum, *Love's Knowledge: Essays on Philosophy and Literature* (New York: Oxford University Press, 1990), 44. Other representative texts in this tradition include Lionel Trilling, *The Liberal Imagination: Essays on Literature and Society* (New York: Doubleday, 1950); Wayne Booth, *The Company We Keep* (Berkeley: University of California Press, 1988); Martin Price, *Character and Moral Imagination in the Novel* (New Haven, Conn.: Yale University Press, 1983); and Susan Feagin, *Reading with Feeling: The Aesthetics of Appreciation* (Ithaca, N.Y.: Cornell University Press, 1996).

5. Wittgenstein, *Culture and Value*, 11.

6. Peter Kivy, *New Essays on Musical Understanding* (Oxford: Oxford University Press, 2001), frames the problem well:

> The question I am raising is how we are emotionally aroused by what the nineteenth century called absolute music . . . It is important to remember this because when the resources of language are added to the musical work, the terms of the argument are radically changed. I have no quarrel, for example, with someone who says that when he attends a performance of *La Traviata*, he experiences real and intense sorrow over the death of Violetta, . . . This is not to say that there is no philosophical problem in just how the emotions of sorrow and love can be aroused by the fates of fictional characters . . . But the presence of language, with all its potential for conveying concepts, and the presence of delineated characters, such as Violetta and Alfredo . . . provide materials for arousal of garden variety emotions far exceeding anything that can reasonably be postulated in absolute music. And that is why absolute music poses a problem far beyond opera, oratorio, song and programme music to those who wish to claim that it arouses the garden variety emotions. (101–2)

For further discussion and motivation along these lines, see Derek Matravers, "Expression in Music," in *Philosophers on Music: Experience, Meaning, Work*, ed. Karen Stock (Oxford: Oxford University Press, 2007), 95–116. While the problem of expression of emotion in music dates back to Pythagoras, Plato, and Aristotle, and extends through nineteenth-century philosophy, it was revived in its current inflection by Macolm Budd's influential *Music and the Emotions* (London: Routledge and Kegan Paul, 1985).

7. Roger Scruton (*The Aesthetics of Music* [Oxford: Oxford University Press, 1997], 96, 141) characterizes musical expressiveness as irreducibly metaphorical and inexplicable, which simply restates the problem: why emotional terms are so readily and communally attributed to passages of music and audiences' responses to them, where these emotion terms apparently are being used with their usual meanings. Understanding musical properties as response-dependent averts this impasse: see Paul Boghossian, "Explaining Musical Experience," in *Philosophers on Music: Experience, Meaning, Work*, ed. Karen Stock (Oxford: Oxford University Press, 2007), 122–24. For a recent argument, drawing on empirical work in cognitive science, that musical structure "represents" environmental affordances for emotional responses, see Charles Nussbaum, *The Musical Representation: Meaning, Ontology, and Emotion* (Cambridge, Mass.: MIT Press, 2007).

8. Jerrold Levinson, "Emotion in Response to Art: A Survey of the Terrain," in *Emotion and the Arts*, ed. M. Hjort and S. Laver (New York: Oxford University Press, 1997), 27–28.

9. The qualifications couched in terms like "understanding" or "appropriate" listeners are intended to allow for the fact that cultural factors may play a role in the success of the disposition. For versions of the arousal theory, see P. Mew, "The Expression of Emotion in Music," *British Journal of Aesthetics* 35 (1985): 33–42; and Derek Matravers, *Art and Emotion* (Oxford: Oxford University Press, 1998).

10. Jenefer Robinson, *Deeper Than Reason: Emotion and Its Role in Literature, Music and Art* (Oxford: Clarendon, 2005), 291–92 (original emphasis).

11. Ibid., 366.

12. There are other problems with the theory that should merely be mentioned here. First, the arousal theory is neither necessary nor sufficient for expression. It is not necessary, because "dry-eyed critics" experience music as expressive without experiencing the affective feeling (see O. K. Bouwsma, "The Expression Theory of Art," in *Aesthetics and Language*, ed. William Elton [Oxford: Blackwell, 1954], 73–99). It is not sufficient, because many things arouse a feeling without one's finding them expressive. One might feel anxiety at an unexpected noise without finding the noise expressive (see next note). Lastly, the arousal theory seems to violate the experienced epistemology of the emotional response: rather than an immediate experience, the theory analyzes hearing music as sad, for example, as hearing the music and then feeling sad: that is, as two separable experiences (see Derek Matravers, "Expression in Music," in *Philosophers on Music: Experience, Meaning, Work*, ed. Karen Stock [Oxford: Oxford University Press, 2007], 95–116).

13. This example comes from Ridley, "Mr. Mew on Music," *British Journal of Aesthetics* 26 (1986): 69–70.

14. See Paul Boghossian, "Explaining Musical Experience," in *Philosophers on Music: Experience, Meaning, Work*, ed. Karen Stock (Oxford: Oxford University Press, 2007), 117–29. Compare Wittgenstein: "The understanding of a [musical] theme is neither sensation nor a sum of sensations. Nevertheless it is correct to call it an experience inasmuch as *this* concept of understanding has some kinship with other concepts of experience. You say 'I experienced that passage quite differently this time.' " Wittgenstein, *Zettel*, §165. "Aesthetic questions have nothing to do with psychological experiments, but are answered in an entirely different way"; "You could say: 'An aesthetic explanation is not a causal explanation' "; "The sort of explanation one is looking for when one is puzzled by an aesthetic impression is not a causal explanation, not one corroborated by experience or by statistics as to how people react." Ludwig Wittgenstein, *Lectures and Conversations on Aesthetics, Psychology and Religious Belief*, ed. Cyril Barrett (Berkeley: University of California Press, 1966), 17, 18, 21.

15. Robinson, *Deeper Than Reason*, 403.

16. Other arousal theorists bite the bullet here and concede that music can only induce affective "feelings," not genuine emotions. See note 3 to this chapter.

17. Robinson, *Deeper Than Reason*, 403, 405. Stephen Davies, *Musical Meaning and Expression* (Ithaca, N.Y.: Cornell University Press, 1994), chap. 6, and Davies, "Artistic Expression and the Hard Case of Pure Music," in *Contemporary*

Debates in Aesthetics and the Philosophy of Art, ed. Matthew Kieran (Oxford: Blackwell, 2006), 186–88, also invokes "emotional contagion" and "mirroring responses" without any intentional object or property.

18. Compare Levinson's judgment regarding theories of musical expression that invoke exclusively the "sensory, or cognitively unmediated route": "if the capacity of music to elicit emotion were exhausted by the direct effects of sensing basic musical features, it would be a poor thing, falling far short of the evocation of *emotions proper*, or even the semblance of such" (Levinson, "Emotion in Response to Art: A Survey of the Terrain," 28).

19. Robinson likewise accepts the unwelcome consequence that no "higher-order" or "cognitively complex" emotions can be attributed to the expressiveness of the music, as opposed to the "cognitive monitoring" and context of the listener. This is a revision of her earlier attempt to attribute a complex emotion—"false hope"—to a musical work: see J. Robinson and G. Karl, "Shostakovitch's Tenth Symphony and the Musical Expression of Cognitively Complex Emotions," *Journal of Aesthetics and Art Criticism* 53 (1995): 401–15; and Davies's objections in his *Themes in the Philosophy of Music* (Oxford: Oxford University Press, 2003), 161–66. Jerrold Levinson offers several persuasive suggestions of how music can express cognitively complex emotions: (1) the overall totality and interrelatedness of non-cognitive aspects (physiological, phenomenological, behavioral, etc.) readily expressible and inducible by music might be determinative of a specific complex emotion; (2) expressive music can evoke intentional object-types (if not specific tokens); (3) musical features and their implications, including the temporal progression of variably expressive passages, can provide a determinate context for individuating a specific emotion. This last point comports well with the narrative dimensions of some emotions (such as grief, hope, etc.) discussed at the outset of chapter 6. See Levinson, "Hope in *The Hebrides*," in his *Music, Art, and Metaphysics: Essays in Philosophical Aesthetics* (Ithaca, N.Y.: Cornell University Press, 1990), 336–75.

20. Levinson, "Emotion in Response to Art," 28.

21. These theories are presented, respectively, in Bruce Vermazen, "Expression as Expression," *Pacific Philosophical Quarterly* 67 (1986): 196–224; Jenefer Robinson, "The Expression and Arousal of Emotion in Music," in *Musical Worlds: New Directions in the Philosophy of Music*, ed. P. Alperson (University Park: Pennsylvania State University Press, 1998), 13–22; and Robert Stecker, "Expressiveness and Expression in Music and Poetry," *Journal of Aesthetics and Art Criticism* 59 (2001): 85–96.

22. For criticism of inferentialist or "judgment-based" theories of musical expression, see Jerrold Levinson, "Musical Expressiveness," in his *The Pleasures of Aesthetics: Philosophical Essays* (Ithaca, N.Y.: Cornell University Press, 1996), 98–102, and his "Musical Expressiveness as Hearability-as-Expression," in *Contemporary Debates in Aesthetics and the Philosophy of Art*, ed. Matthew Kieran (Oxford: Blackwell, 2006), 199–201.

23. See Stephen Davies, *Musical Meaning and Expression* (Ithaca, N.Y.: Cornell University Press, 1994) and his "Artistic Expression and the Hard Case of Pure Music," in *Contemporary Debates in Aesthetics and the Philosophy of Art*, ed. Matthew Kieran (Oxford: Blackwell, 2006), 179–91. Another resemblance-based theory is that of Malcolm Budd, *The Values of Art: Pictures, Poetry, and*

Music (London: Allen Lane, Penguin Press, 1995). Peter Kivy advanced a similar "contour theory" in his *Sound Sentiment* (Philadelphia: Temple University Press, 1989), but has voiced dissatisfaction with the theory subsequently in his *New Essays on Musical Understanding* (Oxford: Oxford University Press, 2001).

24. Davies, *Musical Meaning and Expression*, 228.

25. Ibid., 229. "I think music is expressive in recalling the gait, attitude, air, carriage, posture and comportment of the human body." Davies, "Artistic Expression and the Hard Case of Pure Music," 182.

26. Davies, *Musical Meaning and Expression*, 239.

27. Boghossian, "Explaining Musical Experience," 124.

28. Davies, "Artistic Expression and the Hard Case of Pure Music," 181.

29. Levinson, "Musical Expressiveness as Hearability-as-Expression," 197.

30. Boghossian, "Explaining Musical Experience," 125.

31. Levinson, "Musical Expressiveness as Hearability-as-Expression," 197.

32. Jerrold Levinson, "Musical Expressiveness," in his *The Pleasures of Aesthetics: Philosophical Essays* (Ithaca, N.Y.: Cornell University Press, 1996), 107.

33. Levinson, "Musical Expressiveness as Hearability-as-Expression," 201.

34. A form of this objection is raised by Robert Stecker, "Expressiveness and Expression in Music and Poetry," *Journal of Aesthetics and Art Criticism* 59 (2001): 91–94.

35. Levinson, "Musical Expressiveness as Hearability-as-Expression," 193. Levinson dropped the qualification of "sui generis manner" due to objections of obscurantism, but these objections are not pertinent to my line of argument here.

36. Levinson, "Musical Expressiveness as Hearability-as-Expression," 198.

37. Peter Kivy, *The Corded Shell: Reflections on Musical Expression* (Princeton, N.J.: Princeton University Press, 1980), 14–15. Kivy is relying on the careful exposition of the argument in Alan Tormey, *The Concept of Expression: A Study in Philosophical Psychology and Aesthetics* (Princeton, N.J.: Princeton University Press, 1971), 39–62. See my discussion of Tormey in chapter 3.

38. Wittgenstein, *The Blue and Brown Books*, 178. See also the rhetorical question posed: "I.e., can I separate what I call this experience of pastness [caused by hearing a specific Schumann *Lied*] from the experience of hearing the tune?" (184); and the rhetorical question posed in *Culture and Value*: "If art serves 'to arouse feelings,' is, perhaps, perceiving it with the senses included amongst these feelings?" (42).

39. It might be helpful to think of this constitutive relationship in dispositional or ability terms. The disposition or ability to speak Russian, say, does not preclude one's occasionally making mistakes or intentionally feigning a lack of or imperfect mastery of the linguistic ability.

40. My thoughts in this paragraph are indebted to Aaron Ridley, "Expression in Art," in Jerrold Levinson, ed., *The Oxford Handbook of Aesthetics* (Oxford: Oxford University Press, 2003), 211–27.

41. Levinson, "Musical Expressiveness as Hearability-as-Expression," 201. Jenefer Robinson, like Levinson, holds that we hear expressive music as the expression of emotion of a persona in her *Deeper Than Reason*, 320.

42. Wittgenstein, *Zettel*, §234.

43. Wittgenstein, *Philosophical Investigations*, §527. See also Wittgenstein, *Zettel*, §161, §175; Wittgenstein, *Culture and Value*, 59, 63, 93. For an extension

of Wittgenstein's likening music to the audible appearance of speech acts, see Jerrold Levinson, "Musical Thinking," *Midwest Studies in Philosophy* 27 (2003): 59–68.

44. Wittgenstein, *Culture and Value*, 83. See also Ludwig Wittgenstein, *Remarks on the Philosophy of Psychology*, vol. 1, ed. G. E. M. Anscombe and G. H. von Wright, trans. G. E. M. Anscombe (Oxford: Blackwell, 1980), §§435–36.

45. Wittgenstein, *Remarks on the Philosophy of Psychology*, vol. 1, §660; see also Wittgenstein, *Zettel*, §158.

46. Wittgenstein, *Philosophical Investigations*, §281.

47. I make this argument in greater detail in my "Towards a Disjunctivist Conception of Aesthetic Expression" (unpublished manuscript). On epistemic disjunctivism, see John McDowell, "The Disjunctive Conception of Experience as Material for a Transcendental Argument," in his *The Engaged Intellect* (Cambridge, Mass.: Harvard University Press, 2009), 225–40.

48. Wittgenstein, *Culture and Value*, 67.

Conclusion

The epigraph for the conclusion is from Wittgenstein, *Culture and Value*, 38.

1. Tolstoy, *What Is Art?* 39–40 (original emphasis).

2. For instance, in cases of collective or vague authorship, the "persona" theory might be required. Recall that two of Tolstoy's examples of successful artworks are a traditional peasant wedding song and a Siberian shamanistic performance (see chapter 3, section 2): such cases might require the audience's projection of a persona or implied author.

3. Wittgenstein, *Culture and Value*, 49.

4. Wittgenstein, *Philosophical Investigations*, part II, 183.

5. Wittgenstein, *Remarks on the Philosophy of Psychology*, 1: §434.

6. Contrary to Roger Scruton, "Wittgenstein and the Understanding of Music," *British Journal of Aesthetics* 44 (2004): 1–9, who argues that Wittgenstein advocates merely the expressiveness of art and denies that art can express an emotion.

7. "Here is a possibility: I hear that someone is painting a picture 'Beethoven writing the ninth symphony.' I could easily imagine the kind of thing such a picture would shew us. But suppose someone wanted to represent what Goethe would have looked like writing the ninth symphony? Here I could imagine nothing that would not be embarrassing and ridiculous." Wittgenstein, *Philosophical Investigations*, part II, 183. "I hear a melody completely differently after I have become familiar with its composer's style. Previously I might have described it as happy, for example, but now I sense that it is the expression of great suffering. Now I describe it differently, group it with quite different things." Wittgenstein, *Last Writings on the Philosophy of Psychology*, 1: §774.

8. Wittgenstein, *Lectures and Conversations*, 4.

BIBLIOGRAPHY

Abrams, M. H. *The Mirror and the Lamp: Romantic Theory and the Critical Tradition*. New York: Oxford University Press, 1971.

Adams, Fred, and Ken Aizawa. "Causal Theories of Mental Content." *Stanford Encyclopedia of Philosophy*. http://plato.stanford.edu/entries/content-causal/.

———. "'X' Means X: Semantics Fodor-Style." *Minds and Machines* 2 (1992): 175–83.

Alexandrov, Vladimir E. *Limits to Interpretation: The Meanings of "Anna Karenina."* Madison: University of Wisconsin Press, 2004.

Altieri, Charles. "Cavell and Wittgenstein on Morality: The Limits of Acknowledgment." In *Stanley Cavell and Literary Studies: Consequences of Skepticism*, edited by Richard Eldridge and Bernard Rhie, 62–77. London: Continuum, 2011.

Anscombe, G. E. M. *Intention*. Cambridge, Mass.: Harvard University Press, 2000.

Aristotle. *Rhetoric*. Translated by W. Rhys Roberts. In *The Complete Works of Aristotle*, edited by Jonathan Barnes. 2 vols. Princeton: Princeton, N.J.: Princeton University Press, 1984.

Austin, J. L. *Philosophical Papers*. 3rd edition. Edited by J. O. Urmson and G. J. Warnock. Oxford: Oxford University Press, 1979.

Baehr, Stephen. "Art and 'The Kreutzer Sonata': A Tolstoian Approach." *Canadian-American Slavic Studies* 10 (1976): 39–46. Reprinted in *Tolstoy's Short Fiction*, edited by Michael Katz, 448–56. New York: W. W. Norton, 1991.

Bagnoli, Carla. "Introduction." In *Morality and the Emotions*, edited by Carla Bagnoli, 1–21. Oxford: Oxford University Press, 2011.

Baier, Annette. "What Emotions Are About." *Philosophical Perspectives* 4 (1990): 1–29.

Barran, Thomas. "Rousseau's Political Vision and Tolstoy's *What Is Art?*" *Tolstoy Studies Journal* 5 (1992): 1–12.

Bennett, M. R., and P. M. S. Hacker. *Philosophical Foundations of Neuroscience*. Oxford: Blackwell, 2003.

Bennett, Maxwell, Daniel Dennett, Peter Hacker, John Searle, and Daniel N. Robinson. *Neuroscience and Philosophy: Brain, Mind, and Language*. New York: Columbia University Press, 2007.

Billington, James. *The Icon and the Axe: An Interpretive History of Russian Culture*. New York: Vintage, 1970.

Blackburn, Simon. "Errors and the Phenomenology of Value." In *Essays in Quasi-Realism*, 149–65. New York: Oxford University Press, 1993.

———. *The Oxford Dictionary of Philosophy*. Oxford: Oxford University Press, 1994.

Boghossian, Paul. "Explaining Musical Experience." In *Philosophers on Music: Experience, Meaning, Work*, edited by Karen Stock, 117–29. Oxford: Oxford University Press, 2007.

Booth, Wayne. *The Company We Keep*. Berkeley: University of California Press, 1988.

Bouwsma, O. K. "The Expression Theory of Art." In *Aesthetics and Language*, edited by William Elton, 73–99. Oxford: Blackwell, 1954.

Brandom, Robert. "Insights and Blindspots of Reliabilism." In *Articulating Reasons: An Introduction to Inferentialism*, 97–122. Cambridge, Mass.: Harvard University Press, 2000.

Brennan, Teresa. *The Transmission of Affect*. Ithaca, N.Y.: Cornell University Press, 2004.

Brentano, Franz. *Psychology from an Empirical Standpoint*. Edited by Oskar Kraus. Translated by Antos C. Rancurello, D. B. Terrell, and Linda L. McAlister. London: Routledge and Kegan Paul, 1973 [1874].

Brink, David. *Moral Realism and the Foundations of Ethics*. Cambridge: Cambridge University Press, 1989.

Budd, Malcolm. *Music and the Emotions: The Philosophical Theories*. London: Routledge and Kegan Paul, 1985.

———. *The Values of Art: Pictures, Poetry, and Music*. London: Allen Lane, Penguin Press, 1995.

Burnyeat, M. F. "Aristotle on Learning to Be Good." In *Essays on Aristotle's Ethics*, ed. A. O. Rorty, 69–92. Berkeley: University of California Press, 1980.

Carroll, Noël. *Philosophy of Art: A Contemporary Introduction*. London: Routledge, 1999.

Casati, Roberto, and Christine Tappolet, eds. *Response-Dependence*. Stanford: CLSI Publications, 1998.

Cavell, Stanley. *The Claim of Reason: Wittgenstein, Skepticism, Morality, and Tragedy*. Oxford: Oxford University Press, 1979.

———. *Must We Mean What We Say?* Cambridge: Cambridge University Press, 1976.

Clough, Patricia Ticineto, and Jean Halley, eds. *The Affective Turn: Theorizing the Social*. Durham, N.C.: Duke University Press, 2007.

Coetzee, J. M. "Confession and Double Thoughts: Tolstoy, Rousseau, Dostoevsky." *Comparative Literature* 37 (1985): 193–232.

Collingwood, R. C. *The Principles of Art*. Oxford: Clarendon, 1938.

Conant, James. "Must We Show What We Cannot Say?" In *The Senses of Stanley Cavell*, edited by R. Fleming and M. Payne, 242–83. Lewisburg: Bucknell University Press, 1989.

———. "Varieties of Scepticism." In *Wittgenstein and Scepticism*, edited by Denis McManus, 97–136. New York: Routledge, 2004.

Connolly, William E. *Neuropolitics: Thinking, Culture, Speed*. Minneapolis: University of Minnesota Press, 2002.

Crane, Tim. "Intentionality as the Mark of the Mental." In *Current Issues in Philosophy of Mind*, edited by Anthony O'Hear, 229–51. Cambridge: Cambridge University Press, 1998.

———. *The Mechanical Mind: A Philosophical Introduction to Minds, Machines and Mental Representation*. 2nd edition. London: Routledge, 2003.

Dal', Vladimir. *Tolkovyi slovar' zhivogo velikorusskogo iazyka*. Moscow: "Russkii Iazyk," 1981 [1881].

Damasio, Antonio R. *Descartes' Error: Emotion, Reason, and the Human Brain*. New York: Putnam, 1994.

———. *Looking for Spinoza: Joy, Sorrow, and the Feeling Brain*. New York: Harcourt, 2003.

———. "William James and the Modern Neurobiology of Emotion." In *Emotion, Evolution and Rationality*, edited by D. Evans and P. Cruse, 3–14. Oxford: Oxford University Press, 2004.

D'Arms, Justin. "Two Arguments for Sentimentalism." *Philosophical Issues* 15 (2005): 1–21.

D'Arms, Justin, and Daniel Jacobson. "Anthropocentric Constraints on Human Value." *Oxford Studies in Metaethics* 1 (2006): 99–126.

———. "Sensibility Theory and Projectivism." In *The Oxford Handbook of Ethical Theory*, edited by David Copp, 186–218. Oxford: Oxford University Press, 2006.

———. "Sentiment and Value." *Ethics* 110 (2000): 722–48.

———. "Sentimental Values and the Instability of Affect." In *The Oxford Handbook of Philosophy of Emotion*, edited by Peter Goldie, 585–613. Oxford: Oxford University Press, 2010.

———. "The Significance of Recalcitrant Emotion (or, Anti-Quasijudgmentalism)." In *Philosophy and the Emotions*, edited by Anthony Hatzimoysis, 127–36. Cambridge: Cambridge University Press, 2003.

Darwall, Stephen. "Empathy, Sympathy, Care." *Philosophical Studies* 89 (1998): 261–82.

Darwall, Stephen, Alan Gibbard, and Peter Railton. "Toward Fin de Siècle Ethics: Some Trends." *Philosophical Review* 101 (1992): 115–89.

Davies, Stephen. "Artistic Expression and the Hard Case of Pure Music." In *Contemporary Debates in Aesthetics and the Philosophy of Art*, edited by Matthew Kieran, 179–91. Oxford: Blackwell, 2006.

———. *Musical Meaning and Expression*. Ithaca, N.Y.: Cornell University Press, 1994.

———. *Themes in the Philosophy of Music*. Oxford: Oxford University Press, 2003.

Davison, R. M. "Wittgenstein and Tolstoy." In *Wittgenstein and His Impact on Contemporary Thought*, edited by E. Leinfellner, W. Leinfellner, H. Berghel, and A. Hübner, 50–53. Vienna: Hölder, Pichler, Tempsky, 1978.

Deigh, John. "Concepts of Emotions." In *The Oxford Handbook of Philosophy of Emotion*, edited by Peter Goldie, 17–40. Oxford: Oxford University Press, 2012.

———. *Emotions, Values, and the Law*. Oxford: Oxford University Press, 2008.

Denner, Michael A. "Accidental Art: Tolstoy's Poetics of Unintentionality." *Philosophy and Literature* 27 (2003): 284–303.

Deonna, Julien, and Fabrice Teroni. *The Emotions: A Philosophical Introduction*. London: Routledge, 2012.

Derrida, Jacques. "The Force of Law: The 'Mystical Foundation of Authority.'" In *Deconstruction and the Possibility of Justice*, edited by D. Cornell, M. Rosenfeld, and D. Carlson, 3–67. New York: Routledge, 1992.

———. *Limited, Inc.* Translated by Samuel Weber and Jeffrey Mehlman. Evanston, Ill.: Northwestern University Press, 1988.

———. *Of Grammatology*. Corrected edition. Translated by Gayatri Chakravorty Spivak. Baltimore: Johns Hopkins University Press, 1997.

———. *Speech and Phenomena and Other Essays on Husserl's Theory of Signs*. Translated with introduction by David B. Allison. Evanston, Ill.: Northwestern University Press, 1973.

———. *Spurs: Nietzsche's Styles*. Translated by Barbara Harlow. Chicago: University of Chicago Press, 1981.

De Sousa, Ronald. *The Rationality of Emotion*. Cambridge, Mass.: MIT Press, 1987.

Dewey, John. *Art as Experience*. New York: Putnam's, 1934.

Diamond, Cora. "Ethics, Imagination and the Method of Wittgenstein's Tractatus." In *The New Wittgenstein*, edited by Alice Crary and Rupert Read, 149–73. London: Routledge, 2000.

Diffey, T. J. *Tolstoy's "What Is Art?"* London: Croom Helm, 1985.

Dixon, Thomas. *From Passions to Emotions: The Creation of a Secular Psychological Category*. Cambridge: Cambridge University Press, 2003.

Döring, Sabine. "Seeing What to Do: Affective Perception and Rational Motivation." *Dialectica* 61 (2007): 363–94.

Dretske, Fred. *Explaining Behavior: Reasons in a World of Causes*. Cambridge, Mass.: MIT Press, 1988.

Ducasse, Curt John. *The Philosophy of Art*. New York: Dover, 1966.

Dunn, Barnaby D., Tim Dalgleish, and Andrew D. Lawrence. "The Somatic Marker Hypothesis: A Critical Evaluation." *Neuroscience and Biobehavioral Reviews* 30 (2006): 239–71.

Eikhenbaum, Boris. "Tolstoi i Shopengauer: K voprosu o sozdanii 'Anny Kareninoi.'" *Literaturnyi Sovremennik* 11 (1935): 134–49.

———. *Tolstoi in the Sixties*. Translated by Duffield White. Ann Arbor, Mich.: Ardis, 1982.

———. *Tolstoi in the Seventies*. Translated by Albert Kaspin. Ann Arbor, Mich.: Ardis, 1982.

Ekman, Paul. "All Emotions Are Basic." In *The Nature of Emotion: Fundamental Questions*, edited by Paul Ekman and Richard Davidson, 15–19. New York: Oxford University Press, 1994.

———. "Biological and Cultural Contributions to Body and Facial Movement in the Expression of Emotions." In *Explaining Emotions*, edited by A. O. Rorty, 73–102. Berkeley: University of California Press, 1980.

———. "Expression and the Nature of Emotion." In *Approaches to Emotion*, edited by K. Scherer and P. Ekman, 319–43. Hillsdale, N.J.: Lawrence Erlbaum, 1984.

———. "Universals and Cultural Differences in Facial Expressions of Emotion." In *Nebraska Symposium on Motivation 1971*, edited by J. Cole, 207–83. Lincoln: University of Nebraska Press, 1971.

Emerson, Caryl. "Tolstoy's Aesthetics." In *Cambridge Companion to Tolstoy*, edited by Donna Tussing Orwin, 237–51. Cambridge: Cambridge University Press, 2002.

Engelmann, Paul. *Letters from Ludwig Wittgenstein: With a Memoir*. Oxford: Oxford University Press, 1967.

Feagin, Susan. *Reading with Feeling: The Aesthetics of Appreciation*. Ithaca, N.Y.: Cornell University Press, 1996.

Felman, Shoshana. "Forms of Judicial Blindness, or the Evidence of What Cannot Be Seen: Traumatic Narratives and Legal Repetitions in the O.J. Simpson Case and in Tolstoy's *The Kreutzer Sonata*." *Critical Inquiry* 23 (1997): 738–88.

Ferrara, Lawrence. "Schopenhauer on Music as the Embodiment of Will." In *Schopenhauer, Philosophy, and the Arts*, edited by Dale Jacquette, 183–99. Cambridge: Cambridge University Press, 1996.

Ficker, Ludwig von. "Rilke und der unbekannte Freund." *Der Brenner* 18 (1954): 234–48.

Finkelstein, David H. *Expression and the Inner*. Cambridge, Mass.: Harvard University Press, 2003.

Fischer, Michael. *Stanley Cavell and Literary Skepticism*. Chicago: University of Chicago Press, 1989.

Fodor, Jerry. *A Theory of Content and Other Essays*. Cambridge, Mass.: MIT Press, 1990.

Fogelin, Robert. *Wittgenstein*. 2nd edition. New York: Routledge, 1995.

Forbes, Graeme. "Skepticism and Semantic Knowledge." In *Rule-Following and Meaning*, edited by A. Miller and C. Wright, 16–27. Montreal: McGill-Queen's University Press, 2002.

Friedlander, Eli. *Signs of Sense: Reading Wittgenstein's "Tractatus."* Cambridge, Mass.: Harvard University Press, 2001.

Frijda, Nico H. *The Emotions*. Cambridge: Cambridge University Press, 1986.

Gasché, Rodolphe. *Inventions of Difference: On Jacques Derrida*. Cambridge, Mass.: Harvard University Press, 1994.

———. *The Tain of the Mirror*. Cambridge, Mass.: Harvard University Press, 1986.

Gibbard, Allan. *Wise Choices, Apt Feelings: A Theory of Normative Judgment*. Cambridge, Mass.: Harvard University Press. 1990.

Gibson, John. *Fiction and the Weave of Life*. Oxford: Oxford University Press, 2007.

Ginzburg, Lydia. *On Psychological Prose*. Translated by J. Rosengrant. Princeton, N.J.: Princeton University Press, 1991.

Glover, Jonathan. "Anna Karenina and Moral Philosophy." In *Well-Being and Morality: Essays in Honour of James Griffin*, edited by Roger Crisp and Brad Hooker, 159–76. New York: Oxford University Press, 2000.

Gol'denveizer, A. B. "Tolstoi i muzyka." *Literaturnoe nasledstvo* 37–38. Moscow: Akademii Nauk SSSR, 1939.

Goldie, Peter. "Emotion, Reason, and Virtue." In *Emotion, Evolution, and Rationality*, edited by D. Evans and P. Cruse, 249–67. Oxford: Oxford University Press, 2004.

———. *The Emotions: A Philosophical Exploration*. Oxford: Clarendon, 2000.

———. "Grief: A Narrative Account." *Ratio* 24 (2011): 119–37.

———. "Intellectual and Religious Emotions." *Faith and Philosophy: Journal of the Society of Christian Philosophers* 28 (2011): 93–101.

———. "Seeing What Is the Kind Thing to Do: Perception and Emotion in Morality." *Dialectica* 61 (2007): 347–61.

Gordon, Robert. 1987. *The Structure of Emotions: Investigations in Cognitive Philosophy*. Cambridge: Cambridge University Press, 1987.

Gracyk, T., and A. Kania, eds. *The Routledge Companion to Philosophy and Music*. New York: Routledge, 2011.

Graham, Gordon. *Philosophy of the Arts: An Introduction to Aesthetics*. 3rd edition. London: Routledge, 2005.

Gregg, Melissa, and Gregory Seigworth, eds. *The Affect Theory Reader*. Durham, N.C.: Duke University Press, 2010.

Greenspan, Patricia. *Emotions and Reasons: An Inquiry into Emotional Justification*. New York: Routledge, 1988.

Greenwood, E. B. "Tolstoy, Wittgenstein, Schopenhauer: Some Connections." In *Tolstoi and Britain*, edited by W. Gareth Jones, 239–49. Oxford: Berg, 1995.

Griffiths, Paul E. *What Emotions Really Are: From Evolution to Social Construction*. Chicago: University of Chicago Press, 1997.

Gumbrecht, Hans Ulrich. *Atmosphere, Mood, Stimmung: On a Hidden Potential of Literature*. Stanford, Calif.: Stanford University Press, 2012.

Gustafson, Richard. *Leo Tolstoy: Resident and Stranger*. Princeton, N.J.: Princeton University Press, 1986,

Habermas, Jürgen. *Communication and the Evolution of Society*. Translated by Thomas McCarthy. Boston: Beacon Books, 1979.

———. *The Philosophical Discourse of Modernity*. Translated by Frederick Lawrence. Cambridge, Mass.: MIT Press, 1987.

Hall, Robert. "Schopenhauer: Music and the Emotions." *Schopenhauer-Jahrbuch* 83 (2002): 151–61.

Hammer, Espen. *Stanley Cavell: Skepticism, Subjectivity, and the Ordinary*. Cambridge, Eng.: Polity, 2002.

Hanslick, Eduard. *On the Musically Beautiful*. Translated by G. Payzant. Indianapolis, Ind.: Hackett, 1986 [1854].

Hatfield, E., J. T. Cacioppo, and R. L. Rapson. *Emotional Contagion*. New York: Cambridge University Press, 1994.

Haugeland, John. "The Intentionality All-Stars." In *Having Thought: Essays in the Metaphysics of Mind*, 127–70. Cambridge, Mass.: Harvard University Press, 1998.

Hegel, G. W. F. *Aesthetics: Lectures on Fine Art*. 2 vols. Translated by T. M. Knox. Oxford: Oxford University Press, 1975.

Heidegger, Martin. *Sein und Zeit*. Tübingen: Niemeyer, 1986 [1927].

Helm, Bennett. "Emotions and Practical Reason: Rethinking Evaluation and Motivation." *Noûs* 35 (2001): 190–213.

Herman, David. "Stricken by Infection: Art and Adultery in *Anna Karenina* and *Kreutzer Sonata*." *Slavic Review* 56 (1997): 14–36.

Hume, David. *Enquiries Concerning Human Understanding and Concerning the Principles of Morals*. Edited by L. A. Selby-Bigge and P. H. Nidditch. Oxford: Clarendon, 1975 [1777].

———. *A Treatise of Human Nature*. Edited by P. H. Nidditch. Oxford: Oxford University Press, 1978 [1739].

Husserl, Edmund. *Logical Investigations*. 2 vols. Translated by J. N. Findlay. London: Routledge and Kegan Paul, 1970 [1900–1901].

Jacobson, Daniel. "Seeing by Feeling: Virtues, Skills, and Moral Perception." *Ethical Theory and Moral Practice* 8 (2005): 387–409.

Jahn, Gary R. "The Aesthetic Theory of Leo Tolstoy's *What Is Art?*" *Journal of Aesthetics and Art Criticism* 34 (1975): 59–65.

———. "The Image of the Railroad in *Anna Karenina*." *Slavic and East European Journal* 25 (1981): 1–10.

James, William. *The Principles of Psychology*. 2 vols. New York: Dover, 1950.

———. "What Is an Emotion?" *Mind* 9 (1884): 188–205.

Janaway, Christopher. *Self and World in Schopenhauer's Philosophy*. Oxford: Clarendon, 1989.

Janik, Allan, and Stephen Toulmin. *Wittgenstein's Vienna*. New York: Simon and Schuster, 1973.

Kania, Andrew. "The Philosophy of Music." In *Stanford Encyclopedia of Philosophy*. 2012. http://plato.stanford.edu/entries/music/.

Kant, Immanuel. *Critique of Judgment*. Translated by Werner Pluhar. Indianapolis, Ind.: Hackett, 1987.

Kaufman, Walter. *Existentialism from Dostoevsky to Sartre*. New York: Meridian Books, 1956.

Kenny, Anthony. *Action, Emotion and Will*. London: Routledge and Kegan Paul, 1963.

Kivy, Peter. *The Corded Shell: Reflections on Musical Expression*. Princeton, N.J.: Princeton University Press, 1980.

———. *New Essays on Musical Understanding*. Oxford: Oxford University Press, 2001.

———. *Sound Sentiment: An Essay on the Musical Emotions*. Philadelphia: Temple University Press, 1989.

Knapp, Liza. "Tolstoy on Musical Mimesis: Platonic Aesthetics and Erotics in 'The Kreutzer Sonata.'" *Tolstoy Studies* 3 (1991): 25–42.

Knowles, A. V. "Russian Views of *Anna Karenina*, 1875–1878." *Slavic and East European Journal* 22 (1978): 301–12.

Kopper, John. "Tolstoy and the Narrative of Sex: A Reading of 'Father Sergius,' 'The Devil,' and 'The Kreutzer Sonata.'" In *In the Shade of the Giant: Essays on Tolstoy*, edited by H. McLean, 158–86. Berkeley: University of California Press, 1989.

Kosman, L. A. "Being Properly Affected: Virtues and Feelings in Aristotle's *Ethics*." In *Essays on Aristotle's Ethics*, edited by A. O. Rorty, 103–16. Berkeley: University of California Press, 1980.

Kripke, Saul. *Wittgenstein on Rules and Private Language*. Cambridge, Mass.: Harvard University Press, 1982.

Lange, C. G. *The Emotions*. Translated by I. A. Haupt, Baltimore: Williams and Wilkin, 1922 [1885].

Lazarus, Richard. "Appraisal: The Long and Short of It." In *The Nature of Emotion: Fundamental Questions*, edited by Paul Ekman and Richard Davidson, 208–16. New York: Oxford University Press, 1994.

———. "Thoughts on the Relations between Emotion and Cognition." *American Psychologist* 37 (1982): 1019–24.

LeDoux, Joseph. *The Emotional Brain: The Mysterious Underpinnings of Emotional Life*. New York: Simon and Schuster, 1996.

Levinson, Jerrold. "Emotion in Response to Art: A Survey of the Terrain." In *Emotion and the Arts*, edited by M. Hjort and S. Laver, 20–34. New York: Oxford University Press, 1997.

———. *Music, Art, and Metaphysics: Essays in Philosophical Aesthetics*. Ithaca, N.Y.: Cornell University Press, 1990.

———. "Musical Expressiveness as Hearability-as-Expression." In *Contemporary Debates in Aesthetics and the Philosophy of Art*, edited by Matthew Kieran, 192–206. Oxford: Blackwell, 2006.

———. "Musical Thinking." *Midwest Studies in Philosophy* 27 (2003): 59–68.

———. *The Pleasures of Aesthetics*. Ithaca, N.Y.: Cornell University Press, 1996.

Leys, Ruth. "The Turn to Affect: A Critique." *Critical Inquiry* 37 (2011): 434–72.

Loewer, Brian. "From Information to Intentionality." *Synthese* 70 (1987): 287–317.

Lomunov, Konstantin. *Estetika L'va Tolstogo*. Moscow: "Sovremennik," 1972.

Longinus, Dionysius. *Libellus de Sublimate*. Edited by D. A. Russell. Oxford: Oxford University Press, 1968.

Lovibond, Sabina. *Ethical Formation*. Cambridge, Mass.: Harvard University Press, 2002.

Lurz, Robert W., ed. *The Philosophy of Animal Minds*. Cambridge, Eng.: Cambridge University Press, 2009.

Lyons, William. *Emotion*. Cambridge: Cambridge University Press, 1980.

Lyotard, Jean-François. *Des dispositifs pulsionnels*. Paris: Union générale d'éditions, 1973.

———. "The Sublime and the Avant-Garde." In *The Lyotard Reader*, edited by A. Benjamin, 196–211. Oxford: Blackwell, 1991.

Mackie, J. L. *Ethics: Inventing Right and Wrong*. Harmondsworth, Eng.: Penguin, 1977.

Mandelker, Amy. *Framing "Anna Karenina": Tolstoy, the Woman Question, and the Victorian Novel*. Columbus: Ohio University Press, 1993.

Marks, Joel. "A Theory of Emotion." *Philosophical Studies* 42 (1982): 227–42.

Massumi, Brian. "Fear (The Spectrum Said)." *Positions* 13 (2005): 31–48.

———. *Parables for the Virtual: Movement, Affect, Sensation*. Durham, N.C.: Duke University Press, 2002.

Matravers, Derek. *Art and Emotion*. Oxford: Oxford University Press, 1998.

———. "Expression in Music." In *Philosophers on Music: Experience, Meaning, Work*, edited by Karen Stock, 95–116. Oxford: Oxford University Press, 2007.

McDowell, John. "Are Moral Requirements Hypothetical Imperatives?" In *Mind, Value and Reality*, 77–94. Cambridge, Mass.: Harvard University Press, 1998.

———. "Brandom on Observation." In *Reading Brandom: On Making It Explicit*, edited by Bernhard Weiss and Jeremy Wanderer, 129–44. London: Routledge, 2010.

———. "The Disjunctive Conception of Experience as Material for a Transcendental Argument." In *The Engaged Intellect*, 225–40. Cambridge, Mass.: Harvard University Press, 2009.

———. "Meaning and Intentionality in Wittgenstein's Later Philosophy." In *Mind, Value and Reality*, 263–78. Cambridge, Mass.: Harvard University Press, 1998.

———. "Non-Cognitivism and Rule-Following." In *Mind, Value and Reality*, 198–220. Cambridge, Mass.: Harvard University Press, 1998.

———. "Projection and Truth in Ethics." In *Mind, Value and Reality*, 151–66. Cambridge, Mass.: Harvard University Press, 1998.

———. "Two Sorts of Naturalism." In *Mind, Value and Reality*, 167–97. Cambridge, Mass.: Harvard University Press, 1998.

———. "Values and Secondary Qualities." In *Mind, Value and Reality*, 131–50. Cambridge, Mass.: Harvard University Press, 1998.

———. "Virtue and Reason." In *Mind, Value and Reality*, 50–73. Cambridge, Mass.: Harvard University Press, 1998.

———. "Wittgenstein on Following a Rule." In *Mind, Value and Reality*, 221–62. Cambridge, Mass.: Harvard University Press, 1998.

McIntosh, D., D. Druckman, and R. B. Zajonc. "Socially Induced Affect." In *Learning, Remembering, Believing: Enhancing Human Performance*, edited by Daniel Druckman and Robert A. Bjork, 251–76. Washington, D.C.: National Academy Press, 1994.

McLaughlin, Sigrid. "Some Aspects of Tolstoy's Intellectual Development: Tolstoy and Schopenhauer," *California Slavic Studies* 5 (1970): 187–248.

McManus, Denis. *The Enchantment of Words: Wittgenstein's Tractatus Logico-Philosophicus*. Oxford: Clarendon, 2006.

McNaughton, David. *Moral Vision: An Introduction to Ethics*. Oxford: Blackwell, 1988.

Medzhibovskaya, Inessa. *Tolstoy and the Religious Culture of His Time: A Biography of a Long Conversion, 1845–1887*. Lanham, Md.: Lexington Books, 2008.

Meilakh, B. C., ed. *Russkaia povest' XIX veka. Istoriia i problematika zhanra.* Leningrad: Nauka, 1973.

Mew, Peter. "The Expression of Emotion in Music." *British Journal of Aesthetics* 35 (1985): 33–42.

Millikan, Ruth. *Language, Thought, and Other Biological Categories: New Foundations for Realism*. Cambridge, Mass.: MIT Press, 1984.

Monk, Ray. *Ludwig Wittgenstein: The Duty of Genius*. New York: Penguin, 1990.

Morreall, John. "Fear Without Belief." *The Journal of Philosophy* 90 (1993): 359–66.

Morson, Gary Saul. *"Anna Karenina" in Our Time: Seeing More Wisely*. New Haven, Conn.: Yale University Press, 2007.

———. *Hidden in Plain View: Narrative and Creative Potentials in "War and Peace."* Stanford, Calif.: Stanford University Press, 1987.

———. "The Reader as Voyeur: Tolstoy and the Poetics of Didactic Fiction." In *Leo Tolstoy: Modern Critical Views*, edited by Harold Bloom, 175–90. New York: Chelsea House, 1991.

Mulhall, Stephen. *Stanley Cavell: Philosophy's Recounting of the Ordinary*. Oxford: Clarendon, 1994.

Nietzsche, Friedrich. *The Birth of Tragedy*. Edited by Raymond Geuss and Ronald Speirs. Translated by Ronald Speirs. Cambridge: Cambridge University Press, 1999.

Nussbaum, Charles. *The Musical Representation: Meaning, Ontology, and Emotion*. Cambridge, Mass.: MIT Press, 2007.

Nussbaum, Martha. *Love's Knowledge: Essays on Philosophy and Literature*. New York: Oxford University Press, 1990.

———. *Upheavals of Thought: The Intelligence of Emotions*. Cambridge: Cambridge University Press, 2001.

Oakley, Justin. *Morality and the Emotions*. London: Routledge, 1992.

Oatley, Keith. *The Passionate Muse: Exploring Emotion in Stories*. New York: Oxford University Press, 2012.

Oddie, Graham. *Value, Reality and Desire*. Oxford: Clarendon, 2005.

Opul'skaya, L. D. *Lev Nikolaevich Tolstoi: Materialy k biografii c 1886 po 1892 god*. Moscow: Nauka, 1979.

Orwin, Donna Tussing. *Tolstoy's Art and Thought: 1847–1880*. Princeton, N.J.: Princeton University Press, 1993.

———. "What Men Live By: Belief and the Individual in Leo Tolstoy and William James." In *William James in Russian Culture*, edited by Joan Delaney Grossman and Ruth Rischin, 59–80. Lanham, Md.: Lexington Books, 2003.

O'Shaughnessy, Brian. *The Will: A Dual Aspect Theory*. Cambridge: Cambridge University Press, 1980.

Pears, David. *The False Prison: A Study in the Development of Wittgenstein's Philosophy*. 2 vols. Oxford: Clarendon, 1987.

Pickford, Henry. "Towards a Disjunctivist Conception of Aesthetic Expression." Unpublished manuscript.

Pockett, Susan, William P. Banks, and Shaun Gallagher, eds. *Does Consciousness Cause Behavior?* Cambridge, Mass.: MIT Press, 2006.

Pomorska, Krystyna. "Tolstoy—Contra Semiosis." *International Journal of Slavic Linguistics* 25–26 (1982): 383–90.

Price, Martin. *Character and Moral Imagination in the Novel*. New Haven, Conn.: Yale University Press, 1983.

Prinz, Jesse. *The Emotional Construction of Morals*. Oxford: Oxford University Press, 2007.

———. *Gut Reactions: A Perceptual Theory of Emotion*. Oxford: Oxford University Press, 2004.

Pryor, James. "There Is Immediate Justification." In *Contemporary Debates in Epistemology*, edited by Matthias Steup and Ernest Sosa, 181–201. Oxford: Blackwell, 2005.

Putnam, Hilary. *Reason, Truth and History*. Cambridge, Mass.: Harvard University Press, 1980.

Radford, Colin. "Emotions and Music: A Reply to the Cognitivists." *Journal of Aesthetics and Art Criticism* 47 (1989): 69–76.

Radford, Colin, and Michael Weston. "How Can We Be Moved by the Fate of Anna Karenina?" *Proceedings of the Aristotelian Society*, suppl. vol. 49 (1975): 67–93.

Rawls, John. *A Theory of Justice*. Cambridge, Mass.: Harvard University Press, 1971.

Rhees, Rush, ed. *Ludwig Wittgenstein: Personal Recollections*. Oxford: Blackwell, 1981.

Ridley, Aaron. "Expression in Art." In *The Oxford Handbook of Aesthetics*, edited by Jerrold Levinson, 211–27. Oxford: Oxford University Press, 2003.

———. "Mr. Mew on Music." *British Journal of Aesthetics* 26 (1986): 69–70.

———. *Music, Value, and the Passions.* Ithaca, N.Y.: Cornell University Press, 1995.

———. "*Persona* Sometimes *Grata*: On the Appreciation of Expressive Music." In *Philosophers on Music: Experience, Meaning, Work*, edited by Karen Stock, 130–46. Oxford: Oxford University Press, 2007.

———. *The Philosophy of Music: Theme and Variations.* Edinburgh: Edinburgh University Press, 2004.

Rizzolati, G., and L. Craighero. "The Mirror-Neuron System." *Annual Review of Neuroscience* 27 (2004): 169–92.

Roberts, Robert. *Emotions: An Essay in Aid of Moral Psychology.* Cambridge: Cambridge University Press, 2003.

Robinson, Douglas. *Estrangement and the Somatics of Literature: Tolstoy, Shklovsky, Brecht.* Baltimore: Johns Hopkins University Press, 2008.

Robinson, Jenefer. *Deeper Than Reason: Emotion and Its Role in Literature, Music, and Art.* Oxford: Clarendon, 2005.

———. "The Expression and Arousal of Emotion in Music." In *Musical Worlds: New Directions in the Philosophy of Music*, edited by P. Alperson, 13–22. University Park: Pennsylvania State University Press, 1998.

———. "Startle." *Journal of Philosophy* 92 (1995): 53–74.

Robinson, Jenefer, and G. Karl. "Shostakovitch's Tenth Symphony and the Musical Expression of Cognitively Complex Emotions." *Journal of Aesthetics and Art Criticism* 53 (1995): 401–15.

Rorty, Amélie. "Explaining Emotions." In *Explaining Emotions*, edited by A. O. Rorty, 103–26. Los Angeles: University of California Press, 1980.

Ryle, Gilbert. *The Concept of Mind.* New York: Barnes and Noble, 1949.

Schachter, Stanley, and J. Singer. "Cognition, Social, and Physiological Determinants of Emotional State." *Psychological Review* 69 (1962): 379–99.

Schopenahauer, Arthur. *On the Basis of Morality.* Translated by E. F. J. Payne. Providence, R.I.: Berghahn Books, 1995.

———. *On the Fourfold Root of the Principle of Sufficient Reason.* Translated by E. F. J. Payne. La Salle, Ill.: Open Court, 1974.

———. *Parerga and Paralipomena.* 2 vols. Translated by E. F. J. Payne. Oxford: Clarendon, 1974.

———. *Prize Essay on the Freedom of the Will.* Translated by E. F. J. Payne. Cambridge: Cambridge University Press, 1999.

———. *Sämtliche Werke.* Edited by Wolfgang Freiherr von Löhneysen. Frankfurt: Suhrkamp, 1986.

———. *The World as Will and Idea.* 2 vols. Translated by E. F. J. Payne. New York: Dover, 1969.

Schultze, Sydney. *The Structure of "Anna Karenina."* Ann Arbor, Mich.: Ardis, 1982.

Scruton, Roger. *The Aesthetics of Music.* Oxford: Oxford University Press, 1997.

———. "Wittgenstein and the Understanding of Music." *British Journal of Aesthetics* 44 (2004): 1–9.

Searle, John. "Putting Consciousness Back in the Brain." In *Neuroscience and Philosophy: Brain, Mind, and Language*, by Maxwell Bennett, Daniel Dennett, Peter Hacker, and John Searle, 97–124. New York: Columbia University Press, 2007.

Sedgwick, Eve Kosofsky. *Touching Feeling: Affect, Pedagogy, Performativity*. Durham, N.C.: Duke University Press, 2003.

Sellars, Wilfrid. *Empiricism and the Philosophy of Mind*. Cambridge, Mass.: Harvard University Press, 1997.

Shusterman, Richard. *Pragmatist Aesthetics: Living Beauty, Rethinking Art*. 2nd edition. Lanham, Md.: Rowman and Littlefield, 2000.

Silbajoris, Rimvydas. *Tolstoy's Aesthetics and His Art*. Columbus, Oh.: Slavica, 1991.

Singer, T., B. Seymour, J. O'Doherty, H. Kaube, R. J. Dolan, and C. D. Firth. "Empathy for Pain Involves the Affective but Not Sensory Components of Pain." *Science* 303 (2004): 1157–62.

Skaftymov, Aleksandr. "Idei i formy v tvorchestve L. Tolstogo." In *Nravstvennye iskaniia russkikh pisatelei*. Moscow: Khudozhestvennaia literatura, 1972.

Slote, Michael. "Moral Sentimentalism and Moral Psychology." In *Oxford Handbook of Ethical Theory*, edited by David Copp, 219–39. Oxford: Oxford University Press, 2006.

Smith, Adam. *The Theory of Moral Sentiments*. Oxford: Clarendon, 1976 [1759].

Smith, Michael. *The Moral Problem*. Oxford: Blackwell, 1994.

Solomon, Robert. "Emotions and Choice." In *Explaining Emotions*, edited by A. O. Rorty, 251–81. Berkeley: University of California Press, 1980.

———. "Emotions, Thoughts and Feelings: What Is a 'Cognitive Theory' of the Emotions and Does It Neglect Affectivity?" In *Philosophy and the Emotions*, edited by Anthony Hatzimoysis, 1–18. Cambridge: Cambridge University Press, 2003.

———. *The Passions: Emotions and the Meaning of Life*. Indianapolis, Ind.: Hackett, 1993.

Sontag, Susan. "Against Interpretation." In *A Susan Sontag Reader*, 95–104. New York: Vintage, 1983.

Staten, Henry. *Wittgenstein and Derrida*. Lincoln: University of Nebraska Press, 1984.

Stecker, Robert. "Expressiveness and Expression in Music and Poetry." *Journal of Aesthetics and Art Criticism* 59 (2001): 85–96.

Steiner, George. *Tolstoy or Dostoevsky: An Essay in the Old Criticism*. New York: Knopf, 1959.

Stenbock-Fermor, Elisabeth. *The Architecture of "Anna Karenina."* Lisse: Peter de Ridder, 1975.

Stocker, Michael. "Psychic Feelings: Their Importance and Irreducibility." *Australian Journal of Philosophy* 61 (1983): 5–26.

———. "The Schizophrenia of Modern Ethical Theories." *Journal of Philosophy* 73 (1976): 453–66.

Stocker, Michael, and Elizabeth Hegeman. *Valuing Emotions*. Cambridge: Cambridge University Press, 1992.

Stokhof, Martin. *World and Life as One: Ethics and Ontology in Wittgenstein's Early Thought*. Stanford, Calif.: Stanford University Press, 2002.

Stone, Martin. "Wittgenstein on Deconstruction." In *The New Wittgenstein*, edited by Alice Crary and Rupert Read, 83–117. New York: Routledge, 2000.

Taylor, Charles. *Hegel*. Cambridge: Cambridge University Press, 1977.

Taylor, Gabriele. *Pride, Shame, and Guilt: Emotions of Self-Assessment*. Oxford: Clarendon, 1985.

Thompson, Caleb. "Wittgenstein, Tolstoy and the Meaning of Life." *Philosophical Investigations* 20 (1997): 98–116.

Todd, William Mills, III. "The Responsibilities of (Co-)Authorship: Notes on Revising the Serialized Version of *Anna Karenina*." In *Freedom and Responsibility in Russian Literature*, edited by E. C. Allen and G. S. Morson, 159–69. Evanston, Ill.: Northwestern University Press, 1995.

Tolstoy, Lev N. *Anna Karenina*. Translated by Richard Pevear and Larissa Volokhonsky. New York: Penguin Books, 2000.

———. *A Confession and Other Religious Writings*. Translated by Jane Kentish. New York: Penguin Books, 1987.

———. *The Gospel in Brief*. Edited by F. A. Flowers III, translated by I. Hapgood. Lincoln: University of Nebraska Press, 1997.

———. "The Kreutzer Sonata." In *"The Kreutzer Sonata" and Other Stories*, translated by David McDuff. New York: Penguin Books, 1985.

———. "The Memoirs of a Madman." Translated by Louise and Aylmer Maude. In *Tolstoy's Short Fiction*, edited by Michael Katz, 295–303. New York: W.W. Norton, 1991.

———. "O tom, chto nazyvaetsia iskusstvom." *Literaturnoe nasledstvo* 37–38. Moscow: Akademii Nauk SSSR, 1939.

———. *Polnoe sobranie sochinenii*. Edited by V. G. Chertkov. Moscow: Gosudarstvennoe izdatel'stvo khudozhestvennoi literatury, 1928ff.

———. *Tolstoy's Diaries*. 2 vols. Edited and translated by R. F. Christian. New York: Charles Scribner's Sons, 1985.

———. *Walk in the Light and Twenty-Three Tales*. Translated by Louise and Aylmer Maude. Farmington, Penn.: The Plough Publishing House, 1998.

———. *What Is Art?* Translated by Richard Pevear and Larissa Volokhonsky. New York: Penguin Books, 1995.

Tooby, John, and Leda Cosmides. "The Evolutionary Psychology of the Emotions and Their Relationship to Internal Regulatory Variables." In *Handbook of Emotions*, edited by M. Lewis, J. Haviland-Jones, and L. Feldman Barrett, 114–37. New York: Guildford, 2008.

Tormey, Alan. *The Concept of Expression: A Study in Philosophical Psychology and Aesthetics*. Princeton, N.J.: Princeton University Press, 1971.

Townsend, Dabney. *An Introduction to Aesthetics*. Oxford: Blackwell, 1997.

Trilling, Lionel. *The Liberal Imagination: Essays on Literature and Society*. New York: Doubleday, 1950.

Velleman, David. *Practical Reflection*. Princeton, N.J.: Princeton University Press, 1989.

Vermazen, Bruce. "Expression as Expression." *Pacific Philosophical Quarterly* 67 (1986). 196–221.

Walsh, Harry. "The Place of Schopenhauer in the Philosophical Education of Leo Tolstoi." In *Schopenhauer*, edited by Eric Von der Luft, 300–311. Lewiston, N.Y.: Mellen, 1988.

———. "Schopenhauer's *On the Freedom of the Will* and the Epilogue to *War and Peace*." *Slavonic and East European Review* 57 (1979): 572–75.

Walton, Kendall. *Mimesis as Make-Believe: On the Foundations of the Representational Arts*. Cambridge, Mass.: Harvard University Press, 1990.

Weir, Justin. *Leo Tolstoy and the Alibi of Narrative*. New Haven, Conn.: Yale University Press, 2011.

Wiggins, David. "Moral Cognitivism, Moral Relativism and Motivating Moral Beliefs." *Proceedings of the Aristotelian Society* 91 (1990): 61–85.

———. "A Sensible Subjectivism?" In *Needs, Values, Truth*. 3rd edition, 185–214. Oxford: Clarendon, 1998.

Williams, Bernard. *Ethics and the Limits of Philosophy*. Cambridge, Mass.: Harvard University Press, 1985.

———. "Morality and the Emotions." In *Problems of the Self: Philosophical Papers 1956–1972*, 207–29. Cambridge: Cambridge University Press, 1973.

Wilson, A. N. *Tolstoy*. New York: W. W. Norton, 1988.

Wispé, Lauren. "History of the Concept of Empathy." In *Empathy and Its Development*, edited by H. Eisenberg and J. Strayder, 17–37. Cambridge: Cambridge University Press, 1987.

Wittgenstein, Ludwig. *The Big Typescript: TS 213*. Edited and translated by C. Grant Luckhardt and Maximilian A. E. Aue. Oxford: Blackwell, 2005.

———. *Blue and Brown Books*. New York: Harper, 1958.

———. *Cambridge Letters: Correspondence with Russell, Keynes, Moore, Ramsey and Sraffa*. Edited by Brain McGuinness and G. H. von Wright. Oxford: Blackwell, 1995.

———. *Culture and Value*. Revised edition. Edited by G. H. von Wright in collaboration with H. Nyman, revised edition by A. Pichler. Translated by Peter Winch. Chicago: University of Chicago Press, 1998.

———. *Last Writings in the Philosophy of Psychology, Preliminary Studies for Part II of Philosophical Investigations*. Vol. 1. Edited by G. H. von Wright and H. Nyman. Translated by C. G. Luckhardt and M. A. E. Aue. Oxford: Basil Blackwell, 1982.

———. "A Lecture on Ethics." In *Philosophical Occasions 1912–1951*, edited by J. Klagge and A. Nordmann, 37–44. Indianapolis, Ind.: Hackett, 1993.

———. *Lectures and Conversations on Aesthetics, Psychology and Religious Belief*. Edited by Cyril Barrett. Berkeley: University of California Press, 1966.

———. "Letter to Ludwig von Ficker." In *Wittgenstein: Sources and Perspectives*, edited by C. Grant Luckhardt, 34–35. Ithaca, N.Y.: Cornell University Press, 1979.

———. *Notebooks 1914–1916*. Edited by G. E. M. Anscombe and G. H. von Wright. Translated by G. E. M. Anscombe. Oxford: Basil Blackwell, 1961.

———. *On Certainty*. Edited by G. E. M. Anscombe and G. H. von Wright. Translated by G. E. M. Anscombe. New York: Harper, 1969.

———. *Philosophical Investigations*. Translated by G. E. M. Anscombe. Oxford: Blackwell, 1958.

———. *Remarks on the Foundations of Mathematics*. Edited by G. H. von Wright, R. Rhees, and G. E. M. Anscombe. Cambridge, Mass.: MIT Press, 1983.

———. *Remarks on the Philosophy of Psychology*. Vol. 1. Edited by G. E. M. Anscombe and G. H. von Wright. Translated by G. E. M. Anscombe. Oxford: Blackwell, 1980.

———. *Remarks on the Philosophy of Psychology*. Vol. 2. Edited by G. H. von Wright and Heikki Nyman. Translated by C. G. Luckhardt and M. A. E. Aue. Oxford: Blackwell, 1980.

———. *Tractatus Logico-Philosophicus*. Translated by D. F. Pears and B. F. McGuinness. London: Routledge, 1961.

———. *Werkausgabe*. Frankfurt: Suhrkamp, 1984.

———. *Zettel*. Edited by G. E. M. Anscombe and G. H. von Wright. Translated by G. E. M. Anscombe. Berkeley: University of California Press, 1967.

Wollheim, Richard. *On the Emotions*. New Haven, Conn.: Yale University Press, 1999.

Zagzebski, Linda. "Emotion and Moral Judgment." *Philosophy and Phenomenological Research* 66 (2003): 104–24.

Zhdanov, V. A. *Ot Anny Kareninoi k Voskreseniiu*. Moscow: Kniga, 1967.

Zurek, Magdalene. *Tolstojs Philosophie der Kunst*. Heidelberg: C. Winter, 1996.

INDEX